2 —

# Soviet Signoras

**FIELDWORK ENCOUNTERS AND DISCOVERIES**
A series edited by Robert Emerson and Jack Katz

# Soviet Signoras

*Personal and Collective Transformations
in Eastern European Migration*

MARTINA CVAJNER

*The University of Chicago Press   Chicago and London*

The University of Chicago Press, Chicago 60637
The University of Chicago Press, Ltd., London
© 2019 by The University of Chicago
Published 2019
Printed in the United States of America

28 27 26 25 24 23 22 21 20 19     1 2 3 4 5

ISBN-13: 978-0-226-66225-1 (cloth)
ISBN-13: 978-0-226-66239-8 (paper)
ISBN-13: 978-0-226-66242-8 (e-book)
DOI: https://doi.org/10.7208/chicago/9780226662428.001.0001

Library of Congress Cataloging-in-Publication Data

Names: Cvajner, Martina, author.
Title: Soviet signoras : personal and collective transformations in Eastern
    European migration / Martina Cvajner.
Other titles: Fieldwork encounters and discoveries.
Description: Chicago ; London : The University of Chicago Press, 2019. |
    Series: Fieldwork encounters and discoveries
Identifiers: LCCN 2019012199 | ISBN 9780226662251 (cloth : alk. paper) |
    ISBN 9780226662398 (pbk. : alk. paper) | ISBN 9780226662428 (e-book)
Subjects: LCSH: Women immigrants—Italy—Social conditions. | Women
    foreign workers—Italy. | Italy—Emigration and immigration. | Former
    Soviet republics—Emigration and immigration. | Europe, Eastern—
    Emigration and immigration. | Assimilation (Sociology)—Italy.
Classification: LCC JV8138.C837 2019 | DDC 305.48/4120945—dc23
LC record available at https://lccn.loc.gov/2019012199

♾ This paper meets the requirements of ANSI/NISO Z39.48–1992
(Permanence of Paper).

# Contents

# Prologue

Something wrong was unfolding before my eyes and I could not help feeling badly about it. The party intended to celebrate my return was not going as expected. I had been looking forward to that night for weeks. For many years, I had been doing fieldwork with a group of post-Soviet women employed as care workers in the northern Italian city I call Alpinetown. I had subsequently spent quite a bit of time abroad, staying in touch with "the women," as the set had been known, only through Skype and occasional emails. I was looking forward to a great reunion.

I had pestered some of them to organize a welcome back party. Dasha had eventually given in. Some years before, she had married Gianfranco, the son of the old woman for whom she had done care work for many years. Small entrepreneurs of some means, they lived in a beautiful chalet with a view onto the entire town encircled by chains of mountain peaks. She had been adamant, however, in inviting only a small number of them, justifying this by saying that "A large bunch of people is no fun, Martushka." We decided to invite the women who had become the main subjects of my ethnographic project in the early 2000s; they had been the collective core of Eastern European women pioneers in Alpinetown.

Late Sunday, Iryna, my closest friend in the group, arrived to pick me up in her car. She was already in full regalia, with heavy makeup, high heels, skinny black jeans, a white lace see-through shirt, and a large red belt. As always, even before greeting me, she scolded me for my sloppy, unfeminine dress.

After a short drive, we entered the gate of the chalet and parked the car. We were in a pleasant garden overlooking the river. The weather was warm, and the smell of a delicious borscht emanated from the kitchen.

Dasha was waiting for us on the patio. She was radiant, elegantly dressed, with short hair, little makeup, and no heels. Although like Iryna she was in her midfifties, she definitely looked younger. Dasha was proud to show off her wealth; Iryna was equally happy to constantly remind her about the origins of it. The gross humor, the constant bickering, and the blatantly invidious comparisons: that was precisely what I had grown to appreciate and enjoy as a token of friendship. I felt at home.

A bottle of wine later, I asked when the other guests would arrive. Dasha smiled and replied that the "Ukrainians, as usual," would be late. Iryna did not laugh.

Other women arrived. One of them quickly noticed that there was no vodka available. Dasha replied that Gianfranco did not like it. As some of his friends were among the best winemakers in the region, she explained, she was giving the women a chance to try out some of the very best Italian wines. It was at that moment that I started feeling some creeping uneasiness. I suddenly felt that the party was not something that would have happened without my pressure.

I asked what the women were planning to do during the summer. Dasha was proud to state that they would go to an Italian resort on a Mediterranean island, where they would be able to relax. When you go back to your hometown, she said, there is no rest. "Everybody wants to drink with you. Nobody minds his business." Some other women said they were planning to spend a few days in a working-class holiday destination on the Adriatic coast. In recent years, they had found it increasingly difficult to persuade their adolescent sons and daughters to travel back to Ukraine or Moldova. The kids would complain that "nothing ever happens there."

Iryna, who planned to spend her holidays in the house she had slowly built in her Ukrainian hometown, decided it was time to draw a clear line against all the others. She said the kids needed to go back as much as possible, to practice their language and to stay with their own. She declared proudly that Lena, her daughter, had always spent all her holidays with her grandmother. To prove the effectiveness of her educational strategy, she claimed Lena's boyfriend was Ukrainian, not Italian. Another woman immediately retorted: "Good luck! You will be happy the first time he gets drunk and beats her!" Other women nodded and laughed. Iryna, who was one of the very few women in the group who had an Eastern European partner, felt isolated and on the verge of defeat. She suddenly shifted registers, trying to recast her trips home as a patriotic duty. Pointing a finger at Dasha and the other women, she said they would be sunbathing among Italians while the Russians occupied their homeland. "You have already forgotten Maidan," she said despairingly.[1]

A few minutes later, I entered the kitchen precisely as Iryna was accusing Dasha of living as a "signora," having married "an idiot who despises us all." Dasha retorted that Gianfranco had not been an idiot when he had hired "that drunkard." She was opening an old wound that had laid dormant for a long time. Some years before, Iryna had asked for Dasha's help in finding a job for Andriy, a newly arrived cousin who could not find a job and was unable to repay his many debts.

Iryna started shouting that she had no reason to be grateful to Gianfranco. "Should I thank him for treating Andriy like an African? For giving him a hard job, paying him as a Moroccan?" I was accustomed to the deep ambivalence the women felt toward *signore*, those immigrant women who had attained, usually through marriage, what they considered a middle-class status. It was the first time, however, in which the difference between the "women" and the *signore* had been presented as so wide as to be unredeemable.

The bell rang and another batch of women arrived. Dasha rushed to open the gate, and Iryna whispered it was time to return to the garden to the "old Italian prick." In a swift change of temperament, she had gone back to the usual teasing mood. Speaking in a low voice, she said that Dasha, at least, "has a nice house now . . . she does not need to wash old asses anymore. Only the ass of her old husband!" I laughed and hoped for the best.

The arrival of the other women improved the climate considerably. We had some more drinks, we started eating, and we exchanged further rounds of salacious jokes. I could not help feeling we had matured together. I had met the women when most of them were in their thirties and a few in their forties. Nearly all of them were now in their fifties, and a few of them were in their sixties.

Suddenly, Maria asked Sofia if she had thought about her proposal to buy a flat that Sofia owned in their hometown. Maria's daughter lived in an adjacent unit, was pregnant with her second child, and had sought to expand her living space by buying Sofia's unit. Sofia lived in Alpinetown; no one occupied the flat.

In Alpinetown, Maria and Sofia had been practicing very different lifestyles. Maria had been among the most involved in the life of a local Romanian Orthodox Church. She defined herself above all as a mother.

She was a critic of women of "loose morals." Sofia was single and largely uninterested in religion or family ideology. Still, they had always been very close and had helped each other on many occasions.

But Sofia thought that she could surely gain more from selling it later. Maria was furious. "Sofia does not even have children," Maria moralized, as if this fact disqualified her from wishing to keep her flat.

Iryna supported Sofia. After all, she had also earned it with her many years of work as a *lavaculi*. Others rushed to Sofia's defense. They had emigrated to Italy, worked in demeaning jobs, and supported their parents and children. "The flat is hers, and she can let it rot if she wants," one woman said defiantly. I could see the widening gulf between those women who still thought of themselves only as sacrificing mothers and those who now thought of themselves in a different way.

Dasha sided with Maria and delivered a final blow by saying that Sofia did not need money because "all she needs is at the bus station!" She was referring to the waiting room of the bus station in Alpinetown, where we had congregated during the many years in which the women had no other place to meet and where many casual affairs had sometimes been consummated. As everybody understood perfectly, Dasha was accusing Sofia of having remained the same person as in the most destitute days, to have failed—maybe not even to have really tried—to gain a new, respectable self. It was the last time all of these women would have a party together.

I had thought my presence in town would have made everything as I remembered in the beginning, when we met for the first time and became friends. I suddenly realized that I could well be the only person who remembered those years fondly. I had always known that my initial fieldnotes contained a detailed chronicle of the very formation of the group. I had recorded how the group had slowly emerged out of random encounters in the streets among women who had recently migrated alone and independently to the town. Now, I realized that my last years of fieldnotes also contained a chronicle of its dissolution.

When we arrived back at my place I invited Iryna to come in. We sat at the table and opened a bottle of vodka, and I told her how badly I felt about what had happened. After a while, Iryna gave me the usual look she reserved for what she regarded as my naïveté. "Martushka, as usual you do not understand anything. We are not the same people anymore. We have just become different people now. We have learned to think in a different way."

# Introduction

This book chronicles the transformations in the individual and collective lives of women who migrated from the territories of the former Soviet Union to work as care workers in a northeastern Italian city I call Alpinetown.[1] When I met them, just weeks or months after their arrival, their lives were remarkably similar. They all regarded themselves as survivors, their previous middle-class lifestyle shattered repeatedly into pieces by the various waves of destruction brought about by what Vladimir Putin famously defined "the greatest geopolitical catastrophe of the century," the breakdown of the Soviet Union.[2]

They were all "pioneers," having migrated alone, without relying on any established network of already settled relatives or kinsfolk, to an area with no previous history of immigration from their lands. They were all unsponsored, having arrived without any formalized recruitment program. All were irregular migrants, or bound to become so as soon as their ninety-day tourist visas expired. Their presence was still largely unrecognized, and most natives, including their employers, had only rudimentary ideas about who they were.

They had all found jobs in the lowest segment of the local market for household services: they were *badanti*, live-in care workers, entrusted with around-the-clock care of elderly people. They all had debts to repay and remittances to send, out of their meager salaries, to their parents and offspring. They spent the few hours they did not work nearly always banded together, in a new urban environment they felt was unknown and, not infrequently, hostile. Above all, they were all women.

For more than a decade, I had the chance to observe and participate regularly in the processes that made them a stable presence in the urban environment and gradually differentiated them into several cliques, supporting different social identities and often divided by strong moral cleavages.

My focus is on how small, everyday interactions slowly forced each of them to fashion new selves, new ways of feeling, thinking, and acting about who they were, what they should be, and what would, in the new circumstances, make them worthwhile people.

Dealing with new challenges opened up by emigration, the women learned—sometimes in a picaresque manner, often in conditions of considerable duress—to define their relationships (with emigrants and natives alike) in new ways, to establish new criteria for allocating—or claiming—status and honor and to draw new moral distinctions between them and others. In short, they created a set of new social worlds, where they can uphold a positive view of themselves and repair, or at least try to repair, the damage emigration so frequently imposes on themselves and their social relationships.

## Migration as Lived Experience

Over the last decades, we have acquired a considerable amount of information on international migration. Information technologies have greatly enhanced the capacity of economically developed states to monitor their populations and collect data on those who cross their borders. A variety of international bodies have struggled to standardize, thus making comparable, these data. Both in Europe and in the United States, many carefully designed, large-scale surveys have provided a wealth of important information. Today we have detailed knowledge of the main demographic and socioeconomic features of many immigrant populations, and we are able to employ sophisticated statistical models to explain how these affect their decisions to leave or to stay, the type of movement they pursue, and their prospects for social and economic mobility. A growing number of studies provide us with a picture of the activities that migrants undertake in their places of origin, the strength of their personal connections with relatives and friends left behind, and the ethnic affiliations they claim or despise.

Our knowledge, however, is largely focused on identifying the many individual characteristics of migrants that, prior to or during emigration, make more (or less) likely their successful participation in the new context of reception.[3]

We tend to see geographical mobility as a "matching process" of sorts, where ready-made individuals, already endowed with certain preferences, skills, and resources, struggle to locate themselves in the ready-made slots available in the social structure of the receiving context. We know little about how these struggles change their very way of perceiving themselves. We have only a rudimentary understanding of how migrating individuals "make sense" of the meaning of their new experiences and of their struggles to create out of these experiences a new image and enactment of self.[4]

Migrants have often remarkably different biographies, one from the other, prior to emigration. They clearly move with different ex ante resource endowments, skills, competencies, and aspirations, vis-à-vis the new context and other migrants. Still, these endowments are not the only explanation for their subsequent migration trajectories. Migration does not simply transport people. It also changes them.

Migration should *also* be seen as an experiential process, a complex set of interactional encounters through which emigrants construct a new meaningful social world out of the new conditions. Emigration triggers the restructuring of the lives of emigrants and of their families, as well as of the symbolic frames they employ to make sense of these changes. Dealing with employers, finding places they may call home, learning how to locate themselves in new worlds of consumption, encountering new kinds of lovers and friends, attending new churches, and fighting to maintain a foothold in their original towns and villages, migrants do not only "adapt," "adjust," or "integrate." They also, and maybe above all, enter new terrains of experience where they must work out who they are and who they are to each other, what they can expect, and what others can expect from them.

It is not only a matter of knowledge or information. It is a matter of a sensual, bodily encounter with a different universe of objects, people, relationships, and ideas. The outcome of these experiences, and the ways in which migrants understand them, also shapes their subsequent trajectories. Previously similar individuals may end up living within different worlds of consuetudinary practices and conceive of themselves according to very different conceptions of personal worth.

Migration changes migrants, but not necessarily along similar lines. A multitude of everyday decisions, each of them understood as merely practical, imperceptibly sort migrants along different tracks, their lives increasingly defined by different priorities, social networks, and self-perceptions. Some of these decisions, such as attempting to leave live-in domestic service for hourly-paid work, may be excruciatingly difficult to make and be pondered for a long time. Some, such as becoming a regular in the town's open market instead of staying within communitarian outlets, are hardly ever matters of explicit deliberation or discussion. They just happen. Some others—such as "getting papers" through amnesty or meeting a suitable partner—are events largely beyond the control of migrants. Each of these events transforms, over time and in unforeseen ways, both their social world and the ways in which they can make sense of it. Small and inconsequential in the beginning, these interactional changes are the breeding ground for different ways of understanding one's life, embedded in different networks, grounded in different lifestyles, and policed by different notions of decency and moral worth.

## Pioneers and Followers

The experiences of unsponsored pioneers, the first wave of migrants moving to a new location, represent strategic research materials for the study of migration as a transformative experience.[5] The processes through which the very first wave of migrants learn how to fashion new identities—T. S. Eliot's "new faces to meet the faces they meet"—make observable a set of processes that, although endemic in all migration experiences, operate in a less visible way in subsequent waves.[6]

The key assumption of any sociology of migration is that mobility is not a set of independent individual choices and actions but an iterative process, where each movement alters the social context within which subsequent movements take place. The previous emigration of relatives and friends—and sometimes merely acquaintances—triggers emulation and reduces the costs and risks of migration, thereby modifying the conditions for future migrants.[7] In the beginning, there are the pioneers, a scattered group of individuals who end up in a largely unknown, far-away land without the information and support of earlier immigrants. They are the ones who explore the new setting, learn how to survive in the new environment, identify opportunities, and gain a foothold in the new location.

When and if their travel acquires a certain stability and control, their very same existence may trigger the movement of a wider range of early followers, who rely on their presence to lower the costs and risks of their own migration. Through personal contact with pioneers, these early successors move to the same locations and gradually expand the presence of the group in one or more occupational niches.[8] If successful, their presence increases the number of migrants and contributes to solidifying a wider set of social networks and a stronger migration infrastructure. This expanding presence lowers the costs and risks associated to further mobility, triggering subsequent waves of arrivals. These late followers migrate along a well-known path, moving to a location where they can anticipate the presence of a significant number of people they personally know.

Pioneers and early followers set many key parameters for subsequent migration.[9] It is through them that information circulates and news of job opportunities spreads. They often work as models, living proof that migration is desirable and, indeed, feasible. They often channel, through information and recommendation, new arrivals into the occupational niches in which they are already active. They provide help with housing, economic assistance, and inclusion in new sociability networks, thus making further migration more or less likely.[10]

Given the importance of pioneers, it is surprising that we do not know much about their migration experience or the ways in which it is different from the experiences of later arrivals. Available accounts tend to draw on (mostly theoretical) psychological distinctions, seeing pioneers as adventurous risk-takers, while defining followers as more passive and risk-averse. The existing profiles are shaped by a heavily rationalistic emphasis, portraying pioneers as having less to lose, in comparison to followers, from a failed trip and more to gain from a successful one.[11] The few attempts to empirically ascertain their socioeconomic profile have produced meager results. Pioneers are said to be usually male, younger, more educated, and less bounded by familial duties than followers. While convincing in certain cases, this portrait is often contradicted by many large-scale migration flows: in the case of this book, for example, the pioneers are women, middle-aged, and bound by strong responsibilities to their children and parents. We know little about the ways in which pioneers, migration's absolute beginners, experience the new environment and the contingencies through which they shape—and are, in turn, shaped by—their new emigration world. We know little about how pioneers find a footing in the new location and how their experiences solidify in taken-for-granted options by those who follow them.[12]

The main difference between pioneers and followers is that the latter enter a field that is, to various degrees, already crowded by the former. They arrive in places where the presence of people "like them" is already publicly recognized, where there are available exemplars of what may happen to them, and where they may rely upon, or avoid, groups that have already developed a minimal infrastructure to promote their definition of the good life and have available a modicum of resources to police deviance.

Much of the literature on migrant networks has a strong instrumental bias. It has emphasized nearly exclusively the various material resources through which previous immigrants support, constrain, or exploit newcomers.[13] Researchers tend to see networks as mechanisms through which the presence of earlier immigrants lowers the economic costs and social barriers to further settlement. Aside from some lip service, the social psychological dimension of social networks seldom receives its due. The material resources channeled through immigrant networks are, however, only one side of the coin.[14] It is equally important that the presence of already settled migrants and the functioning of the informal institutions they have created play a key role in alleviating and making manageable the traumas and shocks associated with geographical mobility.

For women leaving the ex–Soviet Union, migration has often been a profoundly transformative event, a trauma, a break in the perceived continuity between previous experience and current intentionality. It nearly always involves moments in which experiences challenge a person's basic understanding and image of oneself in ways perceived by one who experiences it as beyond her control. Such trauma is seldom a "lay trauma," a set of events inherently and automatically traumatic to the individuals who experience them. It is rather a "cultural trauma": a socially shared interpretation of events that narrates their impact as marking a group memory forever and changing its future identity in fundamental and irrevocable ways.[15] The severity and meaning of trauma is contingent upon the narrative available to migrants to make sense of what they experience and by the circles of recognition—the social interactions and relationships—that guide, sanction, validate, or contest one's standing within each particular narrative. This makes the study of pioneers crucial for any understanding of migration as lived experience: pioneers shape the narratives and the social worlds that subsequent followers will encounter as practical options.

Pioneers must learn, often by trial and error, the local distinctions between approved and improper acts. Followers arrive in a social world that appears much more ordered. They encounter from the beginning what was once the unsteady outcome of a much more serendipitous process. They are, to varying degrees, sheltered from the direct impact of the acculturation shock, thanks to the very existence of previous immigrants.[16]

Cognitively, newcomers encounter the varying terrain of experiences embodied in different cliques of earlier arrivals as potentially distinguished, and perceived-as-natural, recipes. They have access to a vocabulary of motives and a whole nomenclature of possible identities. They have templates to follow (or to challenge), exemplars to use as benchmarks, boundaries to maintain, and outcomes to fear. To be sure, followers experience the ambivalences and strains arising from competing interpretations of their mobility, from a more detailed distinction between "us" and "them," among various groups of immigrants and "natives." They are, however, somewhat protected by the most radical challenge to their own meaningful presence in the world.

I encountered the most vivid example of the differences between pioneers and followers the day I visited Nastya, one of the very first women who had arrived in Alpinetown. A few weeks before my visit, a younger cousin, Olysa, had arrived to work for one of Nastya's previous employers. I had promised Nastya that I would bring Olysa out for a stroll, to show her around. Olysa was late, and Nastya, a very down-to-earth, severe woman, who hardly ever spoke about herself, offered me a coffee while we waited for her to arrive.

We had been meeting regularly at all kinds of social occasions, without ever speaking of anything remotely intimate. The arrival of Olysa had triggered something, because Nastya suddenly started reminiscing about her first days in town. I remembered that her initial living and working conditions, as for many of the very first pioneers, had been particularly awful. She had arrived in Alpinetown with a huge debt, and the only work she had been able to find had been with an old couple living in a very small flat. She had to sleep in the very same bedroom, in cramped conditions. She was poorly paid, and the woman she was caring for had occasional bouts of dementia during which she could become violent.

I remembered we had celebrated together when, after having lived in these conditions for more than a year, she had been able eventually to find another family to work for. I was consequently surprised that her reminiscences hardly mentioned her material tribulations. These were somewhat taken for granted. What triggered her emotionally was recollecting how in those days she had felt, in her own words, "horribly naked."[17] She had felt "skinless," as, almost literally, everything she encountered in the new environment seemed to have the power to penetrate her. She mentioned that she was constantly tired, as every single sensation she experienced was extraordinarily powerful, overwhelmingly so. She said that the occasional gaze of an unknown passerby could leave a sensation that would last for hours. She felt constantly clumsy, even the most mundane operations being fraught with unknown dangers. She had once panicked in front of a billboard, exposing an ad with a vaguely Eastern European theme, as she thought it contained a message directly targeted to her. "I was out of place anywhere, even at night in my bed, close to mama and papa."[18] She felt void of any protection. She remembered being constantly ashamed of herself, without being able to know what she had done to feel ashamed.[19] She would wake up fearing she would not be able to "recognize myself anymore."

While speaking slowly and softly about those days, Nastya was busy making coffee in her spotless kitchenette, where every single item had its place according to an ironclad logic. Many years had passed, and Nastya had been one of the most successful of the women, both economically and socially. She had a steady job in a decent household, where the pay was good and everybody treated her nicely. Her Italian husband was taking a nap on the sofa in the adjacent living room. Her daughter had joined her a year before, after having passed the entrance exams for the local college. Still, I could feel the shadows emanating from the memory of those early years and the powerful pressure it still exercised on her. The atmosphere had become tense, Nastya was on the verge of crying, and I felt we were both relieved when the bell rang and Olysa eventually arrived, putting an effective end to Nastya's reminiscing.

While strolling in the cold fall weather with Olysa, whom I had never met before, I did my best to engage in small talk. I asked her how her first days in Alpinetown had been. She felt stressed and tired, and she had no problem with telling me she felt lonely. It was hard for her to be far away from her children and to spend most of the day in the flat of a family she barely knew. She felt destitute, and she complained about rude people. She also complained, however, that she had no time for herself because she was too busy.

Still under the spell of Nastya's tale, it took me some time to realize she was not talking about how devastating around-the-clock care work could be. She was actually complaining about the fact that her minimal free time was eaten up by a demanding set of social obligations. She said many women had invited her, to explain to her how life was in Alpinetown. She appreciated their caring for her, but as she smiled, she pointed out she had already known many of these things from the conversations she had already had with many women during their holiday returns.

I quickly realized that in trying to describe and make sense of her recent experiences, she was able to draw on a rich set of comparisons, which contributed to make her new experiences manageable. She considered herself lucky, as the family she was working for was less demanding than the ones Nastya and Valentina had worked for when they had arrived. She acknowledged that her salary was lower than Iryna's, but still higher than Iryna's first job. She hoped her children were getting along as well with her mother, to whom she had entrusted them, as those of Maria, who were of the same age. She feared they could end up like the children of Yaneta, who had grown up "wild." She wondered if she was too old to go to a certain disco where many Moldovan women had recently started to go, as Oksana had told her. Maybe she was too young and in need of fun to spend her Sundays only engaged in church activities, as Inna had advised her. She planned to send her mother 250 euros a month, an amount she judged as slightly higher than the amount other recently arrived women sent. She described herself as baffled, pressured by her lack of understanding of many things. She was not, however, radically lost or clueless. In everything she said, it was clear she was embedded in a wide circle of recognition that she could use as a reference to orient herself and determine what was right to do.

I decided to dare to ask her what she wanted to do in Alpinetown. At the very beginning of my fieldwork, I had learned never to ask this question. The pioneer women would stare at me puzzled; the politest of them would just reply, "Who knows?" Most times, they would accuse me of being utterly silly and insulting. They were *rab* (slaves) or *lavaculi* (ass washers), people not entitled to have plans or choose a future for themselves.[20] Olysa, on the contrary, found my question plain and reasonable.

She said she needed seven or eight months to repay her debts. Reaching a working level of proficiency in Italian would have taken at least a year. Once she had repaid her debts, she wanted to rent a bed in a shared flat, so that she could have a bit of a private life. In three years, she would have to decide whether to ask the children to join her or to have them stay put and sustain them from abroad. Things would look different if she could find a nice Italian husband in the meanwhile.

I suddenly realized that all the things that the women I had lived with had gone through, all the events they had encountered serendipitously and with great pain and shock, appeared to Olysa as neatly arranged in possible trajectories, as scenarios that had not to be created, but chosen and acted upon. Notwithstanding the difficulties she was experiencing at the moment, she could recognize her own potential future as one of a recognizable and socially shared set of types. Olysa felt her future was a choice among different scenarios, each defined by well-defined social markers: getting her papers, discharging the debts, renting a room in an independent flat, dating someone reliable, and applying for family reunification.

Like most of the women I knew, she was surely underestimating the time necessary to achieve any of these markers. Moreover, she likely overestimated the amount of control over her life she could achieve in emigration.[21] Still, the difference with Nastya could have not been more salient. Nastya had been overburdened with a completely open future, in which she felt that anything could happen. She also felt that she had to face such an unknown future alone. Olysa had migrated within a socially structured sense of migration time, her scenarios and markers widely shared with others she could easily benchmark.

The difference between Nastya's and Olysa's experiences may explain why so many researchers, focusing on well-established communities largely comprised of followers, end up neglecting the importance of migration as a transformative experience. The experience of pioneers, in fact, masks itself over time. Once the differentiation among their trajectories moves beyond a certain threshold, their new selves solidify retrospectively into a repertoire of taken-for-granted differences. The new selves are projected well into the past, and differences—as occurred at my wretched party—become heavily moralized, perceived as natural attributes of specific individuals and their cliques. The various groups justify their separation as a matter of having always had different standards, different priorities, different projects, and different dreams. The outcome modifies the path that has brought them there and negates all the other possible paths the very same women could have taken. What has become is now what was bound to be.

As most migration research relies on retrospective interviews, researchers often access accounts of reality where purpose plays a large, defining role and events are narrated teleologically. In this study, by contrast, I provide a natural history of the changes based on direct observation of what occurs during the process itself.

I have also been helped in this task by the chance of observing the same women over many years. Much research on migrant communities is inevitably based on relatively short spans of observation, thus turning a movie into a still photograph. The processes of transformation of the self, however, can be observed only over long periods. Not only do such changes usually mature slowly, but only extended observation can help disentangle the natural changes brought by the life course from the impacts of contingent experience and protracted practices.

What defines the experience of unsponsored pioneers is that they must build a new self, relying only to a minimal degree on established narratives and uncontested norms. Their attempts to perceive themselves (and present to others) as decent and worthy, to manage their stigma,

and to restore a modicum of social status represent experiments under-
taken from a liminal location where clinging to the old self is already self-
defeating and new templates for the self are not yet available. They must
build some tentative ways of interacting with others from scratch and try
them out. When I met them, the pioneers in this study were constantly
unsure about which aspects of their previous biography could still be
meaningful, what they should make public, and what they had to keep
hidden. They did not know which elements of their previous lives had to
be maintained, reinterpreted, or discarded. They often discovered, sometimes painfully, that what they held dearest could be a liability, while
features they regarded as trivial could become precious public resources.
Since the very beginning, they discovered that migration both forced and
made it possible for them to be different *women.*

## Women Pioneers

A striking feature of the group of migrant pioneers I studied is that all were
women. In the first wave of Eastern European migrants arriving in Alpinetown, there was not a single man. The size of the group grew quickly,
with new migrants arriving every week, virtually all women. After four or
five years, when the number of women had already reached several hundred, I counted no more than twenty-five men. Except for two, they had
arrived independently from the women and were frowned upon by them.
The story I tell is definitely a story of *women* migrant pioneers.

Today, nearly two decades after the very first arrivals, men are still a minority in Alpinetown, representing about one quarter of the local population sharing the same origin. They are, moreover, nearly always sons who
have joined their mothers or partners in couples of followers who have
migrated together, often through the help of the mother or the mother-
in-law. A few are new partners, met by the women during their holidays or
at various communitarian occasions. In all these years, even now that the
group consists of more than one thousand women, the number of preexisting husbands who have joined their wives in Alpinetown is negligible.

The group I spent time with is part of a much larger phenomenon,
usually labeled as the "feminization of migration." Scholars and international bodies have coined this label, at the turn of the twenty-first century,
to provide a (rather tardy) acknowledgment that there is nothing strange
about a migrant woman. Actually, approximately half of the world's migrants are women. Nor is the movement of women a structural novelty

of recent decades: they have been a significant part of migratory movements for many decades, the gender composition of many immigrant populations having shifted toward higher percentages of women for much of the last century.[22] In 1960, women accounted for 47 out of every 100 migrants living outside of their countries of birth and around half of the migrants directed at economically developed societies.[23] The current emphasis on migrant women is not a matter of shifting numbers. It is above all a change in the way we frame them.[24]

The classical view of migration defined pioneers and early adopters exclusively as young males. The Chinese railroad worker, the Western European *Gastarbaiter*, and the Mexican bracero worker have become exemplars of the "normal" migration pattern. Other historic forms of migration, such as the Irish and German migration to the United States, where women played a much larger and independent role, have been considered anomalous and marginalized.[25]

An entire narrative has evolved on these bases: men initiate migration and settlement; women follow, after having passively waited for the return of their men or even actively resisted moving. Men were considered heroic innovators, women conservative elements.

The seminal text in the sociology of migration, Thomas and Znaniecki's *The Polish Peasant in Europe and America*, published between 1918 and 1920, codifies in detail this gendered vision of the distinction between pioneers and followers. Thomas and Znaniecki, outspoken members of the progressive elite, had no doubts in defining male migrants as active and women as passive; they treated the migration of the former as voluntary, and that of the latter as forced by the decisions of their husbands. In their view, moreover, women did not only resist migration. They assumed that when women arrived in the new location, following along the tracks already established by husbands or parents, they would bring with them a more traditional interpretation of the "backward" customs of the sending area. Either they would become the inertial force slowing down the assimilation of their husbands and children, or they would suffer a far heavier toll of psychological strain and social disorganization.[26]

The vision of the "immobile woman" was so powerful that it was still presented as obvious in the main theoretical summaries of migration processes in the 1960s.[27] The standard expression "migrant workers and their families"—endemically used in the policy papers of international bodies—carried well into the 1980s an unequivocal meaning: it referred to male workers and to the women and children that followed them.[28] It is only in the last few decades that a large wave of new research has challenged the vision of women as passive followers.[29]

There are obviously cases in which the male-pioneer model is consistent with empirical evidence. For example, in many phases of the Mexican migration to the United States, a large proportion of women have traditionally migrated following their husbands or parents, in a journey that often involves crossing boundaries not only between countries, but also between rural and urban life and between unwaged and waged labor.[30] Even in these cases, it is hard to describe the women involved as recalcitrant and passive.[31] The male-pioneer model, however, is far from being a model of the "natural" order of migration.

In fact, there are numerous migratory systems in which many of the migrants are women, moving independently from their fathers or husbands.[32] Flows largely comprising women are documented in a variety of migration corridors: from the Dominican Republic, the Philippines, and India to the United States and Western Europe; from Eastern Europe to Western Europe and the Mediterranean rim; and from South and Southeast Asia to the Gulf countries and the newly industrialized countries of Southeast Asia.[33]

Flows of women pioneers may trigger the subsequent arrival of male relatives, whose trajectories are at least partially shaped by the conditions created by the settlement of the women.[34] In other cases, the arrival of women pioneers establishes conditions for the development of migration chains that positively select other women.[35] In both cases, women pioneers do not migrate toward already well-established communities, in locations defined by dense networks of coethnics. There is little chance they may play a conservative, inertial role. They will not mimic the "cake of custom" prevailing in the sending area, as Robert Park would have expected.[36]

On the contrary, as I document in this book, women pioneers must struggle to establish a seminal infrastructure and a shared language to give form to their own experiences. Doing so requires an explicit difference from, and sometimes an outright hostility toward, the role of women and the rules about presentation of the self that have defined their previous lives. Even when they enact homeland-related performances in the new setting, the same symbols cover very different meanings.[37]

## Women Migrants, Women Pioneers, and the Shifting Boundaries of Gender

The current research on women migrants has not yet paid adequate attention to the ways in which the changes in the gender order triggered by migration vary according to the role played by women in the migration process. Busy with debunking the myth of the passive woman, researchers have often conflated pioneers and followers in a single category of "women migrants," thus making latent how the experience of migrant women located at different points of the sequence must reckon with different sources of strains, challenges, and opportunities.

Feminist scholars are correct in stressing that—even in male-initiated movements—the pressures deriving from the incorporation of migrants (and migrant households) into new conditions of production and reproduction trigger changes in the relationships between men and women.[38] Their work has documented how emigration *potentially* empowers women, thus altering the "traditional" gender balance within their families and communities. During emigration, many emigrant women experience— through the combined effect of urbanization, wage labor, and access to a social service infrastructure—a stronger influence in household decision-making.[39] The experience of emigration may also play a significant role in favoring the adoption of more egalitarian gender and marriage norms not only in emigrating communities but in the places of origin as well.[40]

The direction of change, however, is often murky. Potential empowerment does not necessarily translate into greater personal satisfaction, as the possibilities of greater egalitarian intimacy are often squeezed by the working and living conditions of immigrant households.[41] In other cases, male partners may resent the increased autonomy of their women, particularly if they become the main breadwinners. Women may thus have to compensate for their increased autonomy outside the household with a stricter and more emphatic affirmation of traditional roles within the household and in their public presentation within the community.[42]

This ambivalence operates also in migration systems in which the gendered sequence of settlement is starkly different.[43] This is precisely the case in the many migratory systems where women come first, acting as pioneers or providing auspices for subsequent arrivals. In recent decades, several studies have brought an increasing awareness of the numerical and structural significance of these types of flows, in the academic literature as well as in a number of policy debates. Many accounts have nonetheless mirrored the classical narrative of male-triggered migration, only inverting the sequence of the movements of family members. They have described women pioneers as triggering subsequent movements of male migrants, according to a reversed logic of family reunification. Therefore, scholars' appreciation of women pioneers has not challenged enough the assumption that migration unleashes gender changes altering the power balances within ethnically homogeneous households.

As for the case of male pioneers, there are surely cases in which this assumption is more than appropriate. Some flows of women pioneers do indeed activate family reunification, producing gender-balanced communities over the long term. In such communities, there are cases in which husband-followers regain their status as primary breadwinners, compensated for their late arrival by wider access to job opportunities open to them in highly gendered labor markets.[44] In contrast, there are cases in which husbands find themselves much more dependent on their wives, who have migratory seniority and much better knowledge of the new environment.[45]

My point is that, exactly as with male pioneers, family reunification and ethnic community formation are not automatic outcomes. To a degree still underappreciated, women pioneers do not necessarily trigger the subsequent arrival of male followers.[46] In fact, when and if they sponsor new arrivals, women pioneers often sponsor the arrival of other women, before—or even instead of—the arrival of male partners.[47] Two important elements contribute to the development of migration systems in which women pioneers are (largely) followed by women followers. First, as Katharine Donato has convincingly shown, marital status is an often-neglected variable that plays a powerful role in explaining women's propensity to migrate as well as to be active in the labor market during emigration.[48] There is no reason to assume that women pioneers will be "normally" married women or single women with homogamic preferences. Actually, one of the reasons for the contemporary mobility of women is precisely the growing pool of women who choose migration as a way of dealing with the consequences of single-parent motherhood, an unsatisfactory union, or a failed marriage.[49]

Moreover, as it is for the women discussed in this book, women pioneers may subscribe to a variety of cultural norms discouraging the selection of male compatriots as worthwhile candidates for migration. As already seen in the account of my ill-fated party, many of the women I lived with had an explicit exogamous preference. Those of them, like Iryna, who dated compatriots were often classified at the bottom of the mating stratification.[50]

A second important factor is the expanding global labor market for household services, care work, and low-paid service work. As this market is highly gendered, most of the opportunities women pioneers may hoard for subsequent migrants are de facto reserved for other women.[51] Women pioneers may consequently open the way to women followers.

## On Why Care Work is Different from Manufacturing and Construction

The specific features of the expanding global labor market for household services, care work, and low-paid service work have important impact on the experiences of migrant women, sharply differentiating them from those of the "classical" male pioneers of the past. The perceptive strength of the classical framework, built around the implicit image of the male foreign worker employed in manufacturing and construction, has made latent the peculiarities of the migration experiences of women pioneers employed in household services. The classical framework describes the initial social life of immigrants as marked above all by segregation and lack of interpersonal contacts with natives. The ethnic slum, the assembly line, the construction site, the crowded barrack, and the factory hostel are all spaces where segregation is high and contact with natives is limited.[52]

Unsurprisingly, the classical theory of assimilation has located migrants' "normal" sociability as intragroup, oriented to the "old world transplanted," and has tried to identify the conditions for triggering personal relationships across ethnic boundaries. It has described settlement as a process that slowly shifts the interaction from group-mediated to that of a more individualized kind.[53]

In the case of immigrant care workers, the situation is just the opposite. They work, often indeed live, in strict contact with their individual employers, while spatially and temporally isolated from other immigrant workers of similar origins.[54] Because care work is above all bodywork, migrant women are constantly exposed to close, physical, intimate experiences with natives.[55] No matter how sophisticated their (and their employers') attempts to keep between them a degree of social distance, they spend a significant amount of the daytime hours, and sometimes whole nights as well, in an environment defined by the presence of individuals that perceive the same space as intimate and personal. They have plenty of chances to observe each other and often they cannot help doing so, no matter how much they try to avoid it.

Such a process of mutual observation is pressing on both sides. In care work, no job description can offer guidance, and the boundaries between worker and person are inevitably blurred.[56] Employers worry about the quality of the work, but they are even more concerned about the moral character of the worker. Conversely, workers are worried about living in an unknown household and receiving pay for their work, and they fear their employers will fail to deliver the required papers when the time for amnesty arrives. It is a dense cluster of personal interactions, and workers must manage them without relying on the presence of other migrants in the workplace.

In the case of the Eastern European women I spent time with, the interactional complexities of domestic work were further escalated by two additional conditions. Firstly, the women had usually no previous experience of domestic work, particularly in its live-in form. They had to learn quickly how to manipulate appearances in ways that reassured prospective employers about both their skills and their general moral trustworthiness. As they catered to the least desired segment of the market—the elderly from working- and lower middle-class backgrounds—their employers were also often undergoing their first experience with salaried help, uncertain as to what they could expect from the women. This perilous navigation had to be accomplished alone, in a job situation where there is no backstage to relax and no alternative audience to validate an "authentic" self as distinguished from the one shown to employers.

In short, the women had plenty of contact with natives, while struggling to keep some form of differentiated social identity and circle of recognition.[57] Not by chance, the women were literally scared of their occupation becoming their only identity. They placed great emphasis on claiming they were "not *sidelki* but women who worked as *sidelki*."

The women, even in the very early stages of their migratory careers, were quite interested in feeling recognized as morally worthy. As I detail in the next chapter, they strongly resisted arrangements and stereotypes they felt were degrading. Even under conditions of considerable duress, they struggled to be recognized—by the other women, by the natives, by their relatives and acquaintances back home—as deserving respect.

Since the very beginning, a whole roster of dignity claims was part of the social life of the group. They reacted to the negative narratives about their emigration widespread in their homelands, claiming they deserved to be considered good mothers sacrificing themselves for the sake of their children. They expected, most of the time unsuccessfully, that their employers would recognize not only their hard work but also their generous labor of love in taking care of their frail parents. They wanted to appear in the public space not as destitute immigrants but as former middle-class professionals, cultured and with refined manners, hit by a hard fate.

Finally, and importantly, they wanted to be considered decent women, sharply differentiating themselves from both Italian women—whom they regarded as manly and androgynous—and from the public image of the "Slav" as a promiscuous, immoral gold digger.[58] Since the very beginning of their migratory careers, they struggled to find a moral order that could make sense in their conditions, a ground upon which to assert, to themselves and to others, the intrinsic dignity of their selves. For the women, building a network of friends, exploring the consumption opportunities available in the new environment, learning the proper ways of dating potential partners, and building their own "ethnic" infrastructure were all difficult tasks that required a form of experimentation radically different from the everyday practices documented by the classical framework.

If any migration involves a process of social disorganization (and reorganization), they experienced it in a highly individualized way. As in the experience of Nastya recounted earlier, the women experienced a pressing need to learn how to shape—with a significant dose of trial and error—a new face, a new positive self-image that they could hold when interacting with others in the new environment.[59]

It is plainly impossible to understand their process of settlement within the template developed to make sense of male-centered migrations to Fordist economies. It took me quite a while to understand the importance of attitudes and habits in emigration processes and to take seriously their key concern with issues of recognition and respect. It took even more time to conceive of my own work as a plea to see migration also as an experiential process of personal transformation.

## Women Pioneers from Eastern Europe

The women who attended my ill-fated party, as well as all the other events described in this book, have a common pre-emigration history worth narrating. How had such a large number of middle-aged women— nearly all of them mothers, many of them grandmothers—left their countries, outside of any recruitment program? How had they migrated to an unknown city, where no relative or friend was waiting for them? How had they arrived in Alpinetown, more or less during the same years in which hundreds of thousands of other women from the same regions were migrating all over Europe, from Cape Finisterre to Istanbul, from Oslo to Palermo?[60]

As evident in most of our jokes, small talk, and big debates, the key biographical fact is that all of them had been born and raised in the Soviet Union, a reality that, at the time of their youth, they took for granted. Even if difficult to remember today, the Soviet Union was the world's largest state, covering a sixth of Earth's land surface, comparable in size to the whole of North America. It spanned across eleven time

1   The women's origin areas

zones, where 293 million inhabitants, routinely classified in more than a hundred "ethnic" groups, lived, more or less easily, together.

For seven decades, from 1917 to 1991, Eastern European populations lived through one of the most radical projects of social engineering in human history, one that—with various intensities and degrees of repression—was meant to implement at the same time a planned economy, a detraditionalized society, and an imperial project. It is consequently not surprising that a quarter century after its demise, the Soviet Union is still very much alive in the biographies of the women, providing a common stock of experiences and tacit knowledge that links together middle-aged women who now hold different passports.

More precisely, almost all of the women I studied had grown up along the western fringe of the Soviet Union, in the territories that had often been contested in modern and contemporary history by a variety of European powers, from the Polish-Lithuanian Commonwealth to the Ottomans, from the Hapsburgs to the Romanovs. Nearly all of them now have the passports of the Soviet successor states of Moldova, Russia, and Ukraine.[61] All of them, even the most nationalist, are fluent in Russian, which functioned many times as our common language.

A majority of the women emigrating to Alpinetown had lived most of their previous lives in territories that are part of what Timothy Snyder has called "the Bloodlands"—the area between Berlin and Moscow where, from the 1920s to the 1950s, the European totalitarian powers had done their best in unleashing the worst horrors in recent European history.[62] This period has left traces in their family memory, many of them having had relatives who perished during the war, disappeared for years (or forever) in the gulags, or were killed by starvation and famine.

At the same time, nearly all of the women were born in the late 1950s or later (some during the late Khrushchev and most during the early Brezhnev era), when the Soviet regime had lost much of its ferocity and had accustomed itself to a slow decline. They grew up in a period where the regime was sending different, often contrasting, messages. It was an economy of scarcity, where even the supply of basic goods often appeared unpredictable. Concurrently, the Brezhnev regime increasingly adopted the promise of a rising living standard as an instrument of legitimacy and a symbol of modernization. One of the main consequences of such ideological transformation was that the regime now largely tolerated, if not encouraged, the adoption of an active search for a better life on an individual and family basis.[63]

Nearly all the women pioneers grew up in families belonging to the new Soviet middle class, composed of skilled and semiskilled professionals who—even if they could not enjoy the privileges of the ruling *nomenklatura*—could still expect a lifestyle marked, as many women keenly remembered, by "an independent flat, a car, some shopping, and some days of summer vacation." Commerce and services, once considered politically suspicious, were by then respected trades, sought after both for privileged access to scarce goods and for serving as a symbol of modernity. Many of the women already practiced in their youth some commercial activities, as employees of the state-run enterprises or as informal traders in the burgeoning black market (and sometimes both).[64] The Khrushchev and Brezhnev eras also introduced significant changes in the Soviet Union's gender regime. The USSR had always emphasized the importance of the full participation of women in society, defined mostly in terms of their active participation in the labor force. It also had a long-standing interest in the public education of children, but it had been more ambiguous in its vision of family life. Early Soviet family policy was modernist and emancipatory, championing a progressive family exclusively based on companionship and affection. Subsequently, from the 1920s to the early 1950s, it increasingly swung back to a traditional "Slavic" conception of the family as centered above all on motherhood. From the early 1960s, the pendulum swung again in a more liberal direction, maintaining both the emancipatory view of the woman as an equal worker and the traditionalist definition of the woman as, above all, a mother.[65]

Weaving together such views was not an easy task. In fact, the regime accepted a double register of public discourse. As explicit policy, it would prescribe and require complete equality between men and women (and a vision of the couple as a relationship between equally modern individuals). At the same time, it tolerated, when not actively sponsored, a large variety of concerns on the societal dangers of women's emancipation. The dangers of women's emancipation was one of the very few areas where social criticism of Soviet society was largely possible, practiced even in official newspapers.[66] Public discourse progressively absolved men of most responsibilities in the lives of their families. Women, as "natural" family leaders, were responsible for any of the shortcomings. In the tightly controlled Soviet press, women were routinely blamed for failing to discipline their husbands, to properly raise their children, and to provide a hygienic household and nutritious diet. Unsurprisingly, most of the women I encountered grew up with a double standard of epic proportions.

A related aspect of gender discourse in the Brezhnev era concerned the promotion of a vision of the Soviet woman worker/mother who depreciated her sexuality and physicality.[67] Fashion privileged grey colors, padded shoulders, and shapes that did not stress a woman's figure. The general tone of public discussion was prudish, and sexuality was treated exclusively as a health issue.[68] Starting in the early 1970s, the opposition between the modest and chaste Soviet woman and the careless Western one become an endemic trope of Soviet propaganda.

One of the first consequences of the breakdown of the Soviet Union was thus the backlash against whatever recalled the Soviet past. One of its forms was the adoption of hyperfeminine, doll-like images of womanhood, signifying a refusal both of peasant life and of Soviet oppression.[69] Many years later, a common complaint among the women who had emigrated was that their employers openly despised the flashy clothes and heavy makeup that they cherished as a sign of modernity and self-respect.[70]

When the Soviet Union collapsed, all the women were busy with their professional and family lives. The breakdown implied a sudden and dramatic change both in living standards and in the gender regime. The transition affected the condition of livelihood for large sectors of the population, but it also brought about a dramatic change in the definition of the situation. Ukraine, from 1992 to 1999, lost nearly half of its GDP, and Moldova more than a third.[71] The professional middle class, particularly those employed in education, health, and social services, took a hard hit. Savings disappeared owing to hyperinflation, salaries were crippled or even not paid at all, prices went up, and most of the luxuries of a middle-class Soviet lifestyle became suddenly unaffordable. The first years of the transition were so difficult that life expectancy rates showed a marked decrease.[72]

Given the severity of the transition, Western European governments expected a large number of arrivals from the territories of the former Soviet Union. There were talks of an "Eastern invasion" and the fear of the incoming flows from the East dominated policy discourse in the European Union.[73] Such fears were largely unfounded, as most movements took place across the borders of the former Soviet bloc. Besides the facilitating role of Russian as a common language, the Iron Curtain had been quite an effective containment tool. The West was terra incognita, while eastward movements could take place along the well-established infrastructure of the former Soviet Union.

The first wave of migration from the western fringe was consequently eastward, toward Russia. It did not involve a significant number of women, as most job opportunities there were concentrated in the heavily masculine sector of construction work. The few women who moved were followers, joining their husbands or brothers in the new Russia.

Many pioneer women, especially those with an upper middle-class background, experimented with another form of mobility in which they could be self-organizing actors: petty trade, also called shuttle trade. Building on the skills already developed during the Soviet era, many women from Belarus, Western Ukraine, and Moldova started to make use of the opportunities for free travel to acquire clothing items, cosmetics, and small consumer electronics abroad to resell back home. While there are no precise data on the volume reached by this kind of trade, the arrival of post-Soviet "buyers" was large enough that wholesalers specializing in cheap goods for the post-Soviet market appeared quickly in some postsocialist capitals as well as in the global emporiums of the Mediterranean, from Istanbul to Naples.[74] In the recollection of the many early pioneers who had been involved in it, shuttle trade was a successful survival strategy, often providing a substantial amount of savings over the years.

From the point of view of the women, engaging in petty trade was justified as an alternative to migration. They believed "doing business" was compatible both with their previous social status as respectable middle-class professionals and with their womanly duties. It would allow them to support their households while never staying away for too long from the family and the home.

Even if initially meant as an alternative to migration, the experience gained in petty trade would turn out to be a strong factor facilitating it. Among the first small group of women I met in Alpinetown in the late 1990s, all had been active in the early 1990s in the shuttle trade, although to varying degrees. Many of them had been in Italy at least once previously, in Naples, as buyers.

During the second half of the 1990s, Western-style goods became progressively more accessible. Shuttle trade slowly lost relevance, and many women invested their savings in small, family-run businesses. Many other women, less geographically mobile, had to work several shifts, take second and third jobs, and resort to self-production in gardening and animal husbandry. Some experimented with a sequence of short spells of domestic work in Poland, as babysitters, or as seasonal agricultural laborers in Slovakia and the Czech Republic. Many had to sell any property for which they could find a buyer.

For the women in this study, the early phases of the post-Soviet transition were difficult both economically and personally. The difficulties of the transition placed a strain on many couples, often leading to their breakup. High rates of divorce had always been a key feature of Soviet family life.[75] In the climate of the transition, however, conjugal breakup acquired a different, and more stressful, meaning.

Many husbands found themselves unemployed or unpaid, and—at least according to the women—they refused to adapt to a situation in which their wives had become the primary breadwinners. Alcoholism was rampant. Family violence, in the accounts of many women, became endemic and largely tolerated.

Women found themselves in charge of both their parents (whose salaries and pensions had been slashed) and their children, while husbands completely disappeared or even became a financial burden. All but seven of the women pioneers I met in the early phases of their emigration were widowed or divorced, factually or legally.[76] They felt they had no more chances to create a family. Public discourse tended to impute to them, along the lines of previous Soviet discourse, the failure of their families.

Many of them felt, as one woman recalled, like "damaged goods." The family model of their regions in Eastern Europe has been defined by widespread marriage, early marriage, and early fertility. Sometimes in their late twenties, and automatically by their early forties, the women were regarded as too old, as "babushkas."[77]

The women described a situation in which even the idea of dating someone seemed preposterous. Besides their age, there was simply an utter scarcity of suitable mates. "I was definitely not choosy," Domnica once told me. "I was desperate for a man. Really. Very simply, there were no decent males left. Gosh, it was like shopping in the old [i.e., Soviet] times."

The pains of the transition took a dramatic turn at the end of the 1990s, with the Russian financial crisis known as the "ruble crisis." In the summer of 1998, fears of ruble devaluation and a default on domestic debt brought about a Russian stock, bond, and currency market collapse. The government reacted with a significant devaluation of the ruble and, a month later, made the ruble a freely floating currency. Inflation reached 84 percent. A sovereign default on the state debt and the collapse of the banking sector followed.

The ruble crisis hit the entire world economy, but particularly the Soviet successor states. The ruble was the currency in which many savings were held, and its devaluation, together with the closure of many banks, resulted in a significant number of households across the former Soviet space losing all their savings. The crisis also had heavy consequences for the economies of neighboring countries. Moldova lost more than 5 percent of its GDP just in export contracts. Ukraine had to devalue its currency, the hryvnia, by 60 percent, and domestic prices increased by a further 20 percent. For most Eastern European families, it was like going through the breakdown of the Soviet Union all over again, only worse. This time, moreover, there was very little left to buffer the shock.

The consequences of the ruble crisis represent what the literature on international migration usually calls a "push factor," something that makes migrants willing to move abroad as soon as possible. Another independent factor made possible the rapid transformation of small numbers of isolated pioneers into a mass emigration flow toward Western Europe. In 2000, in Berlin, the German Ministry for Foreign Affairs issued the so-called Volmer directive (named after the junior minister who signed it). The directive, inspired as a sign of goodwill, reformed the conditions for the granting of short-term visas (so-called tourist visas) in Eastern European countries. The directive shifted effectively the burden of proof; embassies in Eastern Europe were instructed, when in doubt, to issue a visa to the applicant rather than deny it.

Table 1 Percentage of women among post-Soviet resident foreigners in some European countries, 2017

| | | Sending country | | | | | | |
|---|---|---|---|---|---|---|---|---|
| | | Belarus | Georgia | Moldova | Russia | Ukraine | Other Soviet successor states | Migrant women |
| | | | | | | | | (*N*) |
| Receiving country | Belgium | 70% | 47% | 62% | 57% | 65% | 59% | 19,057 |
| | Denmark | 72% | 59% | 64% | 67% | 59% | 54% | 18,643 |
| | Germany | 72% | 58% | 59% | 64% | 64% | 61% | 347,944 |
| | Ireland | 60% | 51% | 47% | 56% | 53% | 54% | 38,495 |
| | Spain | — | — | 53% | 66% | 57% | — | 157,690 |
| | Italy | 46% | 83% | 67% | 82% | 79% | 74% | 338,754 |
| | Netherlands | 66% | 59% | 69% | 66% | 65% | 62% | 17,485 |
| | Austria | 74% | 54% | 67% | 57% | 67% | 60% | 33,773 |
| | Portugal | 66% | 46% | 55% | 65% | 61% | 54% | 26,170 |
| | Sweden | 58% | 49% | 66% | 61% | 63% | 52% | 22,674 |
| | Norway | 71% | 58% | 66% | 66% | 71% | 48% | 35,826 |
| | Switzerland | 72% | 56% | 80% | 66% | 76% | 67% | 21,692 |
| | Total | 30,945 | 44,485 | 116,636 | 231,122 | 364,945 | 5,381 | |

*Source*: Author's elaboration on data from Eurostat migr_resvas database.

The policy change had powerful consequences, with the German embassy in Kiev processing nearly 300,000 applications for short-term visas in 2001 alone. As the visa granted by a member state allowed the grantee to travel in all the territories of the European Union, the German reform had European-wide consequences: following the Volmer directive, large numbers of Eastern Europeans, most notably Ukrainians and Moldovans, moved to the irregular labor market of southern European countries, where they had previously been nearly absent.[78]

Just a few years later, the Soviet successor states were already acknowledged as major emigration countries, their struggling economies supported by huge flows of remittances.[79] Already in 2006, a commentator could write, although with some exaggeration, of Ukraine as "Europe's Mexico."[80] In little more than a decade, small clusters of women pioneers have triggered the arrival of large number of followers, making Eastern Europeans among the most sizable groups of new immigrants in the European Union.[81] Even in southern Europe, despite the deteriorating living standards caused by the economic downturn, their number has continued to grow year after year.[82] As shown in table 1, women are nearly everywhere highly overrepresented, with percentages as high as 78 percent in Greece and 76 percent in Italy.

# ONE

# A Room of One's Own: Managing Spaces, Lives, and Laws in Residential Care Work

When I met the first women in the streets of Alpinetown, their stories seemed (and claimed to be) remarkably similar. They talked of their previous lives as teachers, doctors, nurses, managers of small factories and offices, military junior officials, and engineers in the provincial capitals of the empire. Of their increasingly desperate attempts to find, after 1991, new ways of earning a livelihood. Of the consequences of the ruble crisis. Of the breakdown of their families. They spoke incessantly about their children, left behind with their parents.[1]

They all claimed they wanted the same things: to work, to save some money, to improve the living conditions of their families, and to return as quickly as possible to their "real" lives. They all worked as live-in care workers, providing around-the-clock care and assistance to working- or lower-middle-class elderly.[2] Their lives were structured by the same rhythm, by the pressures of similar problems, and by the need to deal with similar risks.

Over the years of my fieldwork, however, a significant differentiation has occurred. Some women have remained in the live-in sector, maximizing the amount of income and energy targeted at their sending areas, to their "real" homes *there*. Although they are only a small fraction of the women who had originally wanted to do so, some of them have left Alpinetown and returned to their hometowns. Some have succeeded in creating new, hybrid homes with the elderly they assist, taking on ersatz family roles, developing complementary emotional attachments to the *here* and the *there*.[3] Still others have maintained their work in the care sector, complementing it with the building of communal, shared spaces with other women. Many others have left the live-in sector, looking for a space of their own and slowly putting down roots *here*.

The causes of these transitions have been varied and sometimes unpredictable. It has been a matter of being employed by the right (or by the wrong) household, facing yet another family emergency that has required stepping up their remittances, finding better schools for their children in Alpinetown or the offer of a room available at a discounted rent, finding a lover, or breaking up still another relationship.

Starting from very similar conditions, the women have entered quite distinct trajectories in the social space, which I call "careers," each accompanied by a different set of constraints, opportunities, expectations, and fellow travelers.[4] Each of these careers has constituted an experiential environment that has often shaped their new understanding of themselves in an increasingly differentiated way. Such trajectories have rarely started, and even less subsequently grown, out of carefully laid plans. The women have crafted such trajectories out of uneven materials, out of encounters, expedient actions, adaptation to new conditions, and imitation of other women. Very often, wishes and desires have followed, rather than preceded, their actions. Over the years, the cumulative consequences of such trajectories have been quite remarkable, slowly fragmenting the initial community into increasingly separate lifeworlds.

A special role in differentiating these trajectories has been played by the various ways through which the women have tried to manage the problem, intrinsic and endemic in residential care work, of securing a private, personal space over which they can exercise some degree of control.

## Reaching Alpinetown

The first women who arrived in Italy from territories of the former USSR had travelled along a very similar path. They acquired tourist visas, usually through an agency. Very few women paid for it with their savings, and only a handful of them pawned or mortgaged whatever property they had left. Most of them borrowed the necessary money, from a variety of sources. As the rate of interest was usually high, repaying the debts was the most pressing priority upon arrival.[5]

They boarded a bus, very often headed for Naples, in southern Italy. Upon arrival, they would face different situations according to their age, economic resources, language skills, amount of connections, and sheer luck.[6]

Most women would start working very quickly, sometimes even the same day, as live-in care workers.[7] Conditions in southern Italy, however, were particularly tough. Salaries were low and working conditions demanding. Families regarded women as quick-fix solutions, and job training hardly ever lasted more than a few minutes. Above all, very few southern families seemed willing to guarantee any adjustment of legal status for their care workers in the future. In reality, many families regarded the irregular status of their employee as a guarantee she would not leave them for a better-paying job. The constant arrival of new women in Naples made competition fierce.

In the early 2000s, many new arrivals were pushed to look for new destinations, and some women tried to get away from Naples as soon as possible, seeking to improve their prospects by migrating again to northern Italy. Alpinetown, a wealthy area with a rapidly aging population, was among the favorite destinations. The labor market of Alpinetown offered slightly higher salaries, some degree of protection, and much higher chances that the family would support their adjustment of status when possible. To move to Alpinetown was not easy. The area did not have anything comparable to the network of sites, agencies, and bus companies already operating in the south.

Most of the first women arrived independently from the others, based on little more than rumors about the availability of jobs in the area. They would disembark at the railway station and ask passersby—including (more than occasionally) startled police officers—where they could go to look for a bed and a job. In many cases, the natives instructed them to visit one of the philanthropic services active in town that often functioned also as informal job centers for immigrant workers.

The women would also walk around the city looking for women "like them" whom they could ask for help and information. These women would provide the newcomers with some basic information—such as the existence of a shelter where they could sleep a few nights, or the best Catholic parishes to go to when asking for a job. But they also provided them with a precious form of emotional support and social recognition. They were the living proof that leaving southern Italy was possible and that they would not be completely alone in the "north." As such experienced women were few and lived dispersed, newcomers faced the problem of finding them. Anastacia, a thirtysomething Moldovan who arrived in Alpinetown among the early followers, found an ingenious solution to the problem. Once she disembarked at the station, she walked through the streets and parks of Alpinetown singing Moldovan songs, confident that any other Moldovan woman, puzzled by her behavior, would start talking to her. She was right; it was exactly what happened. It nevertheless took her most of an afternoon to meet us and, when it happened, she had a sore throat and had started feeling desperate.

Every time I met one of them, I thought their actions required a dose of bravery bordering on madness. Still, to my surprise, and before my very own eyes, the handful of women I had initially met quickly became, in a few years, hundreds, and subsequently thousands.

## Finding the First Job in Alpinetown

A few days after I had met my first Eastern European women in the street, and long before thinking of becoming an ethnographer, I happened to spend several late afternoons in the main local Catholic relief agency. The fact was, like any good emigrant, I was busy refurnishing a house in my hometown, even if I already suspected I would never live in it. The money I was earning with my day job was never enough. One day, somebody asked me if I was willing to work for a project on former refugees from the Balkans, chronicling their lives a few years after their flight. They asked me to stay in the waiting room of the agency, identify possible former refugees, and interview them. The money was good, and I could do it after hours, the ideal moonlighting job.

The Catholic relief agency was at the time one of the best places to go to meet immigrants of all varieties. Operating in the center of the city, it provided a wide range of social services. It enjoyed considerable moral authority that it often employed on behalf of migrants. In addition, it had a reputation of being able to cater to many difficult situations. It was a place nearly anybody, including myself, had used at least once during settlement in the area.

While doing my job there, I happened to meet Piero, a retired man working as a volunteer for the agency. Piero regarded solidarity with the immigrants as a moral duty and enjoyed talking with them. As a native, more at ease with the local dialect than with standard Italian, he was a trusted figure for local families, especially for those working-class households that faced for the first time the need of some paid help for their elderly. Unsurprisingly, he had quickly become a key broker in the local market for domestic services, providing a personalized match between supply and demand.

On one afternoon, I found him particularly stressed. Some days before, he had placed one of the very first Ukrainian women to arrive in Alpinetown, Elena, in what he considered one of "his" best families. He had been extremely proud of having been able to find such a good solution for a newly arrived woman who was badly in need. Now, however, Elena was in his office, sobbing and crying, and he could not understand adequately what had happened. He asked me if I would go to his office and talk with her, hoping this would help ease the situation.

She was a blonde woman in her midthirties, sitting on a chair, head bowed, crying silently. She was modestly dressed, but very neat, with her hair in a bun. When I greeted her in Russian, I suddenly saw a light in her eyes. I introduced myself as a friend of Piero, and we quickly briefed each other on our biographies. She was a former child psychologist from a small town in Western Ukraine, the mother of two and the wife of a schoolteacher. The orphanage she used to work for had stopped paying her years before, and she had been unable to find another job, no matter how much she had tried. Her husband was also unemployed, and for years, they had barely survived, moving in with his parents, selling all their belongings, growing as much of their own food as possible, and getting whatever odd jobs were available. Her attempts at earning some money going to buy goods in Poland to resell in her hometown had been utter failures. In the beginning, they had planned to emigrate together, entrusting the children to her mother. They had been unable to borrow enough money for two visas, and she had decided to go alone to Italy, where she expected to find a job more easily. She had arrived in Naples, and a woman had dispatched her to a job in a small village just on Italy's heel, with a severely disabled man who could hardly speak. She had taken care of him, in the solitude of his flat, without speaking to anyone for weeks. Her only contact with the outside world had been the television.

When the man she assisted died, she found herself suddenly unemployed, with no savings, and hardly more fluent in Italian than the day she arrived. The son of the man, who had always paid her late, refused to pay her for the last month of work (not to mention any severance pay) as his father was by now dead and she was useless. When she complained, he threatened to report her to the police. Elena called the woman who had found her the job. The woman said she could find her a new job, but she had to move to another nearby village and again pay a month's salary for the new contract.

Desperate, Elena had called an acquaintance in Rome and asked for advice. Her friend told her there were just too many Ukrainians in southern Italy and suggested she take a train. She told her she had heard that in Alpinetown there were few women, and locals paid salaries on time. She said Elena should "go to the priests" and ask for a job. Elena had taken the train, scared somebody would ask for her papers, and after many hours, she had reached Alpinetown and gone straight to the agency. She had met Piero, and she had discovered that he did not expect a bribe. She said that the day she had entered her new employer's house had been the happiest of her life.

She had done her best to make him happy. Her life in the new workplace had nonetheless quickly become miserable. Gianni, her employer, criticized her constantly, whatever she did, from morning to dawn. The very same morning, he had said he wanted to fire her. She said that keeping the job was her only hope of repaying her debts, helping her husband, sending remittances to her children, and giving meaning to all her solitude and distress. I briefly summarized the situation to Piero and he suggested we make a visit all together to Gianni and see if something could be done.

While we walked toward Gianni's flat, Elena kept chatting constantly. She seemed hungry for talk. She wanted explanations regarding what she felt were bizarre Italian folkways. She was particularly interested in why Italians used so many different kinds of soap in their homes. She found it strange, slightly uncanny: *Soap is soap*, she kept insisting for most of our walk. We walked close to each other, with her holding my arm as if it were a last ditch promise of a better life. Piero tactfully walked a few steps behind.

After a while, we reached the building where Gianni lived. It was a gray, five-story building, likely built at the end of the 1960s. I joked about how the building was the Alpinetown variant of a Khrushchyovka, the mass produced five-story apartment buildings that defined Soviet urban landscapes in the early 1960s. Elena was not in the mood to see any similarity between her previous life and the current situation. She rang the bell and we waited a long time. She smirked and said that Gianni had walking difficulties. I asked her if she had forgotten the keys. She replied that Gianni did not like to give anybody else the keys to his house. Every day, when she returned from her grocery shopping, she had to ring him and wait—sometimes in the rain—for him to open the main door. Finally, we heard a croaking voice asking who it was. Elena answered—in broken Italian—that it was she. The main door unlocked, and Elena went in first.

We climbed three floors. Everything was clean and reasonably maintained, but impersonal, faded, and gray. Even without evidence of it, I felt it was a building still inhabited by the original owners, the young couples who had arrived in Alpinetown from the countryside at the peak of the Italian economic miracle in the 1960s. The building had been aging with them. Gianni opened the door of his flat and welcomed us. He was a man in his late eighties, with a weary expression. Elena took our jackets. She hung them in the hallway leading to the tiny living room. Everything in the flat seemed to be there from time immemorial. I was brought back to my own experience as a care worker many years before, as the dark brown furniture of Gianni's flat was very similar to that in the flat of the couple I had assisted. The flat also had the same slightly moldy smell. I was seriously tempted to ask Elena if Gianni always complained about the cost of heating every time she opened a window, as the elderly man and woman I cared for used to do.

Gianni invited us to sit on the perfectly preserved sofa, while he sat on a chair, as it required, he explained, less effort to get up. He asked if we wanted a coffee and, even before our answer, told Elena to prepare one. He quickly added, in dialect, that he wanted coffee and not dirty water. I was shocked by the rude comment, but Piero seemed rather amused by the situation. Elena rushed to the kitchen to prepare the coffee while Gianni started voicing a long list of complaints about her.

Talking mostly to Piero, he complained that Elena was indeed "a good woman," but silly and primitive. I could not help smiling when he stressed the fact she had been using the same soap to clean the dishes, the glass of the windows, and the floor. The main scandal, however, concerned her cooking. When he had asked her for a simple dish of pasta with tomato sauce, Elena had just boiled the canned tomatoes, added water, and cooked the pasta in the liquid. "She cries every night," he added. He was fed up with her. Piero told him he should be patient; he should not expect her to know how to cook Italian dishes properly. The first reaction to such proposition was quite aggressive.

Gianni said that Elena should know these things by heart. He paid her to do what a wife, any wife, does. How was it possible that "she says she is a wife and a mother and she cooks pasta and canned tomatoes together"? Gianni, who had never had any domestic worker in his house before, let alone a foreign one, clearly acted on the premise that Elena had been hired as a substitute for Maria, his beloved wife who had died a few weeks before.

He was neither willing, nor able, to make a distinction between Maria's former knowledge and practices and what he could expect from any other woman, Italian or Ukrainian. For him, if Elena did not do things in the same way, it was an indicator not of ignorance but of sloppiness. Piero kept explaining to Gianni how Elena simply did not know many of the things he wanted and how she was often not even able to understand what he had said. When Elena returned with the coffee, Gianni was quick to stress that, as expected, it was not coffee but dirty water. Elena apologized and, with eyes ready to cry, turned to me whispering in Russian that she desperately needed this job. Everything among us four was frozen and I could see Gianni was on the verge of a big fuss.

I got up, put my arm around Elena's waist, and walked her toward where I presumed the kitchen was. I told her that we would prepare coffee together as the Italians like it and told Piero and Gianni to chat a little bit while we did so. We entered the kitchen, tiny but well kept, with all the appliances clearly worn by many years of use. I felt as if I were in my grandmother's kitchen, where I always expected a strudel and hot chocolate served in a chipped flowery mug. I quickly taught Elena to use the *moka* (coffeepot), with the right amount of water and coffee powder. This time, Gianni was satisfied and asked ironically if it was really so difficult to prepare a simple coffee. Elena did not answer but smiled smugly.

With Gianni apparently calmed down, Elena seized the occasion to take me to her small room. The room was tiny and sparsely outfitted: a cot, a small wardrobe, and a cupboard where Elena kept a photo of her family close to a snapshot of Gianni's wife Maria. Elena explained that Gianni wanted the room to remain exactly as it was when Maria used it. She added she did not mind the photo of his dead wife in her room, as she seemed a merry person. We sat on the bed to look at photos of her children. I tried to reassure her that I would help her to quickly learn the Italian folkways, and I promised to invite her out with my Italian friends. She replied that she was more interested in the first than in the second offer. She just needed to learn how to manage an Italian household. "I came here to work for my children, and I will go back as soon as possible to my own place among my own folks," she said firmly. I would learn, in the decade since that visit, that most newly arrived women would strongly take such a stance on their relationship with the new environment. I would also discover how often such a stance quickly dissipated with changing circumstances.[8]

We returned to the living room where Gianni, now relaxed, was telling stories about his life. After a while, he returned to the original focus of our visit to state that Elena was a nice woman and they would manage well together. They could go to church together and he could teach her to cook decent pasta. We cheered, and Piero winked at me, signaling that we had accomplished our mission. We left both Gianni and Elena our telephone numbers, telling them to call us if they needed some consultation. Just before leaving, Gianni approached me and said softly, "I would just love her to stop crying . . . can you tell her that I am not a bad person?" I explained to him that she cried because she missed her children, but that she was more than happy to work for an honest man like him.

While we were walking back to the office, I asked Piero how often he was involved in that kind of visit. He said it was common, especially with working-class people like Gianni, who did not really know how to behave with someone who cared for them without being a relative. They simply could not conceive that somebody would be unaccustomed to cooking pasta. Within a few weeks, Elena was able to work out a balance with Gianni. She worked for him until his death a few years later.[9]

In some other cases, entry—and subsequent survival—in the local market for care work was even more difficult. On a Sunday morning, I was in the parking lot that, as I will explain in the next chapter, was slowly becoming a main gathering site for the women. There I met Maria Angela, whom nobody had seen before. In fact, she had arrived from Moldova a few weeks before. During our small talk, she was constantly worried about missing the last bus available to reach the family she was working for. I offered to drive her home, as I was curious to understand exactly what Maria Angela considered "good" working conditions. She happily accepted, saying that it had been a long time since she had had a lift in a car. After leaving the city and entering a nearby valley, we drove for twenty minutes on a back road, until we reached a semidirt road narrowly winding toward the top of the mountain: she pointed out the direction and said that there was still some way to go.

After another spell of road, we reached a beautiful alpine lawn that suddenly opened in front of us. She pointed to the isolated house on the other side of the lawn, saying that she worked there for an old farmer couple. I told her it was an amazing place to live and she agreed with that. She cheekily added that it was amazing provided the place was in Moldova and you had a car. In fact, she had to take care of a very old couple, and the house was actually only a kitchen, a living room, and a bathroom without hot water. They slept all together in the living room. They seldom spoke to her, and she felt isolated. Even if they granted her a half day off each week, she was seldom able to use it, as it took more than three hours to go back and forth from Alpinetown by public transportation. "I had never been on a farm in Moldova," she said. "I have always been a city girl. Now I am in Italy, and I live on a ruined farm."

I was thinking about asking her if I could visit her employers. The answer arrived before I even started. I heard the irritated voice of a woman shouting at Maria Angela that she knew she could not bring people into her house. Maria Angela rocketed up, pushed me away, and told her employers that I was on my way. She said goodbye hurriedly and quickly disappeared into the house.

## The Quest for Private Space

Elena and Maria Angela, in different ways, were dealing with an endemic feature of live-in care work. Their work took place in a space defined obsessively by the lives and biographies of their employers. They lived in flats that had acquired a marmorized meaning. To use Mary Douglas's catchphrase, the flats were homes because they were "memory machines."[10] They were the location of a long series of unspoken routines that the women had to respect in full.[11] They were expected to know such routines without being explicitly taught, as Elena had discovered with Gianni. Such meanings and practices were actually what made those flats "home" for the elders they cared for and for their relatives. They deeply resisted any modification that the women could introduce, intentionally or not.

The feelings of "home" were linked to unspoken sensory experiences or hidden routines that had acquired normative value. Employers consequently often complained, sometimes bitterly, about the women using soap with a different smell, placing butter on a different shelf in the fridge, forgetting to place a chair in the proper position after washing the floor, or wrongly folding socks. The elderly often perceived as aggressive such violations of the normative layout of the sensory experience of "their" flats and any disruption of their routines. They expected the women to know, or to learn quickly, the vast body of tacit knowledge they took for granted, to assimilate unquestioningly the definition of the situation that sustained their employers' domesticity.

Acquiring the ritual knowledge of the space on the terms requested was a process that confirmed both to the employers and to the women that they were alien to them, "temporary," "accidental" presences. Many women said they were, in the best cases, tolerated guests. They felt that they lived in a space they would never be able to call their own. Whenever I visited the women, for whatever reason, in their workplaces, it was evident they suffered from the lack of a private space they could rightly feel inhabitants of.[12]

There were obviously wide differences in the families who inhabited such flats. Some families were more welcoming, willing to greet me or letting us chat a little bit in the living room. Some others would treat my presence as a kind of further invasion of their privacy, making clear that they were looking forward to my quick departure. These differences notwithstanding, it was evident that having any degree of control over a portion of space the women could define as their own was a very rare occurrence, something that had to be fought for, continuously and assertively.

Many of them slept on a sofa in the living room, sometimes in the kitchen. When Iryna, a forty-five-year-old Ukrainian woman working around the clock for a very old "signora," told me she was sleeping with her in the same queen-sized bed, I initially assumed it was a way to monitor her constantly. Iryna explained to me that it was just that the flat was small and her employer simply did not want to buy another bed. Over the years, I realized it was a frequent arrangement.

Many other women did not have even a cupboard or a drawer in which to keep their things. Sometimes there was no wardrobe the women could use; very often, there were physically wardrobes in the flats, but they were full of the clothes and items of the elderly or, not infrequently, of their deceased spouses. I noticed more than once that the women I was visiting, even after years in specific flats, were still keeping their things in the suitcase they had arrived with, and many women had to buy additional pieces of luggage for the items they acquired while in Alpinetown.

A few women could enjoy the privilege of a separate room, but even in this case, many often complained they had no privacy. Even when employers promised a certain spatial autonomy and seclusion, such promises would quickly fade away through a long series of small, everyday encroachments. Most of the elderly, and more than a few of their relatives, regarded their rooms as part of the family space and behaved accordingly. "They always enter without knocking" was a common complaint among the women. Many employers, moreover, resented any attempt by the women to mark "their" space with some personal meaning. For example, one of the earliest desires of the women was to find a place in their flats to display some framed pictures of their families, sometimes accompanied by small icons or postcards of their hometowns. Such a place, which the women often called a "shrine," was highly important to them.[13]

Although the necessary space was small, most employers perceived it as an attempt to colonize and reacted aggressively. Some women had to place the pictures on their bedside tables before going to bed and close them in a drawer during daylight hours. Very simply, the space, saturated by the previous life of the owners, resisted any change, and the women had to adapt to its given configuration.

The utter lack of private space, as well as living always under the sight of those they cared for, made the time spent congregating among themselves particularly important for the women. In the beginning, it was a loose network of personal appointments for strolling together. As most women were free during the same time slots—Thursday afternoons and Sunday mornings—we would start walking in a small group and, along the way, we would often meet others. Walking in a large group was impractical, and we started meeting in the waiting rooms of the train and bus stations.

Centrally located, they were relatively large spaces, rarely used by natives during our times, especially on Sundays. They were free, there was heating, and there were toilets available close by. Without any explicit decision, we switched from individualized appointments to hanging out in what quickly became "our" places.

Whoever happened to be free would visit the waiting rooms, confident that somebody else would soon arrive. It was a flexible group, where participation was highly variable. News of the place slowly circulated, and it became common for the newly arrived women, as well as for the old-timers, to join us there. The women would go there to chat, to relax, to voice grievances, and to collect information and advice. With time, they also became places where women could sell items or sign deals. Subsequently, other locations became equally important as sites where the women could experience an autonomous sociability among themselves. There was a section of the public park nearby, particularly handy during summer.

On Sundays, a deserted parking lot became an open-air market attended regularly by many of the women. Some benches on the riverside were particularly pleasant for Sunday communal meals. Some benches in a corner of one of the main squares of Alpinetown became a good meeting point for strolls. Each of us, when we had some free time, would simply tour such places, clustered in the same area of the town, being sure that we would find women there we could spend time with.

The behavior of the women in such spaces developed into something special. In the previous phase of small groups strolling around, the women had always tried to look as inconspicuous as possible. They feared that the police would identify them as irregular migrants. Perhaps even more importantly, they took for granted, and resented, that the natives, if they identified them as care workers, would have looked down on them as poor and destitute. They reproached one another for talking too loudly, and they always tried to be overly, sometimes ostentatiously, polite to passersby.

When we started meeting in the waiting rooms—and in all subsequent places—the attitude shifted remarkably. They used their bags, their coats, and their own bodies to draw boundaries around them and adopted loud voices and defiant postures to discourage natives from entering their spaces.[14] The women, literally, created their own intimate spaces, their oases of privacy and control, carving them from the tissue of scarcely used public spaces.

## Why Employers Are Always Mean

In the beginning, and for many years, the criteria to judge how good a specific job was were minimal: if the elderly person could take at least minimal care of him- or herself, if payments were regular, if no one in the family attacked or harassed the worker, then it was a good job. The women took for granted that all their employers were mean and despicable, that they were suffering a humiliating ordeal.. In fact, they regarded their work as polluting them, as placing them outside of the world of decent people.

There were at least three reasons for such a gloomy view of their occupation and of themselves. First, they felt it was not a "proper" job, as it was not a position within an organization (what they called *a real job*) nor was it a self-entrepreneurial activity, a business.[15] For the women, working for a family, with the personal dependence it entailed, was something that lacked any intrinsic dignity, a morally doubtful way to earn a living. Many women, when complaining about their conditions, had no difficulties with adopting analogies between their conditions and slavery or prostitution.[16]

From the point of view of the women, the experience of care work in the privacy of their homes could not, no matter how hard they tried, be reconstructed as something noble or altruistic. Taking care of family members in their homes was morally acceptable only as a labor of love. It was the duty of close relatives. In Italy, these relatives escaped from their duties thanks to their money, which allowed them to hire women to do for money what they should do for love. Vika, a Ukrainian woman who had been a manager of a brewery, once explained to me in detail why she resented her condition. She was working for a nice, old man who was in comparatively good health. He was kind and respectful. He even sometimes added a generous tip to the salary his daughter paid Vika. He regularly gave her a gift during holidays. She liked him, and she was proud of providing him with the best care she was able to provide. She could not accept, however, that such a nice man would not receive the care he deserved from his children, from whom he was entitled to expect it. She felt it was morally wrong that they had entrusted him to her, somebody doing it for money. "He has two daughters and even three granddaughters!" she kept reminding me.

Taking care of somebody for a salary was something that polluted both the workers and the employers.[17] For Vika, it was almost as wrong as leaving her own children behind so that she could work in somebody else's home. It was something that could be justified only as a heroic sacrifice performed on behalf of their children.

Here, however, a further problem emerged. The women felt constantly humiliated by the fact that their employers—usually the daughters of the elders they were taking care for—expected them to behave as if they were somewhat "part of the family," showing a genuine affection for the elderly entrusted to them. At the same time, however, they basically showed no interest in the care workers' motherhood. Their employers did not value them for their sacrifice, nor feel the duty to support them emotionally. Once, very early in my fieldwork, I met Nica, a Moldovan in her late thirties who had arrived a couple of months before. Usually a very cheerful person, that afternoon Nica had clearly sad eyes. After some small talk, she said that in the late morning, Paola, the daughter of the elderly man she was caring for, had visited them. Nica had just returned from the minivans, and she was thrilled about having received a small red plastic picture book sent by her two children. They had made drawings on the cover and filled it with pictures of them. Nica wanted to share the joy of having received such a gift, and she had rushed to show it to Paola. Paola, in her account, had a mere glance at just a couple of pictures and quickly moved on to what mattered to her, providing Nica instructions on what to cook for her father in the evening. "She did not even care to have a look at the drawings," Nica said sorrowfully. These interactional signs of disrespect for their motherhood were endemic in the accounts the women provided each other.

Sometimes, motherhood could even work against them. Certain women reported to the group that the elderly people they assisted, when they wanted to be mean to them, would resort to blaming them precisely for having left their children behind. I found it difficult to believe such accounts, until one day I met Vasylyna in the main square of Alpinetown. Vasylyna, entrusted with the care of Anna, a very old and frail woman, stopped pushing her wheelchair in order to greet me. Anna, growing irritated, started saying she was in a hurry. After no more than a couple of minutes, when we were wishing each other goodbye, I heard Anna blaming Vasylyna for not understanding that she was waiting for her son who had promised to visit her. With an unabashed form of senile cruelty, she concluded her reprimand by looking at Vasylyna reproachfully and saying, "I love my son. I have had a very difficult life, but I have never left him alone, not even a single day." Vasylyna's humiliation was palpable.

The demeaning nature of their working conditions and the disrespect for their motherhood were openly and frequently admitted by the women, who supported each other in their sufferings. A third, equally strong but less publicly proclaimed, source of humiliation derived from the very practice of care work. Most women—given their age and the fact they had been able to emigrate precisely because they had parents in relatively good health to whom they could entrust their children— were utterly unprepared for the very physical experience of doing care work for elderly persons.[18]

They had to learn quickly to take care—often within hours or days of their arrival—of an old, often ill, smelly, and ugly body. Many of them experienced high levels of emotional stress while quickly learning to hide their feeling of disgust. When I met Yanina, who had arrived only a few days before, she was still reeling from the impression of the first time she had disrobed and washed her "mama." "Her skin seems to fall from her, her nails are yellow and hard . . . she has no hair on her . . . [pointing to her genitalia]! I did not know hair falls out even there! And then, all of her body is stinky . . . stinky of old things. I have been trying to wash her smell away for days, yuck!" She quickly added that, when she had first been in the bathroom on her knees, washing her mama in the old, rusty bathtub in her flat, she had thought "it would have been better to die than to live as a *lavaculi*." Although such a statement could easily appear as an exaggeration, the immediate identification shown in the other women's faces persuaded me the shocking character of her experience was widespread.[19]

The need to cope with this set of tensions made the existence of our group a key arena for venting frustration and receiving emotional support. Care workers could meet with others who would understand the ordeal they were going through. Initially, the dynamic of our communication followed a very simple script: whenever a woman felt the need to express her pain and humiliation, all of the other women had to support her, share their own pain, and praise her for the sacrifices she was making for her children. I quickly realized that an opposite norm was also tightly enforced: women should never admit that they were happy with their jobs or with their employers. There was a sharp distinction between the elderly people they were taking care of and their offspring, usually their daughters, employing the women. It was acceptable to speak affectionately about their "mama" or "papa." The women always claimed to behave like respectful daughters. Spite, annoyances, and even vexation, when coming from the elderly clients, were usually justified or laughed at in a light mood.

Employers, however, especially the daughters of the elderly clients, had to be described always as "spoiled brats," mean-spirited, and occasionally cruel. This norm was strongly enforced. The few times someone happened to portray her employer in a favorable light, the other women immediately denounced her as incurably naïve or, even worse, as lacking any dignity. The same women who would individually boast proudly to me about receiving some token of appreciation from their employers were very careful to keep silent about it while in the group.

The strength of this group norm become evident one Sunday morning, while I was chatting with a group of women in the parking lot where, as I will tell in more detail in the next chapter, some minivans waited for whatever the women wanted to ship home. Drivers would receive the goods, letters, and money from the women and deliver them, for a reasonable fee, to their families a couple of days later. It was a merry occasion, in which the women celebrated the outcome of their sacrifices.

While we were chatting, Snizhana, a fiftyish doctor who had arrived a couple of months before, arrived in the parking lot carrying, with great difficulty, a trolley with a used dishwasher. She had received it from the daughter of the elder she was caring for, who was renovating her kitchen. The women were quite appalled by the scene and started commenting to each other that Snizhana—obviously in difficulty carrying a dishwasher on a rather small trolley—was a shame, a woman utterly lacking any dignity. None of them went to help her, leaving her to push the trolley alone toward the minivan. Reacting to the silence and the obvious disapproval, Snizhana tried to explain loudly that the dishwasher was nearly new, that she was sending it to her quite old parents, and that the costs of shipping it with the minivan were reasonable. She tried to put forward a rational assessment of the item in question. She did not receive any sympathetic feedback.

The tension was palpable, and many women were staring at her aggressively. Luckily, Iryna decided to intervene. She rushed over to the women, shouting an alternative explanation: they, women expert in the ways of Alpinetown, should have understood that Snizhana was not shameless. She was just silly and naïve. She had not yet been in Italy long enough and she was gullible, failing to understand that her employer, in giving her the dishwasher, had meant to humiliate her. The driver (who was to profit from the shipping of the dishwasher) quickly supported Iryna, claiming, "Come on, women, we have all been in the shit here; we were naïve like Snizhana when we arrived."

The other women grudgingly accepted this alternative account, reluctantly accepting the presence of Snizhana and her dishwasher in the parking lot for the time necessary to ship it. Snizhana was not expelled from the group, but she had to accept the role of the novice for quite a long time. What triggered the hostile reaction of the women was not so much that Snizhana had accepted a valuable gift from her employers. I knew for sure that many of them had done the same. It was the fact that, owing to the dishwasher's size, she had not been able to transport it discreetly, thus bringing within the safe space of the parking lot a conspicuous and polluting reminder of their subordinate status. In a place where they could comfortably display themselves as mothers and women, Snizhana had turned them again, although only for a few minutes, into destitute care workers.

## Employers Can Make People Real

Even if expectations toward their employers were remarkably low, the women nonetheless had to place a great deal of trust in them for their legal status. Only employers could make possible their adjustment of status, thus enabling them to become legal residents. Since the very beginning, they worked for families based on the mutual understanding that, when the chance manifested, their employers would support their applications for an adjustment of status.

For the women, to acquire legal status was, as they said, to become "real people," able to live in the open and to visit their hometown.[20] To "get papers" required two preconditions. One was the launch by the Italian government of a special program, an amnesty, for irregular foreign workers. This happened with a certain frequency, often with special provisions targeting domestic workers.

Such amnesties allowed for the regularization of employment relations, transforming an illegal labor contract into a regular, tax-paying one. Residence permits automatically followed. The granting of legal status to immigrants was consequently a by-product of the granting of amnesty to employers for their violation of labor laws.

To "get papers," it was consequently necessary that employers apply for such a program, acknowledging previous employment of foreign workers and paying a fine. Alternatively, employers could pretend the women were still abroad and apply as if they wanted to recruit and sponsor them within the yearly contingent of authorized new foreign workers.[21] The women's hopes to *get papers* were consequently entirely contingent on their bosses' goodwill.

From the point of view of the women, working as an irregular migrant was part of a moral economy in which they exchanged faithful service for the promise of such goodwill. Most women relied on the promise of their employers that they would file the application for them when a new amnesty opened up. Whenever it happened, many women discovered that such promises could be easily broken.

Many employers were reluctant to file their applications. Some thought that the women, once they acquired legal status, would leave for "better" families. Many others feared they would ask for higher wages. Many did not want to pay the fine. Among the oldest and weakest, many assumed, rightly, that the women would use their newly acquired papers to return to their countries for a visit. They worried what would happen to them in those weeks, and they feared the women might not come back again.

When amnesties were launched, the group lived in a state of frenzy. The first question the women asked each other when they met was if their employer had already filed the application. The favorite topic of discussion in our gatherings was how to persuade the elderly, or their relatives, to apply for the amnesty. Many women offered to pay the fine themselves. Some promised they would pay for a replacement out of their own money for the weeks they would spend traveling home. All played hard the card of telling how existentially important it was for them.

If everything failed, the women had to rush to find new families willing to file the application for them. Short of that, the women would fail to become *real people*, often being constrained to keep working every day for the families that had denied them such status. During my fieldwork, I witnessed many successful regularizations, but I also knew several women who had failed to obtain legal status.

One case I witnessed was particularly painful. Valeria was a Moldovan woman in her midforties, who had been working for more than three years for an old man, Beppe, with severe walking limitations. I had always been impressed by how well Beppe and Valeria got along. Valeria, the mother of three children, the youngest of whom was barely three years old when she left, was taking care of him in an admirable way, and Beppe used to refer to Valeria as the "daughter he had never had."

I was consequently quite shocked when I met Valeria and she told me Beppe had decided that he would not file the application, fearing she would never go back to work for him after her trip home. She had tried to reassure him in every possible way, and she had begged for his help to no avail. She asked me to go visit Beppe and try to persuade him to file the application, whose deadline was just a couple of weeks away.

I visited him, and I did my best, but there was no way to change his mind. Beppe claimed he could not trust someone who took care of him just for money and that he could not stay even one week without assistance. I tried to remind him of the care and attention he had received from her over the years, and I tried to make him sympathetic to the plight of a mother who had not seen her children for more than three years. Beppe was, however, unmovable: "Who will stay with me while she is away?" Valeria tried desperately to make a last attempt, suggesting she could pay for the trip to have her sister come to Alpinetown, so that she could take care of Beppe while Valeria was away.

He did not want to have an unknown person in his flat, and anyway, he did not trust Valeria to keep her word. Once she had her papers, he argued, she would be able to leave him at any moment. Valeria cried and implored him to listen to his heart and to her pain. She reminded him he was a parent; he could understand how she felt in not having seen her children for years. Beppe was unaffected by her ardent pleas. He was not filing the application. She could stay as an irregular immigrant or she could leave immediately.

Valeria accompanied me to the door and thanked me for trying. She felt trapped by the necessity of providing for her family and could not believe how heartless Beppe was. That night, sleepless in bed, I could not stop thinking about how it must have been for Valeria to spend the night in the same flat of the man who was denying her rights and the chance to see her children, a man who could nevertheless call her at any time to be helped to the bathroom. Even worse, in the following days, with the deadline fast approaching, I happened to hear similar stories from other women.

Luckily, the case of Valeria turned out, at the very last minute, to be a success story. Just a few days before the amnesty expired, she was able to find—as I will explain shortly—another person who needed her company and succeeded in obtaining her papers.

## Staying Put

The arrival of their "papers" was a point of no return in the lives of the women. Until then, the women had little choice in their lives. The lack of papers sharply reduced their options both in Alpinetown and in their engagement with their place of origin. Without legal status, their lives were remarkably similar. Once they had obtained their papers, their futures became multiple, as a set of paths that antagonized *here* and *there* in a very sharp way.

If they wanted to be able to send a sizable amount of remittances to their families, if they wanted to repair or build a house *there*, they had to keep their living expenses in Alpinetown to the bare minimum. They could achieve such goals only by continuing to work as live-in care workers. Any other solution would have implied a higher level of expenditure *here*. For women who often tried to save (and send as remittances) up to 60 percent, or even 70 percent, of their meager salary, any other option would imply a dramatic change in their budget.

If they wanted to move on to other activities—such as hourly-paid domestic work for a pool of employers—they could expect a higher salary, but they faced much higher expenses. Unless they had a partner, their saving capacity would shrink (at best) to something between 10 and 20 percent of their salary. Live-in care work, moreover, guaranteed more stability: unless the elder died or became hospitalized, the contract would continue at pretty much the same conditions. Other types of domestic services, such as cleaning or babysitting, brought more freedom, but the demand varied rapidly and often unpredictably. Employers could terminate contracts or reduce hours suddenly and for a multiplicity of reasons.[22]

Even if a woman worked, as they usually tried to do, for several employers, her income might vary considerably from one month to the next. The women who had a strong orientation toward *there*, who stayed loyal to their perception of their life in Alpinetown as a mere—and painful—parenthesis, had few alternatives to remaining in the live-in sector. They would change their positions only when their elderly clients died or when "better" families could hire them. Once they received papers, all women would consider only families that would respect their desire to return home regularly, for visits that they felt justified their pains. But they could also leave "bad" employers to become part of "good" families.

The differences between "bad" and "good" families were generally not monetary: besides occasional gifts, the salary was pretty much the same, and it was sometimes slightly lower in the "better" families (for example, if the employer scrupulously paid the statutory contribution for the worker rather than giving a part of it to the employee in cash).[23] The women who worked for relatively autonomous elderly people enjoyed a much better work experience, but it was usually difficult to choose a job on these grounds.

A "good" family was rather a workplace in which the woman could claim to be materially and spiritually respected, treated as a "decent human being." It required the allotment of some space for herself in the flat, such as a room or a cupboard explicitly reserved for her, a certain degree of autonomy in her activities with the elderly, and an understanding of her need to return home regularly during the holidays. Above all, it required that members of the family adopt a way of dealing with the woman that entailed treating her as "part of the family" rather than as a mere worker.

Although the forms through which such sui generis inclusion was often actualized may seem paternalistic and hypocritical to external observers, the women experienced them differently. As they understood housekeeping, and particularly care work, as morally acceptable only as a labor of love, they felt that serving a family, performing domestic chores, and taking care of its elderly members *only for the money* was morally polluting. A "good" family was a family that recognized their emotional and moral commitment, their status as respectful, ersatz daughters.

For these women, the best possible employer was consequently an employer who allowed and actually collaborated actively in building with the woman a hybrid space where she could be at the same time fully committed to fulfill her duties towards *there*, while being treated as a dignified member of the family *here*. A perfect match was difficult but not impossible, as the story of Valeria, after her misadventure with Beppe, documented to many other women.

Three days after our unsuccessful attempt to persuade Beppe to do his duty, and only a few days before the closing of the amnesty program, a volunteer in a local parish received a telephone call asking for a reliable care worker. He shyly suggested Valeria, warning that she did not have her papers and that she was looking for an employer willing to file for her regularization.

To his surprise, the caller replied that *of course* her grandmother would never exploit a worker. She expected to sign a regular contract and to file for her amnesty. Her grandmother wanted, however, to meet the woman to see if they could get along well. He immediately called me and asked if I could accompany Valeria to the appointment, keeping our fingers crossed.

We thus met Ilda, an eighty-year-old *signora* and a former social worker who had been always quite active in the progressive Catholic scene of Alpinetown. The doctor had advised her to look for a care worker, as she had started having difficulties in walking and she fainted repeatedly. She was, nevertheless, largely autonomous, she loved reading and watching movies, and she was looking, as she said in deliciously antiquated Italian, for a *dama di compagnia*.[24]

The two women liked each other, and I was hopeful that Valeria could get out of the mess she was in with Beppe. What really surprised me during the meeting was discovering a very different Valeria. While I had always thought of her as shy and clumsy, Valeria presented herself to Ilda in a very different way, stressing she was an educated woman, a good mother, and a devout Christian.

Although she had asked for my presence as a translator, she insisted on speaking herself, claiming she was looking for an educated *signora*, with whom she would be able to learn "proper Italian and not some kind of dialect." She made frequent allusions to her tastes and connections in Alpinetown, thus giving Ilda the idea that in hiring her she would have access to a wide network of interesting, younger foreign women with whom to chat, walk, dine, watch television, and read books.

As I knew how desperate Valeria really was, I was shocked by her playing ball very hard, insisting that, in order to accept the job, she needed the guarantee of having a separate room for herself, where nobody could enter without knocking, and to be sure that she could enjoy her holidays when she needed to. I was frightened everything could collapse at any moment. Valeria seemed to know better: Ilda appreciated her performance and was more than ready to agree to her conditions. She even asked if she would like to have a TV set in her room. Valeria and Ilda visited the nicely organized flat, and we returned home to pack and say goodbye to Beppe. For once, good had been rewarded and evil punished.

A few months later, Valeria called me to invite me to a party to celebrate her newly acquired papers. I took for granted that we would have a pizza slice at the usual benches in the main square, but she informed me it was a borscht party at *their* flat. When I rang the bell, the voice of a woman asked in Ukrainian who I was and let me in. When I entered, I was amazed. A few women were toasting with a glass of wine. I was immediately given one, and I joined the toast for the new "real person," "the only one we have here . . . at least for now!" Katya said. Ilda greeted me, obviously happy to have "young" people around chatting with her. We sat at the table, and we had a real feast of borscht, Olivier salad, pickles, dried herring, salami, cheese, sausages, and mashed potatoes.

The atmosphere was cheerful, and Ilda and Valeria both performed equally as hosts, one filling our plates with food, the other filling our glasses with wine. Their movements were so simultaneous and gracefully fine-tuned that I found it difficult to remember I was actually visiting a care worker friend, that most of the guests were actually still irregular migrants, and that the old woman was actually her employer. The two really seemed like good friends, and the whole thing seemed like a peculiar family gathering.

After a while, I joined Valeria in the kitchen to prepare some more food. Valeria hugged me and said how happy she was to be able to have a real life with Ilda, as well as being able to visit her family. She now felt "like a daughter" in Alpinetown, and she could still send nearly all her salary to her children and improve their living condition *there*.

She would soon travel there for some weeks, and she would be able to see with her own eyes the house that was being remodeled thanks to her remittances. She opened the fridge and invited me to look inside, stressing that there was no rust anywhere and that all the containers were brand new. She asked if I liked the plates and cutlery we were using for our lunch. Valeria and Ilda had recently gone to IKEA, and they had bought all they needed to modernize the place. They had purchased new furniture for their rooms, carpets for the bathroom, and new appliances for the kitchen. After lunch, she proudly showed us her room, which looked cozy. She also brought us to Ilda's room to appreciate the new furniture. On a table, there were some frames. Valeria said she had given them to Ilda as a present. They contained photos of members of the families of both women.

## Unstable Familiarities

Among the women, Valeria had been especially lucky in meeting Ilda. Her living conditions were markedly above average compared with the

other women. However, many other women succeeded in gaining recognition as "part of the family." Natalka, a Ukrainian engineer in her
forties, had established with Luigi a relationship very similar to the one
Valeria had developed with Ilda. Luigi, although in his (very) late seven-
ties, was largely independent, enjoyed the company of Natalka, and was
always happy when one or more of her friends visited. He sometimes
accompanied Natalka to the parking lot on Sunday morning, and, once
it opened, he sometimes attended Mass at the Ukrainian church with
her. Natalka was also proud to say he had asked if she would bring him
to her hometown sometime, as he had always dreamed of visiting what
he still called the Soviet Union.

The two were so close we always suspected they had become lovers. I
asked Natalka several times if there was any element of truth in such al-
legations. She always denied it, saying that Luigi was more of a father to
her. In addition, she said, Luigi was very religious, and he would never
ever break the promise he had made to Maria, the woman he had married sixty years earlier who had recently died. They were just very close,
and she felt she was taking care of him not only for the money, but
because he deserved it.

Family-like arrangements such as those of Valeria and Natalka were
emotionally satisfying, and they allowed for a strong orientation toward
their families in Ukraine or Moldova. Having obtained their papers,
they were able to improve their lives in Alpinetown while maintaining
a strong connection to their sending areas, which they could now visit
regularly.

These arrangements were, however, quite fragile. After many years,
Luigi died, assisted by Natalka to the very end. Natalka felt a great loss,
compounded by the fact that she had lost both her income and her
home. The women did their best to find her a new job, but she seemed
unable to perform. When I invited her for coffee, she said that for the
first time since she had arrived in Italy, she was frightened. Before Luigi,
she had never worried; she knew that her elder would eventually die
and that she would have to change positions. This time, it was different:
Luigi's death had awakened in her a sense of insecurity about the future.
What was she supposed to do? When her small amount of savings ran
out, she returned to care work, but with a very different, bitter attitude.[25]

Besides the fragility, these care-work arrangements implied a different organization of the women's time. The women who stayed in live-
in care work maintained the original schedule of the group, while the
women who had made different occupational choices acquired—at least
potentially—a different control over their time. Although there were

substantial overlapping areas, and the two groups kept meeting often in the same places, this difference slowly introduced a bifurcation in their friendships, with some women reproducing more or less the traditional pattern of makeshift sociability on Sunday mornings and Thursday afternoons, while others started experimenting with new activities.

Remaining in live-in care work, moreover, shaped their subsequent careers in an indirect but powerful way. Except for extraordinary cases of sympathetic employers, live-in care workers could not fulfill the preconditions for applying for family reunification. To remain in live-in care work implied *not* sponsoring the arrival of offspring. The women who remained in live-in care work could, however, contribute financially to the emigration of other women and provide referrals to other families who needed live-in care workers. Several migration chains started, with some women able to sponsor informally the arrival of several women. Their success in doing so supported the expansion of the group, helping to reproduce its gender and occupational homogeneity.

## Hybrid Spaces

Many of the women, even while remaining in the care-work sector, found it necessary to acquire a private space physically detached from the flats in which they were working. The renting of such a space was sometimes part of the larger project of leaving care work. Most of the time, it was simply the consequence of other pressing necessities. In particular, many women who had started affairs in Alpinetown felt the need to have a space where they could meet their lovers in a safe environment.

Natalya was a plump brunette with a sunny smile, very popular among the women. A former doctor, she had arrived in Alpinetown in 2004, leaving behind two daughters she had entrusted to her sister.[26] She worked hard taking care of Claudia, a ninety-year-old woman with limited mobility. Natalya and Claudia lived in a tiny flat in a working-class neighborhood. Claudia slept in the only bedroom, while Natalya slept on a sofa in a small living room, where the furniture was composed of an old television, a radio with an extendable antenna, and a table with four wooden chairs covered with flowery cushions. In the little kitchen, there was a wood stove still in operation. Claudia lived in a state of semisleep because of her pains and chronic weakness. She was no longer able to walk alone, and she needed help to go to the bathroom and help with eating.

Natalya did not complain about the accommodation, as Claudia always paid on time, and her many relatives—she had seven children, fifteen grandchildren, and nine great-grandchildren—visited regularly, giving Natalya the luxury of a couple of hours free every day. She had always claimed to me that live-in care work, "where you accompany people to die" and "wash up old asses," was exactly what she wanted. Unpleasant as it was, it allowed her to do quickly what she had come to Italy to do.

When she met Leonid, her situation started to appear much less satisfactory. He was living in a very crowded flat with other construction workers. Going there was simply out of the question. He was sometimes able to borrow a car from a friend, which they could park somewhere in the countryside for some moments of intimacy. On other occasions, he was able to pay for a room in a cheap motel on the periphery of Alpinetown. Both solutions were expensive and precarious. For a while, Natalya thought she had found a solution: the evenings Leonid was free, she gave Claudia a reinforced dose of the medication she had to take when she had trouble sleeping. Leonid could thus visit her while the elderly woman was sleeping. Either Leonid had too many free evenings, or the dosage was wrong, but Claudia started becoming increasingly dizzy, and one night, Natalya had to call the doctor. She realized it was time to stop and to look for another solution.

A few months later, she looked for me at the bus station and asked if I could help her to move some boxes with my car. I asked, worried, if she had lost her job, but she replied that she had just found a cozy place to stay when not working. It was cheaper than a hotel, and she could leave some of her things there. I drove the car to the flat where she worked. When we opened the door, I heard a little voice asking in dialect who it was. Natalya gave me a nod, and she moved quickly to her room. She approached the bed, gently touched Claudia's hand, and asked her if she needed anything. She also introduced me to Claudia, who said she did not need anything, but she was tired of life.

Natalya scolded her and told her to enjoy the time she had left with her loved ones. She counted for me the number of Claudia's offspring, something Claudia was obviously proud of. Natalya told her we had come to pick up something, and that she would be back in a couple of hours. She gave Claudia a magazine and her glasses and kissed her on the cheek. Natalya went to the cupboard and started grabbing towels, bedsheets, some clothes, and other items she had been accumulating for years. She placed some in a suitcase. When it was completely full, she started filling some plastic bags. Before exiting the place, Natalya glanced once more at Claudia sleeping peacefully.

We drove for a few minutes, and we stopped to park on a side street in what used to be an industrial area of Alpinetown. We took the bags, and we walked to a ghostly building, a three-story house that seemed deserted. She rang a bell and a woman told us to enter. We climbed the stairs to the second floor, where a Russian woman in her late fifties, Ruslana, welcomed us.

The flat looked shabby, and Ruslana, whom I had never met before, had an unfriendly attitude. She accompanied us to a room and told Natalya to store her things in one of the free wardrobe drawers. She subsequently wrote her name with a marker on the wardrobe, below a long list of crossed-out previous names. She gave Natalya three keys—one for the main entrance, one for the flat, and the third for the room—and told her she wanted to be always paid on time, no excuses accepted. They shook hands, and she accompanied us to the door.

Once we were outside, I could not help asking about what I had seen. I was actually surprised I had never heard of Ruslana, and I did not know anything about such a rental opportunity. Natalya explained to me that nobody had heard about Ruslana until very recently. She had been one of the first Soviet women to arrive in the Italian northeast. She had actually arrived *before* the fall of the Soviet Union, and nobody knew for sure how she had succeeded in leaving the USSR, what she had done afterward, or how she had been able to buy the flat. Natalya knew she had married a *chórnenky*, a vague Ukrainian term that covered blacks and North Africans.

The couple had been renting rooms in the flat informally to North African immigrants for a long time. She had never rented to Eastern European women, both because she seemed to avoid interacting with them and because she did not want trouble with the police for renting to irregular migrants. Now that many women had acquired their papers, however, Ruslana had realized they could be quite an appealing new niche in her market. She had accepted an offer to rent a shared room to three of them, Natalya, Alla, and Sofia.

The three of them would split the monthly cost of the rent (120 euros) and they could use the room at different times, according to an agreed-upon schedule and precise rules enforced by Ruslana herself. Natalya, Alla, and Sofia each had the right to use one of the wardrobes in the room, and they would leave the room clean after each of their visits.

The formula proved popular. A few weeks later, waiting in the parking lot to collect Natalya, I met Ivan there, the husband of a care worker and one of the minivan drivers going back and forth between Western Ukraine and Alpinetown. He told me he had just rented a room from Ruslana. He would be able to sleep there when he was in Alpinetown and he could eventually meet his own wife in his room rather than, as previously, in the minivan. He joked that Aleksandra, his wife, was a healthy woman with a large appetite, and she could not be satisfied with a few quickies in the backseat of the minivan, "like when we were kids." He explained to me they had been thinking for a long time about finding a place in Alpine-town. He was tired of his "gypsy life," as he had been traveling back and forth for a long time. He felt the need to have some proper space.

Renting a flat just for them, however, would have required a change in the plans they had in their hometown: they simply could not afford to invest in both places. The supply of cheap rooms *here* by Ruslana had solved their pressing problems allowing them to keep their commitment to *there* nearly intact. Ruslana's flat was the first instance of a migrant institution I started encountering more frequently during my fieldwork: the shared "service" apartment. With more "real people" in the group, a growing number of women pooled their resources to obtain access to a flat they could use during their free time.

In the case of Natalya and her friends, the purpose of acquiring such a space was linked to their sexual encounters. Therefore, to Ruslana's peace, other women seldom visited them in her flat. In many other cases, the women acquired access to a shared room or a flat collectively, as a place to relax together and to experience a surrogate home. Many of these shared flats were temporary: a woman rented a cheap but spacious place as a way to fulfill the requirements for family reunification. While waiting for the procedure to be complete, many women found it convenient to provide access to the flat to other women, in exchange for a low monthly rent.

The women would hardly ever sleep in the flat—they usually had to stay with their elderly clients during the night—but they would use it during their free time as a base they could feel was their own. Slowly, a network of shared places in the cheaper neighborhoods of Alpinetown developed, and many women had now an alternative to public parks and waiting rooms. In many cases, these flats could be crowded or nearly empty according to multiple contingencies.

With time, each of them acquired a specific identity. Some women rented rooms managerially, similarly to Ruslana. In others, the women jointly elaborated specific rules. In one of these flats, every Sunday, the women would take turns cooking a meal for the others. Each woman, moreover, had the right to invite to these lunches one of her friends. The cooking competition among the women was strong, and the Sunday lunches became real feasts, during which a small crowd could exchange contacts and information. In some shared flats, women could meet their dates provided it was outside the hours of major traffic.

In one of the flats, however, the women who shared it did not allow any man to enter, as they wanted to enjoy their few hours there completely relaxed, "so if you want, you can stay in your underwear if you feel like doing so." In some flats, each woman had her own space, and there were strict rules against invading the privacy of others. In others, the climate reminded me of the Yugoslav artist communes my parents had sometimes whispered about when talking about their youth.

The shared flats had also two important ancillary functions, which somewhat alleviated the inconvenience of living in the employer's flat. First, the women who shared a service flat could host guests for the night. Many women had previously felt humiliated by the fact that their employers would not allow them to host anybody, even close relatives in dire need. If they were members of a shared flat, they acquired the right to host. This was a great resource, particularly for those who had relatives or friends who wanted to join them in Alpinetown. The network of shared flats played an important role in the development of various migratory chains.

Slowly, an increasing number of women arrived in Alpinetown with someone waiting for them and knowing where they would sleep the first nights. Interestingly, the shared flat fostered a second, differentiated type of migration chain. If the women who had stayed in live-in care work could support only other women interested in the same job, women sharing a flat could support both women interested in live-in care work and women willing to go directly to hourly-paid jobs for a pool of households.

Another important function of these shared flats was to enable the women to store their property. Over the years, the women had acquired a sizable number of items—clothes, books, videos, appliances, cutlery, and many other things—that quickly filled any appropriable space. The women were hungry for space where they could store their things, and the shared flats I visited had, unsurprisingly, a large percentage of space devoted to storing boxes and packages.

The shared flats helped many women to subsist within the care-work sector, thus making them able to stay focused on their dreams and aspirations in their home areas. At the same time, the availability of shared flats was also an unexpected platform for those women who rooted themselves more deeply in Alpinetown. When they received nonresidential work offers, they could accept without having to worry immediately about the resources needed to find stable accommodation. They would stay in one of the shared flats for a few weeks and make a decision only once they had tried out the new job.

## Putting Down Roots in Alpinetown

Leaving live-in care work was one of the contingencies that made a woman gravitate more toward life in Alpinetown. As the women (correctly) anticipated, for them changing work would mean changing their lives. It implied an existential shift toward the new location, as more and more energy had to be focused there. There were basically three reasons for doing so, and they were nearly always strictly intertwined: they were tired of living in the home of somebody else; they wanted to hedge their bets, working for a pool of employers rather than for a single elderly person; and they wanted a visa for their children (very rarely for a husband).

To file for a family visa, the immigrant must prove she has regular resident status, an adequate income, and a flat large enough to accommodate the sponsored relatives.[27] If they wanted to call for their children, something that became more and more common with the lengthening of their stay, the women had to start changing their lives and budgeting expenditures years in advance, trying to satisfy such requirements.

Sometimes, the relatives of the elderly the women cared for could turn out to be an unexpected resource for such a transition. When the elder died, some relatives would quickly fire the care worker, as had happened to Natalka and Elena. In other cases, they felt responsible for the fate of the woman who had cared for their dear ones, trying to find another satisfactory arrangement.

Masha was a very popular woman in the group, a witty, nice person who had always a caring word for anyone. She was wholly focused on returning as soon as possible to her native town, where her thirteen-year-old boy was living with her mother. In order to earn more, she had actually chosen to work in the most difficult segment of the care-work market: she worked for very old persons, with limited mobility and little self-sufficiency. As seven of her employers had died in a little less than three years, the women had nicknamed her "super-sidelka," a way of stressing her nearly supernatural strength and motivation. Masha found such an arrangement stressful but she always claimed it was what she needed: she was in Alpinetown to work, and her field was better paid and easier to find.

Over the years, however, she started feeling more and more uneasy with the prospect of Alexej, her son, living alone in Ukraine. She often complained he was too stubborn; she feared that he had taken a wrong path and that her mother was unable to exercise the necessary authority.

She felt guilty about having left him alone. One evening, while we were strolling in the park, she nervously blamed herself for the money she had been sending home all those years. She felt it had been a type of "poison."

Money had turned Alexej into a spoiled brat, with false friends only interested in his high-tech gadgetry. She wanted to go back, but she could not. Most of her savings had gone into buying and renovating a large flat in her hometown, but she would not have any source of income there. She added that it was no good to raise a boy like Alexej in Ukraine. She claimed that "the country was bankrupt" according to any point of view. She did not know what to do.

A few weeks later, the woman she assisted died at ninety-seven. Her son, Loris, who was more than seventy and recently widowed, offered Masha the opportunity to stay in his mother's flat, paying only a nominal rent. He also offered her a job as an hourly-paid cleaner in his own flat. She would clean his flat, do the shopping, cook, and do the laundry for him. He was moreover very active in spreading the news about such a trustworthy housekeeper in the neighborhood. The priest of the nearby parish was also happy to help her find other employers. Masha soon found herself having more work than she could handle, and she quickly realized she was earning more than she had before.

A few months later, Masha called me on a Sunday afternoon saying she wanted me to meet a person who was very important to her. Because many women had, as usual, speculated about the real nature of the relationship between Masha and Loris, I assumed she was going to introduce me to her new partner. When I arrived, I noticed that Masha's surname now appeared on the bell. An overexcited Masha opened the door and quickly dragged me into the kitchen where a young man was having a coffee.

Alexej had arrived by minivan in the morning. He seemed nice but shy: he introduced himself and immediately excused himself. He subsequently sat silent, sipping coffee, smoking cigarettes, and looking out the window. Masha said it was normal that he felt lost in a new environment. She was confident that Alexej would manage now that he had a mother to rely upon. She had already prepared a room for him and signed a contract for an internet connection, while Loris, her employer and landlord, had found him a job in a local factory. Everything would be fine.

It surely was, for a certain number of years, until the death of Loris. Besides the pain, Masha found herself quickly evicted from the flat, now the property of Loris's three children. She briefly thought about returning to care work, but Alexej's presence made such a return nearly impossible. She decided to try to rent a flat, relying on the fact that Alexej had a steady income from his job at the factory. She found a moderately priced flat in a nearby village, from which she could reach Alpinetown by public transportation.

The flat was on the third floor, with no lift, in a gray, square building. It was tiny and very dark: two rooms connected by a living room with a small kitchen in the corner. From the windows, I could see a bleak concrete square, completely deserted. With no shade and a geometry consisting of straight lines and squared angles, it was reminiscent of the loneliness captured in De Chirico paintings. The room on the left was Alexej's room, while on the right, there was a smaller room where Masha slept, with only a French bed and a wardrobe with a mirror attached to a nail.

The bathroom had no windows, the ceiling paint was starting to peel off, and the washing machine was rather rusty. Masha said she knew her place was not particularly inviting, far from the warm, cozy environment she had enjoyed thanks to Loris. At least, she stressed, nobody could kick her out of it. She had proudly placed on her sofa a cloth embroidered by her mother, and she had nailed to the wall some icons and some family photos, including one of Loris. She prepared some pickles, salami, and cheese as a starter, followed by borscht.

Even if worried about the new expenses, she was happy about having her own flat and she was proud of Alexej: he worked hard and he had eventually decided what he wanted to do. They were saving money to buy a minivan, so that he could earn his living driving back and forth from Ukraine. She felt it was a good idea, and reasonably safe: "Ukrainian women will emigrate to Alpinetown for decades," she reckoned. At the time, the idea struck me as farfetched. As with many other forecasts concerning the women, I was wrong.

At the end of 2009, Masha became the first female logistical broker in Alpinetown, providing reliable service to women who needed to travel or safely send goods or money to their families. The business has been thriving since then, and the company currently includes two minivans plus a rented storage place in the countryside and a shared flat where the newly arrived women can rent a bed during their first days.

Masha has been able to finance such a business because, after Loris's death, she soon discovered a new, never exploited, economic niche: providing company to elderly hospitalized people. During her years as "super-sidelka," Masha had acquired quite a reputation for managing elderly people very well under stress. One day, the son of one of Loris's neighbors telephoned her to ask her if she could substitute for him in the daily visits to his father, who had broken his ribs. She only had to visit him, check if everything was all right, chat a bit, and read the newspapers aloud.

Masha already knew the man, who had been on friendly terms with Loris, and she did so successfully. The son employed her frequently, whenever he was unable to perform the daily visits to his father. One day, a woman approached her and asked if she would be willing to do the same with her hospitalized mother, who wanted to take a walk every day. Masha quickly realized she had stumbled onto a potentially vast demand for services.

Many Alpinetown families had trouble visiting their old relatives daily in their frequently long spells of hospitalization. They did not feel at ease leaving them entirely in the care of the hospital staff. Professionals offered efficient care in an impersonal, often brusque, style. Masha was more than willing to leave to the hospital staff all the physically demanding care actions, while focusing instead on emotional support and small talk.

Her customers, however, needed very flexible schedules. She was reluctant to give up any potential customer, and she understood families had to be able to book her on short notice. As she explained to me, "Once they discover they can call me to manage an emergency, they have more and more frequent emergencies." Masha's solution was to identify some other women who could provide the service when she could not supply it directly. She selected a few friends who could speak Italian fluently.

As the elders did not like the other people in the room knowing that their visitors were salaried personnel, she also looked for women who could reasonably perform as respectable family friends or previous, trusted care workers. Sometimes, when she could not find enough personnel, Masha would call me and ask me to fulfill one of her contracts. As she stressed, it was easy money: I had to enter the hospital room, greet the person, explain that I was a friend of a daughter/son/husband, and start behaving like a distant family friend visiting a sick acquaintance.

The first time, she assigned me to Gilda, a ninety-year-old woman hospitalized in the geriatrics unit after having had a stroke. I was worried, fearing Gilda could react badly to my arrival. I approached her, greeted her by kissing her on the cheeks, and proudly announced that I was an office colleague of her daughter Tina. I asked how she felt, made some small talk, and that was it.

Gilda slept on and off a couple of times in the two hours I was with her, and all I had to do was give her a glass of water and accompany her to the bathroom once. In the meantime, Masha was assisting a man in the next room, reading him the local newspaper. When we left the hospital, we went to drink a coffee together, and Masha was clearly proud of what she had achieved. Besides the money, she was doing work she felt was charitable.

She visited the sick and made them feel their relatives cared for them. She simultaneously helped their overworked and time-starved offspring. She was cleaning houses in the morning and spending her afternoons in the hospital. Together with Alexej's salary, they could finally live a decent life, and she could be a *signora*. As she stressed proudly, "I am becoming a *signora*, without having to marry an Italian man."

In many other cases, the trajectory out of care work was considerably more difficult. Tamara was a Ukrainian woman in her midforties who had previously worked as a teacher. She had already assisted two elderly people and accompanied them to their deaths, and she felt her life was miserable. She had realized she would not return to Ukraine anytime soon, as nobody could live there on a teacher's salary.

Her son, Edward, was in high school, and she did not like the idea of him growing up there, where "the only thing he can learn is to get drunk and beat his wife." She also thought that Ukrainian universities were "a waste of time," and she did not want to spend years washing old asses so he could attend a finishing school. She had slowly started to think that bringing him to Alpinetown could be the solution. She did not want to go on living as a care worker. She felt that caring for the elderly was a degrading activity.

Contrary to most other women, her indictment extended to cleaning in private households, which she also considered servile. The only kind of household service she regarded as honorable was taking care of children—something she felt was compatible with her education and work experience. One day, she approached me, asking to help her to find courses in Italian and children's textbooks.

She wanted to improve her Italian so that an Italian mother would trust her children to learn properly with her; she felt any potential employer would want a babysitter only if she was also able to help with the homework. In the end, we found a parish where some volunteers offered a language class designed to be compatible with the schedule of care workers. We also collected some textbooks, which Tamara studied at night, also working to improve her computer literacy. For a long period of time, her growing capacities did not match the scarce opportunities open to her.

Assisting an elderly woman diagnosed with terminal cancer, she had to interact daily with her daughter. Sandra was the CEO of a company based in Alpinetown and a mother of two. When her mother died, she asked Tamara, now unemployed, if she wanted to take care of her house and her two children. She was supposed to show up for work at 7 a.m., bring the kids to school, do the shopping, and clean the house. She would be free from 12 to 4 p.m., when she would have to pick up the children at school, bring them to their sport activities, pick them up again, bring them home, help with the eventual homework, shower them, and prepare them for dinner around 7:30 p.m.

When the family started their dinner together, she was free to go. The salary was good, and she would have most of the weekends free, a rare treat for a former *sidelka*. Tamara was thrilled by the offer, but also scared. She had to start immediately, and she had to find a place to sleep. Luckily, she was already participating in a shared flat, and the other women agreed that she could move there permanently, paying a larger percentage of the rent.

After a year, she managed to garner enough savings to rent a small flat by herself, in the same neighborhood as Masha. It was a run-down flat on the ground floor of a dilapidated building, but it satisfied the requirement for applying for family reunification. Tamara was very proud of having eventually attained a degree of privacy, and, unlike most other women, she never tried to sublet a room to help herself out. She immediately applied for a family reunification visa for Edward. Having completed high school in Ukraine, he needed an extra year in an Italian high school to enroll in an Italian university.

When Edward arrived, Tamara discovered that her life project, when turned into reality, was exhausting. To pay for the new expenses, she was working for Sandra with the usual schedule, while spending her "free" hours visiting patients in the hospital for Masha. Such long hours helped her to stay afloat financially, providing the money she needed to maintain the lifestyle she had promised herself to give to her son. It also meant that she was nearly always absent, while Edward was catapulted into a new country, new friends, and an important exam to struggle with in the last year of high school.

Luckily, Edward learned Italian very quickly, and he was able to successfully complete his last year of high school and enter university on a scholarship. Since then, Tamara has kept working for families with children. When Sandra's children became teenagers, Sandra helped her to find another job with a family with small children. She has acquired a good reputation, and she likes to repeat how "I do not have to look for work anymore; now, it's the work that looks for me."

# TWO

# Practicing Abundance: Immigrant Women and the Challenge of Consumption

During the early years of my fieldwork, one of the main challenges I struggled with was the huge ideological difference between the women I was spending time with and me. We held widely divergent opinions on most personal, moral, and political issues, and I was often uncertain about whether to express my views, triggering lively rows, or to keep quiet or even be hypocritical for the sake of peace. I was constantly feeling that if I really spoke my mind, they would find me unsympathetic and spoiled, and they would become suspicious of my project and me. It took quite a bit of time to discover that my fears helped me to identify some important questions I would have otherwise missed.

A key difference concerned the importance of consumption, both in our view of the social world and in our everyday lives. Despite their tight circumstances with regard to disposable income, the women thought of themselves above all as consumers. They were willing to bestow recognition and esteem on themselves and others based on how much money each individual or family could spend. Although they were all destitute by the standard of Alpinetown natives, differences in material assets largely defined the internal social stratification of the group. Showing off newly acquired goods was the most effective way of garnering respect from their peers both in the spaces of Alpinetown and in their relationships with their places of origin.[1] To tell the truth, the ease with which the women used levels of consumption as the only reliable indicator of personal worth was often shocking to me.[2]

I found equally puzzling how the women's memories and images of Soviet times were different from what I expected. Few of their families had escaped some form of Soviet repression. Some of them knew of relatives who had died in the Ukrainian Holodomor ("killing by hunger"), the politically motivated famine of 1932–33 in which millions of Ukrainian peasants died.[3] They described these episodes of political repression stoically, or at least fatalistically. They treated them primarily as natural events beyond moral evaluation. Some of them even presented what had happened to their ancestors as unfortunate mistakes, as victims of a method of rule that was at least partly justified by historical conditions.[4]

At the same time, however, they were the most severe critics of the Soviet system for its inability to provide a decent supply of consumer goods. Their stories of Soviet life were above all stories told from the point of view of disgruntled consumers.[5]

Marinela, a Ukrainian woman in her fifties, had studied chemistry and subsequently worked for many years in a large factory. When I made a joke about the lack of willingness on the part of the women to queue in an orderly manner, she decided to share with me her memories of consumption in Soviet times. She said her early life had been an endless queue. When not working, most of her time was spent hunting for shops stocking the items she needed and queuing for them.

She introduced me to the complexities of the old over-the-counter system, in which she had to queue with her mother first to ask a rude shop attendant to see the goods. They subsequently had to queue to see another (equally rude) cashier to pay and get a receipt. Then, they had to queue again at another counter to surrender the receipt and collect the purchased goods.[6] Her most vivid childhood memory was queuing with her mother in cold and ugly shops. When she was a teenager, she said, the situation had somewhat improved: there were more self-service shops, there was a wider range of goods, and people like her, with a good family and a good wage, could hope to buy occasionally some special, luxurious items.

Her family "could afford to change some of their domestic appliances even if they were not broken," she said proudly. Still, shortage was omnipresent, and shopping was often a hunt for the unexpected. She had carried with her a string plastic bag at all times, because she never knew what might become available along the way.[7]

When she happened to see some agitation in front of a shop, she would immediately jump to check if something desirable had suddenly surfaced.

As a manager, she had to call off activities because the workers on her team had to rush to the shop to queue for a newly arrived item while it lasted. Queuing ate up a significant part of her life.[8] Most of the available goods were cheaply made and inadequate. Many items were available only in the (increasingly sophisticated) informal market. Many desired items were simply unavailable. She said her family accumulated a large amount of savings because there was not really much they could buy.

For a short time, at the beginning of perestroika, it seemed times were changing, and they would be able to buy whatever they wanted. In the second half of the 1980s, Marinela had once travelled to Moscow for a business meeting, and she had discovered a previously unknown world of luxurious objects, wonderful cosmetics, and trendy clothes. She had returned from her trip with a piece of luggage completely full of stuff, and she had distributed it among all her relatives and friends.

After a while, shortages became more acute, and queues got longer. When at last goods became plentiful, Marinela was no longer able to buy them. The goods were now in the shops, but she could not afford them.[9] Prices skyrocketed. Her salary, once regarded as quite good, was now a pittance and did not arrive for months. Her savings were gone. Sometimes, she would be paid in canned food produced by the very same factory she worked in, which she could hardly sell at a profit.

There were again long queues, in the cheapest shops, in the factory canteen, in the hospital when she accompanied her father for a medical visit. They had to pay for many things that were previously free, such as social security, medical assistance, schoolbooks, even—as she mentioned once—parking.

Quite soon, they had to start selling many of their assets. She thought often about emigrating, but she could not make up her mind. A few months before, she had seen from the window her teenage son imploring his friends to lend him one of their bicycles. She felt so humiliated for not being able to buy even a cheap bicycle for her son that she realized "it was time to go." She was working as a slave, she added. She washed old asses. She had yet to repay part of her debt. Two weeks ago, however, she had been able to ship a bicycle to her son, a brand new bicycle from a good Italian brand. He would no longer be humiliated by his family's lack of consumption power.

Marinela, like most other women, described the purpose of emigration, above all, in terms of improving the standard of living for her family. Although many women sent remittances for improving housing, buying some property, and financing their children's education, such medium-term goals always had to be balanced with "*il comprare belle cose*" (buying beautiful things), the short-term acquisition of desired goods their relatives could show off in their everyday life.

For most of the women, the worst sin they could imagine was a wealthy person, by which they meant anyone who had even a very small amount of disposable income, refraining from shopping. Nearly all of them, for example, regarded their employers as stingy and despised them for that. They reported in contemptuous tones that their employers could—as I actually often did—go for a walk in the center of Alpinetown and return home "without having bought anything." Many of their employers, again like me, could put up with an old TV set or vacuum cleaner rather than rushing to buy the latest model, even if they had a reliable income. They regarded shopping as a moral act.

For the women, Alpinetown appeared to be a vast landscape of commodities. The beauty of different neighborhoods was strictly contingent upon the quality of their commercial establishments. They used the location of the showrooms of luxury brands to orient themselves in space, rather than the names of streets and squares. Given the women's budgets, much of their interest was strictly theoretical. Few women could afford to buy anything more than the bare necessities, and even the most "wealthy" of them had no more than ten or fifteen euros a week for all discretionary expenditures.[10]

On Sundays, when most care workers had the day off, it was common to pool money to buy food for a communal meal. Each participant had to contribute only a couple of euros, yet many newcomers would return to their employer's flat, forfeiting a half-day of freedom, rather than incur this expense. For a birthday party, a cherished ritual, the budget rarely exceeded ten euros, which would provide a couple of liters of very cheap wine and some chips. It was a very spartan life; in the beginning, these women had literally nothing to spend.

Naïvely, I found it surprising that—within a few weeks of their arrival in Alpinetown—the women could psychologically immerse so deeply into the world of consumption from which they were financially excluded. They knew the price of everything, from cars to breast implants, from designer clothes to lunches at fast food outlets. They knew where all the items were on sale. Many had a veritable collection of the menus and supermarket leaflets found in their employers' mailboxes, whose bright pictures allowed them to identify each commodity and learn its name in Italian.

Window-shopping was our preferred pastime, and we frequently compared prices in Alpinetown with prices for similar goods in Ukraine or Moldova, and sometimes with prices in other European destinations. The women, who had relatives in other locations, were quick to highlight their cosmopolitan knowledge, stressing which brands were cheaper to shop for in other European countries. Though their participation in the market was virtual, it was nonetheless pervasive and intense.

## The Morality of Consumption

Over time, nearly all the women built some small capacity for discretionary consumption. In the first years, most of their wages were absorbed by remittances and by the repayment of their debts. The level of remittances was also very high at first, as their family members had to recover from the most pressing emergencies. Still, at a certain point, the women realized they had some money to spend in the new environment.[11]

They could start practicing what they regarded as the most important form of citizenship in the civilized world. I do not mean this ironically. The women fully subscribed to the old Latin saying that "a human being without money is the image of death," avoided by everybody and unable to participate in social life. They regarded their capacity to spend as positive proof that they were gaining a legitimate foothold in Alpinetown. Consumption made them feel empowered.

Becoming a consumer, though eagerly anticipated, was quite stressful. The lived experience of shopping implied a transformation both of the women themselves and of the transitional social spaces they inhabited. On a personal level, it imposed the burden of choice. The women understood sending remittances and repaying their debts as moral duties, beyond their control. Once their budgets had some room for maneuver, the women faced options that were heavily moralized.

The opening of even small consumption possibilities triggered difficult personal questions. How much was "right" to spend on themselves? How much should be sent back home? There was no automatic way to set the correct balance between the demands and desires of the women and their relatives, of *here* and *there*. The women could be criticized both for sacrificing too little and for sacrificing too much.

The constant tension between *here* and *there*, between being an immigrant and an emigrant, between their family duties and their individual right to well-being, was a central feature in the lives of the women. Shopping was a highly valued way of acquiring social status, but it remained fraught with anxiety. The women exhibited to their peers every single item purchased and meticulously described the process of buying it.

Each friend had to touch and express her appreciation of it. Touching items the other women had bought, admiring their texture, looking at them carefully before returning them, were all appreciated sensory ways of expressing solidarity with the buyer. The shared tactile emphasis among us was a way to both gain a small pleasure and to confirm to each other that we had moved from sight to touch, from passive admiration to active ownership.

Consumption was a key tool for gaining respect within the women's network, but it was also a risky activity. In fact, consumption conferred status only if carried out cleverly. To make a shopping mistake—to buy something that was available for less somewhere else or to buy a less prestigious brand for the same price—spoiled a woman's reputation, placing her in the category of the sucker. This was a moral judgment: the buyer had made a mistake because she had not trusted the expertise of the other women in the group; she had not asked for their advice or had not followed it.

Unsurprisingly, criticisms of shopping decisions were the most common source of interpersonal conflict among these women. In the early phases of their socialization as consumers, the women were torn between the desire to show off their purchases and the fear of being criticized. Those who dared to buy something alone would first show the good separately to the women they felt were closer to them and less judgmental and only subsequently, having built a sufficiently strong coalition, to the whole group.

A slower, but more consequential, process took place within the network of migrant women as they learned to be smart consumers by trial and error. Their experiences as care workers in Alpinetown did not provide them with the tacit knowledge necessary to navigate the world of local shopping. Although they were entrusted with a wide range of domestic chores, very few did the shopping for their employers, and those who did were specifically instructed where to go, what to buy, and at what price. Some women who had successfully navigated numerous public spaces in Alpinetown, including churches, offices, libraries, and hospitals, had never visited a shop or supermarket alone.

Paradoxically, the dimension of urban life they cherished the most was also the most alien to them. For all their theoretical knowledge, the women were unsure about proper behavior in stores and constantly worried that some ignorant mistake would reveal their stigmatized position as *lavaculi* to clerks and other customers. Participating in consumption required learning new attitudes and skills and discerning what norms applied in different places. Most women started buying in a few sites largely restricted to other migrant women of similar origin.

From there, their paths diverged. Some kept gravitating to these sites, while others explored diverse shopping venues and eventually shifted to them. Differences in their shopping experiences tended to disaggregate previously undifferentiated networks of acquaintances. The women who privileged sending gifts and remittances home had less room for choice and a much lower level of local consumption, which slowly cut them out from the activities of those willing to spend some money in Alpinetown. The two groups developed different patterns of sociability, and over time, two sets of cliques developed around increasingly divergent notions of moral worth.

## Consumption and Sociability with "People Like Us"

The most important early site of consumption for Ukrainian women was the parking lot in the center of Alpinetown that, deserted by natives on Sunday morning, had become the informal station for the minivans connecting Alpinetown to many Ukrainian villages and towns.[12] Starting at the very end of the 1990s, when a couple of minivans began stopping discreetly on the least visible corner of the parking lot every other week, a well-organized, informal network of transportation had developed, with set prices and reasonably reliable timetables. The minivans provided cheap transportation to the new immigrant women who had secured tourist visas for Western Europe.

They transported in the other direction the remittances and goods the women wanted to send to their families. The drivers would also collect letters and gifts from the women's relatives to deliver to Alpinetown. When women eventually "got papers," they would also use the minivans to return to Ukraine for their holidays. At the apex of this system, between ten and twenty minivans would arrive every Sunday morning, in the parking lot, where a small crowd was already waiting.

On weekdays, it was a gray and impersonal square of concrete. On Sunday mornings, it would come to life with the vibrant sound of several hundred migrant women's voices, the bright colors of their best clothing, and the fragrance of their favorite foods. The parking lot became a Ukrainian-only linguistic and cultural space where nobody was surprised if women wore heavy makeup, a tight bright dress, and high heels in the morning. The women felt such space was a place where they could be themselves, *"po-nashemu,"* without being ashamed. It was a prime location for those who had arrived recently to feel at home and network with those better established in Alpinetown.[13]

The Sunday parking lot quickly became an informal community institution, very important for both practical and symbolic reasons. It was a space in Alpinetown that meaningfully connected women with *there*. Most women would spend two or three hours there, even if they had to do something that only took a few minutes.

Unsurprisingly, the parking lot was the only space the women (who were usually very careful to avoid any kind of confrontation with the authorities) had actually fought with the Italian police to protect. One Sunday morning in 2005, while we were chatting in the corner of the parking lot, a number of police cars arrived. Contrary to my initial fears, the police did not look for irregular migrants. They were interested in the minivans. They suspected, quite correctly, that the minivan drivers were selling goods that did not comply with EU food and safety regulations. They raided the parking lot and seized all the goods in the vans.

As the whole system was informal and based on personal trust, seizing the goods carried by the drivers implied also seizing the remittances and the goods women had just entrusted to the drivers. The same applied to the letters and parcels their relatives had sent them. In all the other instances I had witnessed during my fieldwork, whenever the police approached, the women, many of them undocumented, did their best either to disappear or to look "respectable." That morning they reacted very differently.

When the police started sealing the vans, some women quickly disappeared. Many more, however, became openly contentious. They pushed and shouted, blaming the visibly astonished police officers for stealing the boxes of goods they were shipping back to their families. They shouted that the police were punishing them for being mothers simply trying to send food and clothing to their children. They accused the police of stealing from decent workers and desperate mothers. They shouted, cried, and screamed. The conflict was so intense that the next day local public opinion was full of sympathetic accounts. There have been no new raids since then. The Sunday parking lot had become a safe area.

When the minivans arrived, each driver would enjoy his own captive market. Women regularly related to one driver, and the new arrivals followed the customs of their closest friends. "My" driver of choice was Ivan, the client of Ruslana. He was a respected and resourceful driver, the first to have provided direct regular service between Iryna's hometown and Alpinetown. He was highly respected by the women for the reliable service he provided. When needed, he carried almost anything back and forth, from wine to money, from cold cuts to bridal gowns.[14] Even more, they considered him the loving and faithful husband of a woman working as a care worker in Alpinetown. They judged his level of alcohol consumption quite moderate. Ivan often asked me to help him with the distribution of the parcels he brought to Alpinetown.

These were important and emotionally charged moments. As soon as his minivan entered the lot, the women from "his" area surrounded it, asking whether he had brought something for them. Standing by his side helping him sort letters and parcels, I observed that most women knew precisely what to expect. A few women were uncertain about the answer. These newcomers had not yet established a regular routine with their relatives back home. Ivan's answer made all the difference between a sunny day of rest and a deeper sense of isolation. Some received a letter or a box of sweets. For others, there was nothing. Ivan always tried to console them by saying that next week would be different, but it did not help much. Those who received nothing would shed a few quiet tears, surrounded by their silent but more fortunate peers, and leave quickly.

Even when there was nothing to receive, no woman would visit the parking lot without a chat with "her" driver about what was happening back home. The warmth of these relationships was rooted in the drivers' role in carrying goods and money back and forth between them and their families, a crucial form of connection based entirely on personal trust. The drivers, moreover, were thought of as powerful brokers of gossip and information, able to warn the women if there were troubles with their sons and daughters, or if their parents were aging badly.

Further, as drivers were among the very few respectable Ukrainian males who ventured into Alpinetown, the women considered them safe embodiments of Slavic masculinity. In the safety of the parking lot, women could play at being coquettish and even seductive with their drivers, who were invariably gallant with their women. There was always some degree of erotic tension in the air, and the conversation, helped by the frantic pace of the operations, was saturated with salacious innuendos.

The drivers, connecting *here* and *there*, were in the best position to play with the competing demands of the two worlds. In collecting the remittances the women were ready to send home, Ivan would always joke about their competing duties. He would remark aloud how little they were sending and speculate what they were doing with their money instead.

One day in 2012, Sofia, a fiftysomething blonde in high heels who had been working in Alpinetown for many years, handed him fifty euros to send to her daughter. Ivan replied that, since she was sending such a small sum, he had a duty to tell her daughter about the new red dress she was wearing. He was clearly implying she preferred spending money on clothes rather than supporting her relatives.

Sofia maliciously retorted that Ivan was saying so out of jealousy, as his wife never dressed up as she did. She explained to the other women the morality of her position: "When I left Ukraine to come here, it was because of the money. The kids needed to go to college and I needed to repair the house. The university is now finished. The house can wait. I have just one life and I want to enjoy it. I buy nice dresses. Ivan can joke as much as he wants, but he knows that I work here. I enjoy life here. Not like him, who runs here and there endlessly." Even after many years of work, as in the case of Sofia, women could not escape the pressure to define their choices in terms of their duties toward their relatives in Ukraine, as compared to their willingness to spend money on themselves and on their lives in Alpinetown. It was always a prominent part of their conversation.

They were constantly negotiating the countervailing pressures of giving priority to the welfare of their relatives, which was their main rationale for emigrating, and the cherished possibility of having something for themselves. It is important to note that Ivan was not necessarily acting as an ambassador of *there*. On the contrary, he could (and would) also criticize women for sending "too much" money to their relatives. He scolded the women he thought were living miserably deprived lives in Alpinetown, stressing that they had only one life and that their relatives could well manage with fewer resources. He would claim that sending too much money spoiled their relatives and made things worse.

The parking lot was not only the place where the minivans arrived and departed. It was also an important place of sociability. While the minivans clustered along two sides of the parking lot, small groups of women drinking beer and munching pumpkin seeds together dotted the remaining space. Vendors in the parking lot sold small plastic bags with a can of beer and a bag of pumpkin seeds for one euro. Each cluster began when a woman bought a couple of bags and offered them to two or three other women with the unspoken understanding that they would buy the next round.

A full reciprocal exchange, carefully managed, might last from two to three hours. Each cluster was usually closed, as it would be improper to drink the beer offered by one person and then buy beer for someone else. Very few women could afford to participate in two different drinking cliques on the same day. Women, however, still greeted their other friends and talked with those in other cliques. Two or more groups might also merge temporarily. The conversations focused primarily on life in Alpinetown: women exchanged information about possible new jobs, obtained the latest news about Italian immigration laws, and made plans for their free time. Gossip was equally important, as women told tales about the recent actions and loyalties of other women.

In the parking lot, women could spend hours without buying anything. Even when they were penniless, women could spend time there without feeling any sense of shame. Newly arrived women were customarily exempt from the duty to reciprocate the beer and pumpkin seeds offered to them. In the parking lot, they could obtain much-needed information and some degree of social recognition without having to engage in consumption.

The parking lot was, at the same time, also a site of serious consumption. Initially, minivan drivers carried goods from Ukraine only occasionally, when their families sent gifts to the migrant women. As Ivan explained to me, initially, there was nothing to bring from Ukraine and none of the women had any money to spend anyway. After a few years, the women started to have some money to spend, and the transport of Ukrainian goods became a standard element of the business.

A folding picnic table appeared in front of each minivan, exhibiting what was for sale. A typical assortment included Ukrainian newspapers, books, cheese, DVDs, *kefir*, dried fish, national brands of cigarettes and chocolate, beer, vodka, sweets, and a few kinds of *kolbasy* (sausages). Some drivers sold also medicines, either because they were cheaper in Ukraine or because the women, for items such as birth control pills, trusted their national brands more.

While the drivers were the ambassadors of *there* and provided goods associated with migrants' homelands, another type of seller in the parking lot started focusing on the lures of *here*. Over the years, the clustering of so many women in the parking lot has attracted a number of Ukrainian street sellers. At first, they specialized mostly in goods the women wanted to ship home, such as boxes of pots, cutlery, soap, or detergent. The women could buy them and bring them directly to their drivers for shipping to Ukraine. After a while, some vendors changed their marketing strategy, selling goods more clearly oriented to women's lives in Alpinetown.

Even before starting fieldwork, I had befriended Iryna, the woman I went to the party with as described in the prologue. She was one of the first sellers to appear in the parking lot. A former sergeant in the Soviet Army, Iryna had supported her family—her parents and a daughter—for most of the 1990s through various forms of shuttle trade, with Moscow,

Poland, and Istanbul. All her savings, however, had been lost in the bank crisis of 1998, and she had been among the first to try out the newly available EU tourist visas. A blond, blue-eyed, plump woman in her early forties, Iryna had been quick to leave live-in care work to become an hourly paid housekeeper for a pool of Alpinetown families.

Now she was trying to supplement her income with a much more prestigious activity as a street seller, specializing in a mix of lingerie and cosmetics.[15] She was proud of having entered one of the main direct marketing organizations, the only foreign salesperson among more than 200 operating in the region. When she started her business, Iryna quickly decided to enlist me as her unpaid junior partner. I suddenly found myself acting as porter, sales assistant, model, and security guard for her. In return, she offered me a personalized recovery program for my forgotten Slavic feminine self, obliterated—she contended—by assimilation.

Although Iryna would market her wares in any place in town where Ukrainians congregated, our weekly appearance in the parking lot was the apex of the business strategy. Iryna was convinced that, although many women would refrain from buying the goods there, they would still look for her later in order to buy more discreetly. Our space in the parking lot was meant to be a showroom, an exhibition designed to heighten the women's desires.

Iryna would arrive every Sunday morning around 10:30, when most of the women had already completed their dealings with the drivers and were chatting in the parking lot. After ritually scolding me for not dressing smartly enough, which she regarded as diminishing both my womanhood and her sales, we opened the back of her car, our warehouse, and placed a picnic table in front of it. We would cover it with a pink tablecloth, place a bundle of fake flowers at the center, and surround it with bras, girdles, face scrubs and creams, body scrubs, and a variety of makeup.

Sliced salami or *kolbasy* and, in the best of times, small plastic glasses filled with vodka gave women an incentive to stop, chat, and, eventually, buy. Iryna would call women over to see the newest arrivals. The division of labor between us was straightforward: she would attract potential customers and bring them to the table, while I would help them choose the merchandise and, unless they needed a special payment arrangement, sell it.

Iryna had a very popular selling strategy. She told any woman who was interested in a bra or a skin cream that we understood perfectly that she had little money and had to think of her children first. As the item looked so great on her, however, Iryna was willing to accept an advance payment and collect the remaining money in several weekly installments. This approach worked wonders and earned her the esteem of many women who otherwise would not have dared to spend money on unnecessary yet desired goods.[16]

Like other street sellers, Iryna played a tune that was the opposite of the one played by the drivers. She was one of the sirens of *here*, claiming that migrant women had the right to spend something on themselves. They deserved to feel feminine. They had the right to be admired, to be recognized and respected. They were worth more than the Italians, and the Ukrainian males back home, thought they were. We offered our goods in a way that would not threaten the image of the "good mother sacrificing for her family" but complemented it with a vision of them as full-fledged women entitled to enjoy a few small treats.

Iryna relied on her customers to legitimize her marketing performance. One day, when Jevgenija expressed concern about her wrinkles, Iryna showed her the home laser wrinkle treatment that had recently entered our special-order catalogue. Iryna called Alla, who had purchased it two weeks earlier, and asked her to show Jevgenija the improvements she had seen even after such a short period of use. Alla, who was struggling to repay the forty euros she still owed Iryna, kindly complied, exalting the device's visible benefits. Alla was known to be a good mother who supported several children back home. Her statement certified not only the effectiveness of the laser but also the morality of buying it. Jevgenija was still reluctant, so Iryna tried to lure her by promising she could pay in installments. "We know how difficult it is to pay sixty euros at one time," she said empathetically. She offered Jevgenija her best deal, a two-month repayment plan. It was common practice to use testimonials from previous customers when selling.

Iryna did her best to keep the sale of her goods within a wider matrix of sociability, in which every woman could feel entitled to buy as a statement of dignity. Her strategies employed sophisticated claims about the capacity of her goods to provide fulfillment in the demeaning circumstances of migration. She always cast her sales in terms of rights and duties: women had the right to spend something on themselves and the duty to protect and nurture their femininity, the basic asset that made them worthy of recognition and respect. Full womanhood required both being sexy and being a good mother.

Occasionally, Iryna resorted to scare tactics: as she was selling costumes essential to a successful performance of full womanhood, to abstain from acquiring them would imply not being good, self-sacrificing mothers, but rather a creeping acceptance of being seen as mannish or androgynous, similar to Italian women, whom most migrant women regarded as sloppy and unfeminine.

Iryna skillfully played the themes of *there* in attracting women to consume *here*, selling untraditional goods meant to protect them from dangerous assimilation. She continually emphasized that true Ukrainian women should "wear makeup even when going out to throw out the garbage," that they could not become like Italian women "wearing unsexy garments, sleeping in ugly underwear, behaving as if they were not interested in attracting a man!" She argued, "We need to be sexy even when going to bed alone." She would occasionally add, pointing her finger at me, "Why do you think Martina, at her age, does not yet have a husband and children?" Thus, she completed the nightmare scenario for the most reluctant women.

In Iryna's view, Ukrainians should appear different from local women not in order to be loyal to a previous model of femininity but in order to gain respect in their current setting. If they did not take care of their appearance, she claimed, they should not be surprised that Italians did not respect them. As I will argue in detail in the next chapter, this notion of hyperfemininity was regarded as a key resource for claiming respect from both natives and coethnics.

Iryna presented the goods as objects that could help women escape their current degradation and join the local world of respectability and abundance. One such talisman was the thong, which she had originally stocked as a marginal item and hardly ever advertised in her talks in the parking lot.

One day, she happened to talk to Sofia, who had bought a thong some weeks before. She discovered Sofia regarded the thong as a powerful tool for protecting her self-esteem. Sofia said the thong made her feel always ready to love, if the circumstance ever arose. She had started wearing a thong even when she went to clean flats, as a kind of symbolic protection against the degradation she felt in doing such a menial job in somebody else's house. "I always wear a thong; it helps me to remember that, although I clean old asses, I am a real woman who would never disappoint my man." Endorsing this line of reasoning, Iryna started regularly stocking thongs among her merchandise and prescribing them to whoever lamented the degrading nature of her work.

The parking lot was a place of consumption and sociability where all sorts of contrasts enjoyed a fragile truce. It was an egalitarian space, where seasoned care workers and newcomers would feel equally at home. A few women visited the parking lot only briefly to accomplish specific tasks. They were the *signore*, the much-admired migrant women who had been able to leave care work, usually by becoming the wives or partners of Italian men. They were the embodiment—well groomed, wealthy, detached, involved only with their house and their families—of what the women regarded as a model of satisfied, modern womanhood.[17]

Their presence was a carefully orchestrated performance meant to highlight the boundaries between this small cluster of women and the rest. They would arrive by car with their partners, who stopped in the corner of the lot opposite the minivans and waited for them with the engine running. Dressed expensively but conservatively, the *signore* went straight to the minivan linking Alpinetown with their places of origin. They greeted a few women very formally, delivered remittances or parcels for their relatives, and quickly returned to the waiting car.

In years of visits to the parking lot, I have never seen a *signora* buy, indeed even stop to consider, the Ukrainian goods on sale. They did not need anything from *there*; they had all they needed *here*. Their performances were scripted to indicate that they did not belong to the same class as the others who gathered in the parking lot. When a *signora* arrived, the women (and even the drivers) were torn between admiration and contempt. The *signore* had made it, entering the world of abundance and enjoying the security and respect that comes with an Italian man who can provide for "his" woman and take her away from the polluting world of care work.

This socially prestigious position separated them from other women, even those who had shared their previous difficulties and humiliation. Their temporary presence in the parking lot was a reminder both that it was possible to make it and that the other women had not succeeded in doing so.

When the women started to have some money to spend, consumption also entered the world of the waiting room of the bus station. The waiting room shared with the parking lot the fact that it was available to everyone. Unlike the parking lot, there was no fixed time to be there. The first time I noticed something new was when I heard that Zlata, another of the very early pioneers, had created a shopping list of desired goods. She would write down the names of the women and what they needed: contraceptive pills, medications, makeup, perfumes, cigarettes, undergarments.

Zlata would give the list to her driver, wait for his return, collect the goods, and distribute them to the women when she met them in the waiting room. After a while, Zlata also started keeping a list of "Italian" goods, which she bought in discount markets and resold in the waiting room. When I asked Zlata why she conducted business this way, she explained that most of her clientele were undocumented women who were otherwise unable to acquire such goods. That made little sense to me.

Most of the goods they ordered were easily available in shops, where no one would ask customers for their papers. The risk of being detected while visiting the shop was surely smaller than those they faced spending hours together in a noisy posse in the waiting room of a main transportation hub. The preference for this form of trade was instead rooted in the perception that this form of shopping was interactionally "safe."

I discovered this very quickly, when Iryna enlisted me in her project to make the waiting room part of her commercial empire. Given the layout of the waiting room, she could not hope to create there the shop-like structure she had arranged in the parking lot. Everything had to be delivered out of a huge bag, and customers had to use the restroom to try things on.

Iryna consequently had to develop a different strategy for the waiting room. She would enter the space, well dressed and wearing heavy makeup, sit down on a bench, and start a long monologue vaguely inspired by TV sales pitches. Each week we would concentrate on a single item, although she did not have a problem with sending me to her car to pick up a different item if a prospective customer had asked for it. Our first campaign was a cucumber cream that promised to moisturize, smooth, and brighten dull and tired skin.

The sales process began with a presentation of the product followed by the circulation of a sample so everybody could try it. Iryna revealed the price only at the end, once she was sure that some women were hooked on the product.

Week after week, we sold a wide range of cosmetics and lingerie. The scenes in the waiting room—nearly always involving a smaller group of women who knew each other well—were wilder than in the parking lot. Most women enjoyed our little presentations, and the items we sold were perfect for making jokes and telling salacious anecdotes.

The climate became often carnivalesque, and we had great fun. One day Diana, a forty-year-old Ukrainian, arrived breathlessly. She ran into the waiting room, completely oblivious to the long queue of commuters waiting at the nearby ticket window. She jumped in front of us, lifted her skirt, took my hand, and put it on her sweaty girdle. It was a "real wonder," she said aloud. I had sold her the girdle two weeks before for forty-five euros, as she had insisted that she needed to lose weight because her boyfriend had told her she was becoming chubby. She was not ashamed to show off the girdle in public; instead, she was proud to exhibit her "great new shape" to her friends and other onlookers.

Another day Halyna, who was thirty and rather buxom, decided to try on a "sexy bra" that she had previously dismissed as "appropriate only for whores." She soon emerged from the restroom, lifted her shirt, and asked the other women for their opinion. It felt like I was the only one uncomfortably conscious of the stares of the Italians observing the scene.

As we left the bus station, I asked Iryna if she had found anything bizarre in Halyna's behavior. She replied, "There is nothing to be shocked by. We women all have tits. Hers are just bigger ones." I remarked that my point was not about her tits but the fact that she, like Diana, used the waiting room as their own private theater, showing no concern at all about the presence of other people who, in this instance, seemed rather disturbed.

Iryna said that as usual I did not understand anything, that I was too much of an Italian. "Halyna did not want to disturb anybody. She just wanted to show her bra . . . nothing more. And she showed it to friends in a place where people come and go and do not care about what we do there." The bus station had become a place where women felt safe to perform the consumption game among themselves: for once, they expected native bystanders to adapt to their rules.

## Experimenting in the Open-Air Market

Less than half a mile from the parking lot is the main square of Alpinetown. Every Thursday morning, dozens of stalls selling a wide range of goods fill the square and the nearby streets. The traditional open-air market is divided into sections. In the main square, there are vegetables, fruits, cheese, and flower stalls. In the surrounding streets, there are stalls selling clothing, shoes, and accessories. In each section, one or two well-known kiosks, sometimes operated by the same family for generations, sell various kinds of cholesterol-intensive street food.

Alpinetown's open market has a long tradition in the city and the locals regard it as a cosmopolitan site of encounter, frequented by a wide spectrum of city residents. Customers can shop there for gourmet cheese and environmentally friendly lettuce or a cheap skirt selected from a basket of identically priced clothes. During the past two decades, there have been changes in the market. Some older local business owners have sold their stalls to Southern Italian sellers. More recently, sellers with immigrant backgrounds have started to operate. Locals still predominate in the food section. The changes in the clothing and accessories sections have been more dramatic.

Chinese, Pakistani, and North African vendors now manage a significant number of stalls specializing in low-cost merchandise. The older Italian sellers have retreated to the most prized slots at the corner of the two main streets. They describe themselves as an endangered species, predicting that someday they, too, will sell their licenses to newcomers.

Migrant women hear about the open-air market within days of their arrival. As soon as they can afford to spend some money on voluptuary goods, the open-air market is the first venue many of them try out. Being able to get a couple of hours for themselves on Thursday morning is one of the most popular criteria for assessing the quality of a job. Roaming the market is fun, and newcomers face few barriers; the layout and rules of the open-air market are simple; many women have experience both as customers and as sellers in the large informal open-air markets that are one of the novelties of postsocialism.[18] Sellers and customers share a very tolerant attitude. The market offers fake designer goods and Italian-style clothes, items highly appreciated by the women's adolescent sons and daughters.

Strolling through the market, it has become common to encounter migrant women. Whenever such encounters occurred, we would stop to chat a bit, and then we would start moving together from stall to stall looking for bargains. Although each woman might enter the market alone, we tended to form small, cooperative groups once there. Along the way, we would collect other women or split into smaller groups along divergent trajectories in the crowd. The presence of other women was crucial to the experience. From their point of view, shopping was an existentially important activity in which friends or acquaintances should participate. When we identified an item worthy of consideration, we would show it to the other women, to hear their evaluation.

One morning I met Karina, a forty-five-year-old Belarusian care worker whom I had met several times at the bus station. We quickly moved to a stall where a set of baskets held clothes with similar prices so customers could decide what they could afford and look in the basket for something they liked. This way of selling was popular because it allowed customers the pleasure of touching and commenting upon many items before buying one.

Karina dug through several baskets enthusiastically and analyzed their contents item by item. When I asked whether she was looking for something in particular, she replied she was just looking for "something nice" and added that "great occasions are always awaiting when you least expect them." She asked me to help her check the other baskets, but since I did not know what "nice" meant for her I found it difficult to be useful. While Karina was completing her search, other women slowly joined us. We strolled together for an hour before proceeding to the benches in a corner of the main square to have something to eat with the other women who had been at the market.

Other times, the market visit proved to be more complex and required some negotiation. Especially when they were in groups, the women were very selective in their choice of stalls. Most would go only to the stalls with things in baskets and ignore the other stalls, even those with similarly or lower priced goods. As usual, I discovered the reasons only through a clumsy attempt to be of use.

One day I met Olina on the bus, who was going to the market, and I decided to join her. Olina, a fiftysomething Moldovan woman, was a former nurse. She participated in a shared flat where I had been invited a few times. She was markedly overweight and in poor shape. I was consequently puzzled when we stopped in front of a basket of skirts that would have been hard for even a fit young woman to wear. I tried to persuade her to visit a nearby stall where I had seen clothes with a more generous design.

Olina was usually willing to explore new stalls, but in this instance, she replied with a strong *"ni ni ni."* I mentioned the good prices and great colors of the clothes I had seen there, but she refused to go there and responded to my continued pressure by saying, in a very hostile way, that I was stupid to propose going there because at that stall the seller expected you to try things on. The stall, like many others, had a small, improvised tent used as a dressing room. The women perceived this arrangement as indecent and regarded stripping in such makeshift dressing rooms as unrespectable; Olina commented that anybody could catch a glimpse of a woman while she was undressing. As I was accustomed to the parking lot, where women would go to Iryna's car to try on lingerie in full view of one another, I was intrigued by her remark.

I countered that nobody forced a customer to try on something if she did not want to. I soon realized (both from Olina's remarks and from later conversations with others) that the issue concerned the sellers' expectations as much as the women's own sense of decency. Not trying clothes on before buying them was acceptable in the case of basket buying, but the same behavior would have branded a woman as a sucker in a stall with a dressing room.

Olina explained: "If you go to such a place, you are expected to try on things; every good customer does. You do not blindly buy. . . . I prefer buying things from the baskets so I can look for long time without being asked if I want to try something on, see?" The heart of the problem was that once a woman had tried on something she would be expected to buy it, and a refusal would have made her a look like a poor customer. The pleasure of shopping was tempered by the women's desire to avoid uncomfortable situations. Vika too avoided stalls in which sellers were too active in showing her their merchandise. She complained such vendors disturbed the pleasure of shopping, since if she had to talk with them they would surely realize that her Italian was rudimentary.

Over time, the women would discover which stalls offered a safe and relaxing environment. Vendors were quick to appeal to this new group of prospective customers. One morning, while walking along one of the alleys, I heard a woman yelling my name from a stall selling cheap shirts, low-cut jeans, and a few fake leather jackets.

I was surprised to recognize Ivana, a fortysomething Ukrainian who had been in Alpinetown for more than three years. She was the care worker for an elderly couple who had rented her a small flat immediately below their own. She had acquired her papers several months earlier and her adolescent daughter had recently joined her.

A few days before, she had asked me to help her register her daughter in one of the city's high schools, where she was going to study accounting. This morning, Ivana quickly explained that a friend had called the night before and asked her to substitute for her in the stand run by Majirel, a Tunisian vendor. She was happy to help her friend and to earn some extra money to buy some trendy clothes for her daughter. "She is a young girl and needs good clothes," she explained.

Majirel, Ivana's employer and (as I soon discovered) one of the most popular sellers among Eastern European customers, said he would be delighted to hire Lena, Ivana's daughter, and could easily pay her in clothes from the stand. Ivana did not like the undertone of the offer and replied that she was able to take care of her daughter with the money she earned working for him, even if that meant being in the market at 5:00 a.m.[19]

Majirel explained that he arrived so early because he wanted always to be in the same location so that anybody looking for his wares could easily find his stall. I could not imagine a stable clientele for a stall made up of little more than a collection of metal baskets, each with a colorful poster displaying the low price. I expected his customers to be people just casually surveying the market.

I found it difficult to imagine a committed clientele looking for Majirel as their favorite dealer. Nevertheless, Ivana and Majirel proudly declared that he was the dealer of choice for Eastern European customers, in part because he had been the first to hire a Ukrainian woman and, as he stated glowingly, because he knew how to treat them.

A few minutes later, Sofia approached and smiled flirtatiously at him. He remarked that the deep V-neck shirt she was wearing, which she had bought at his stall the week before, fit her perfectly and insisted that Sofia could still surpass the young girls who usually bought the fancy, see-through clothing he sold. Speaking in Ukrainian, Ivana immediately advised her that a fabulous short dress was on sale for just five euros. Sofia was interested but asserted she could not afford to buy something every week, as she needed money to send home.

Majirel approved but gave the conversation a more suggestive twist by affirming Sofia was right to save money for the other "nice things in life," a coded expression for social activities involving men. Ivana whispered to me that Sofia had recently gone for a beer with Majirel and he might invite her out again, which he soon did. "*Da, da*, for sure and soon," said Sofia, before disappearing into the crowd.

In the meantime, Ivana had started talking with Oksana, an attractive twenty-five-year-old Ukrainian who, besides being among the youngest, was also one of the few Ukrainians in Alpinetown who was not a care worker. She was an apprentice in a beauty salon. Oksana had long, colorful nails that were difficult to forget. The long nails had small bells and little chains that tinkled whenever she moved her hands. Ivana was trying to convince her to buy a sequined T-shirt when she excitedly pulled out a pair of white pants with sequins on the pockets.

Since they looked rather unconventional, I asked her where she would wear them. Oksana told me that she did not buy clothes thinking where to wear them. She bought clothes because she liked them. She added it was difficult for her to come to the Thursday open-air market without purchasing anything. "My boyfriend also criticizes me for the money I spend on clothes. I always tell him that if he wants to have a nice lady, there is a price to pay," said Oksana, while Ivana looked at her approvingly.

Oksana stated that she only bought what cost less than five euros, so there was really no reason to criticize her. Taking advantage of my well-established reputation as naïve person, I asked again why they were buying stuff, no matter how cheaply, that they knew they would wear rarely if at all. The women laughed, and Oksana replied: "Martushka, in Italy everything is cheap, and see how much choice you have! You say it is pointless to buy clothes? But you're crazy."

Ivana said that in Ukraine, little was available and prices were higher. "In Ukraine, you do not leave the house, go for a walk, and come back with a shirt. Of course, you buy things if you need to, but here it is easier." Oksana declared that in Ukraine, "you do not get the money and hence you cannot spend it. Since I'm here and I work, I have the right to spend, don't I?" Quick to follow up her assertion with action, Majirel gave Oksana a plastic bag with the pants she had selected, while she kept digging in search of more treasures.

As I stayed at the stall, I observed a steady flow of Eastern European women greet Majirel by name and stop for a few minutes to look through the baskets. Ivana offered her help in finding "*shchos' harne*" (something nice). I was surprised to find such a concentration of Ukrainian women in the market, but Majirel claimed, "Women know about me and they know that I sell nice things for little money."

"These beautiful women know that as well, right?" I teased him by saying that his stall was just one among the many people could visit, which made his success more difficult to explain. He took my observation seriously and, in a very businesslike way, explained his marketing strategy. He was a businessperson who paid attention to his customers' needs, making an effort to learn their first names and remember their tastes so that customers would experience his stall as "a place where you feel you receive full attention."

I noticed that Majirel tried to establish as many personal relationships as possible, even with women he knew could not buy anything that day. Whenever he saw someone who looked like a newcomer, especially a foreign woman, he introduced himself, asked her name, and engaged in small talk about the market, the weather, or Italian customs.

Playing on the stereotype of the ever-horny Arab, he found a way to make little jokes and compliments with sexual innuendos and stressed that a particular shirt or dress would work wonders with their men. He explained to me that his main asset was to know "what is hot for the season and what is out. All the things I sell are nice and every woman, even those who do not have a lot of money, can afford them." Majirel sold to Italian women in the same way, calling them by name, making jokes, and remembering what they had bought before. At his stand, women emphasized, they felt that they were "treated nicely."

In an effort to better understand the pleasures of shopping, one day while strolling through the open-air market with Sofia and Alla, who regularly patronized Majirel's stall, I asked why they were always buying something even when they did not need to do so. They laughed at me and told me I did not understand anything. Sofia said that she purchased things because she liked buying them.

"I work here and I have the right to spend my money as I wish to. I buy because I like to go around elegant! You see? Elegant!" Sofia stressed the "elegant" to draw a clear distinction between her stylish attire and my shabby "Italian" style. Every woman except me bought clothes, they declared. "Did you notice you are the only woman in the parking lot that is dressed as if you were going to work in the field?" When Sofia had completed the moral destruction of the present writer, Alla added professorially that it was an important asset to have a large and ever-increasing array of clothes from which to choose. The market was a perfect place to satisfy this need.

I observed a similar reaction another day while sitting on the benches with Vanesa, who had just arrived and had not yet learned the migrant women's norms for public behavior. She expressed puzzlement that all the women she saw after the Thursday market were having fun showing off *"kol'orovi hanchirky"* (colorful rags); she did not feel like spending money on useless things, as she wanted to save all she could and send it home. "I do not want to spend my life washing old asses," she asserted. This kind of remark usually triggered heated reactions among the other migrants. This time, perhaps because Vanesa was a newcomer, they replied that Vanesa should wait until she received her first money; then she would discover "how nice it is to buy things."

The women perceived both open-air markets as welcoming, inclusive spaces. Still, they were never completely sure they would be fully accepted in the Thursday market. There was always something adventurous going on there, and the women always felt more at ease when they could stroll in a group. Such sense of adventure explains why it was so pleasant, once our shopping had been completed, to move to the benches where other women would wait for us. On the best days, by lunchtime, a crowd of between twenty and twenty-five women would congregate there.

Eating together was a fundamental form of sociability, an integral part of the visit to the open-air market. Eastern European food dominated the Sunday lunch. Thursday lunch was strictly Italian: usually a slice of pizza bought at a nearby stall. This sort of lunch was considered a fitting conclusion to the women's experiment in consumer citizenship.

The food was shared with friends (as in a restaurant), it was purchased (not home cooked), and it was eaten in the same place where Italian youngsters often congregated. The fact that such food, eaten in this way, was very rare in Eastern Europe automatically made our lunches in the square proof of sophisticated integration into the life of Alpinetown. Lunch was also the time when women exhibited whatever they had found.

Olina, who first brought me to have lunch at the market, emphasized that it was good to have "your hands full of bags so you have something to show to friends." As soon as we arrived at the benches, she started showing everyone the pair of shoes she had bought, asking, "Aren't they cute?"

## Adventures in Consumption

In the Sunday parking lot and the bus station waiting room, the women practiced consumption with their peers in a protective environment and within a matrix of sociability that facilitated but did not necessarily require a purchase. Both sites were informal gathering places where economic exchange was only one of the attractions. The women felt free to express desire but were not frustrated by their limited capacity to buy. In both sites, the experience had as an integral part a personal relationship with vendors.

Being a consumer in these locations meant embracing informality as some modus operandi that entailed certain rules, norms, and expectations. The women considered these places their own, to the point of forgetting—as the episodes of showing off the girdle and the bra demonstrate—that they were also public spaces. The informality and the vendor-customer relationship drove the performance.

The open-air market involved different challenges. Migrant women knew that most of the other customers were Italian. The risk of shame was much higher, and women tried to minimize it by carefully selecting stalls and establishing personal relationships with specific vendors who exhibited the same personal touch and lack of pressure as those at the Sunday market and the bus station.

Many migrant women regarded these as *the* places to shop and deemed all others inappropriate for a care worker. Although many women never ventured further, others began to explore different shopping venues, less defined in terms of their collective status and more contingent upon individual projects.[20]

In Alpinetown, buying food was among the first activities that led women beyond these familiar venues. As live-in care workers, most women ate in their employers' households and few did the grocery shopping. Still, food was among life's simple pleasures, and many women found reasons to shop for items to send home (sweets, wine, and parmesan cheese in particular) or to take to their Sunday lunches.

After the open-air market, the first ethnically integrated place I visited with migrant women was the Lidl supermarket. Lidl is a German discount chain founded in the 1930s that operates over 7,200 stores across Europe. Italians consider it the cheapest chain, catering to the working classes. The well-organized, well-designed supermarket often employs immigrant sales clerks. The migrant women first went to Lidl after the hiring of Galina, a Ukrainian who had arrived in the late 1980s, having married an Italian who had been working in Ukraine.

Although Galina was different from the immigrant care workers—"She was already Italian when she was still in Ukraine," the women said—and the chances of meeting her at the cash register in such a huge supermarket with two full shifts were pretty slim, the presence of Galina meant that the place was not completely hostile.

When I went there for the first time with Olga, she said that it was nice to buy in places where your friends work. A second advantage of Lidl, like other supermarkets, is that it minimized the need for interacting with shopping assistants. Customers felt free to take a product from the shelf, to touch it, to put it in their basket and then, quite often, to put it back on the shelves if they changed their minds. Moreover, prices at Lidl were definitely low. Olga explained that she liked Lidl because the place made her feel like "I can buy everything."

Olga had been very successful in Italy. Slightly younger and prettier than most, she had two children in Ukraine. She had been able to acquire her papers early in her migration career and she had left care work for a job as a house cleaner in a two-star hotel.

When we were at Lidl, she was having an affair with the married son of the elderly woman she had previously taken care of. She did not like to be the mistress of a married man, but she claimed he was more caring than many husbands would ever be. She readily acknowledged that her situation was more secure and psychologically rewarding than that of most of the other women.

Her job in the hotel guaranteed her food and lodging, but she shopped outside for food and drinks she could keep in her room and enjoy when she liked. She was particularly fond of having a beer before going to bed, and her stingy employer charged her for whatever she took from the hotel bar. In addition to beer, Olga wanted to buy food. As her lover did not like to go with her to restaurants, as he feared being spotted by someone he knew, they had plenty of picnics in the Alps.

Although she had discovered Lidl only recently, she already regarded herself as a regular. During our visit, Olga greeted two groups of North

Africans, whom she addressed in Italian, and Ana, a Siberian care worker who spoke Russian.

Olga introduced me to Ana as "a friend doing shopping with" her. Ana was curious about the fact that Olga was carrying a fully loaded basket while my hands were entirely free. Olga joked to Ana that I would never shop in Lidl, as I was an Italian *signora*. Taking this remark seriously, Ana preached the advantages of Lidl: "Nobody feels different while shopping here. It is just cheaper and it makes it possible to shop even if you do not have much money or if you want to keep the money you have for other things."

Olga and I kept going to Lidl regularly, often introducing other women to the place. Despite the fact that it was a German discount supermarket whose clientele as well as staff were sizably comprised of immigrants, most women perceived going there as a perfect "Italian" experience.[21]

Visiting dime stores, which the women called "*shyk shyk*"—apparently, a creative adaptation of the French *chic* and the German *schick*—seemed even more adventuresome. These small shops, which are usually managed by Asian immigrants, are common in the old center of Alpinetown.

They sell a wide range of goods, from luggage, umbrellas, and clothing to flashy knick-knacks. The women loved these shops for the same reason I hated them: they are stuffed with cheap merchandise from floor to ceiling, leaving customers practically no room to move. In addition to the abundance of goods, migrant women appreciated the fact that the shopkeepers waited on them. At the *shyk shyk*, the shopkeepers, who were usually female and called by the women "yellow," would treat them as bona fide customers.

As Iryna put it, "I like to be served by the vendor. I like to enter, and I like to hear somebody saying hello and asking if I need something. Then I like to say that I will look around. When I find something, I like to say that I want this but I need this size." I pointed out that such a scenario was exactly the opposite of what I had observed at the Thursday open-air market, and she replied that the market was different. "When you enter a shop, you want to be treated as a lady: the vendor must be nice, wait for you to choose, offer you nice things, and advise you about what might be interesting and look nice on you."

Entering a Chinese shop made them immediately feel at ease with their role as consumer. Although the interaction was more impersonal than in the market, they did not feel embarrassed, as they did in Italian shops. Most important, the women did not think it possible to establish personalized relationships with Chinese shopkeepers. They felt themselves to be naturally superior to those they called the "yellows," or—at least—entirely different from them. They acted as if they were automatically entitled to respect simply for entering the shop. Indeed, the women treated the *shyk shyk* as a sort of playground.

Entering in groups of five or ten, they commented loudly on the merchandise, touching all the items they came across without asking permission. The lone woman staffing the shop was disconcerted by having a large group of people inside and found it difficult to supervise them. They enjoyed making a scene and joked about how embarrassed the shopkeeper was with their noisy ways.

Their feelings of superiority and freedom and their enjoyment in driving the Chinese shopkeepers crazy did not mean they disrespected the shopkeeper's property. Once, when the women dispersed inside a Chinese shop to try on some cheap fake furs, the shopkeeper started screaming and accusing one of the women of stealing.

Iryna was adamant that we were not thieves and decided that we should leave the shop in indignation. Outside, Maryna, who had arrived recently, said teasingly that the "yellow" had made a great fuss and smiled provocatively while taking a small reddish thong out of her bag. The reaction was not what she expected: the other women started yelling at her, using very harsh words and denouncing her for her shameful action.

They abruptly expelled Natalya from the group. She left angry, while the rest of us stopped at a bench to sit down and mourn the wound to our respectability. The women were all ashamed, and Lesa kept repeating that was not good to behave as Maryna had done; after all, we were not "Albanians or Romanians. We [were] not thieves."

## Shopping Like the Natives

Over the years, I made repeated efforts to convince women to enter the town's ordinary shops. For a long time, these proposals were met with heavy resistance. Even women who frequented Lidl and the *shyk shyk* shops argued, saying, "It is too expensive to go there. It is stupid to spend so much money to buy things we can get at the open-air market." Because the women would not consider visiting a store without buying something, there was a real barrier between the sites in which they felt comfortable and the "Italian shops" they pretended to despise.

Many women continued to stay within the boundaries of communitarian shopping or expanded their shopping options only to the open-air market, the food supermarket, and the *shyk shyk* shops. They saw other shops as belonging to a different tribe and felt uneasy about visiting them. The few Eastern European women who frequented Italian shops were those who had Italian partners and had started behaving like *signore*. As becoming a *signora* usually implied the weakening or severing of ties with other women migrants, their experiences did not circulate in the network but, instead, contributed to their defining those shops as exclusive.

Despite this clear boundary, the transition from refusing even to enter an Italian shop to becoming enthusiastic customers could be quite sudden. When women discovered a shop and reported the joys of shopping there to the others, it quickly became acceptable as a shopping venue.

Over time, I witnessed a diffusion process through which newly arrived women enjoyed a widening range of sites for consumption. The women evaluated a new shop based on two criteria: the availability of cheaply priced goods and an inclusionary climate where the women could feel free to express themselves and still be respected as serious customers.

One day, I witnessed such an exploration first hand. While strolling with Olga and Sofia, the middle-aged women I often met in the open-air market, we stopped in front of a store operated by Pittarello, an Italian chain specializing in footwear, accessories, and leather goods.[22] One branch was very close to the building where Sofia worked, but we had never entered it, and Olga always described it as a place "for buyers, not for lookers."

That day, however, we were celebrating Olga's birthday by having a few drinks and were looking for something memorable and adventuresome to do together. We were in my car, and the very simple fact of driving around made us feel like respectable citizens entitled to whatever the city had to offer.

Sofia suddenly suggested we stop at Pittarello and buy something. In an effort to avoid the possibility of humiliation, I announced that Pittarello was actually perfectly okay to visit even without buying anything. Sofia immediately protested how "looking around is a waste of time. If you go in there, you also buy, Martushka. I have money, I am okay, and today is Olga's birthday! We have to get something for her!" Olga seemed quite pleased with the prospect.

When we entered the shop, Sofia and Olga were uncharacteristically quiet and moved slowly, looking around to see how many people were there and admiring the wide space and the four floors. We walked through the aisles observing how the merchandise was organized. Sofia and Olga stared at other customers to see how they behaved in this unfamiliar place. I jokingly told them that such silence was a real miracle and that we should always go to Pittarello to avoid having perpetual fusses.

The fact that even such a provocation went unheard signaled to me the importance of the moment. When we reached the women's department, many shiny, high-heeled shoes immediately caught our attention. Sofia was amazed: "Did you see this wonder? You see the choice? This is a real shop. Iryna [her daughter] would go crazy here. . . . I must buy something [for her]." I reminded her that we had come to get a small present for Olga, but Sofia cut me off by saying that she was already having fun by herself. As Olga tried on a pair of high-heeled sandals, I asked whether she was serious about purchasing them since I could not imagine anywhere it would be possible to wear them. She replied caustically that she could always "wear them in bed" and that was that. Sofia's eyes sparkled as she touched a glittery shoe as if it were magical. I tried again to draw her attention to the present for Olga without any success. I asked them to tell me the amount of money we could spend for the gift, so that I could look around while they enjoyed themselves.

My attempt at rational planning was interrupted by Sofia's shriek of delight as she turned over the shoe and found from the price tag that its cost was much lower than she expected. Sofia rushed to Olga, exclaiming that such beauty was actually affordable. Their surprise made it clear that they had never believed my protestations that goods at Pittarello were comparable in price to some of the goods sold in the open-air market.

An hour later, Sofia emerged with three pairs of shoes, one for herself and two for her fifteen-year-old daughter, which were all flashy and impractical. Olga came out with two pairs of what she called "horny sandals," one a birthday present for herself and the other a "real Italian shop shoe." She quickly noticed that as usual I had failed to buy anything for myself. When I tried to explain that the choices available were not consistent with my sloppy-by-design graduate-student style, they interpreted it as further proof of my lack of a feminine touch.

We celebrated our experience at Pittarello by emptying the half-bottle of vodka that had survived the birthday celebration preceding our shopping expedition. As we sat on a riverside bench drinking and trying on the new shoes, Sofia and Olga said that they would bring their friends there soon. When I asked why they had never believed me the many times I had said Pittarello was an affordable shop, Sofia pointed out to me that the real discovery was not its prices but rather that they could spend a long time inside without being bothered. Olga said that in most shops, "when you enter, people look at you in a way that makes you feel they are waiting for you to take something and pay." I insisted that it was normal to look around and leave without making a purchase. After all, I asked rhetorically, "you cannot buy unless you have looked carefully at things beforehand, right?" They agreed but made it clear that I was missing the point. Olga explained: "You see, the point is not to buy or not to buy but to feel that they expect you to buy and then, if you do not buy, they say, 'Oh, yes, she is a *lavaculi.'* "

They felt that in Italian shops they had to choose between buying something at a high price or being judged and treated as marginal outcasts. That day they had discovered not only that they could afford to buy something at Pittarello but also that the shop was designed in a way that did not made them feel constantly at risk of being exposed as immigrant care workers.

The news about Pittarello spread quickly, and the next week, many women asked me to drive them to the store. They nearly always framed the request as an emergency linked to an important and worthy goal: a niece needed shoes for her first communion; a daughter needed shoes for her wedding.

Other women then joined the expedition. They responded much as Sofia and Olga did. I soon stopped focusing on the women and instead observed the reactions of other customers to their presence. The customer base of Pittarello was largely made up of working-class Italians, and the sales force was Italian. Many customers looked uneasy with the loud cheerfulness the women displayed, but nobody intervened.

Although several women now included Pittarello among the possible places to shop, many still felt they were in a hostile territory where they had to be on guard, especially against the salespeople. When I visited Pittarello with Nadya and two other friends, I noticed that she interrupted her search for a pair of shoes to wear to a party to watch a sales clerk talking with a customer. When I asked her what was up, she replied that the woman was gossiping about the shoes she was looking at. I tried to convince her that she was mistaken, but she continued in a pissed-off tone: "That ignorant person has no idea about who I am or what I need the shoes for. Probably she never went to a party where you have to dress up in a certain way." She looked again and added despairingly, "Probably she does not even know what a real party is." Although I could not see any sign she was correct, Nadya was upset and insisted that we pay and leave. We went to the cashier, where Nadya said to the cashier, "My dear friend, it's time for you to serve us and tell us how much we have to pay." The cashier did not reply to the provocation and just stated the amount due for the purchase. Nadya kept her eyes on the cashier for the few minutes we stood at the register. As she explained after we left, she felt disrespected by a person who, she contended, was treating her for what she was now, ignoring that she was an educated woman. "The woman clearly had never read a book. I know what I am here. I know why I came here and I know who I was in Belarus. I am not an Albanian! I have a degree, and I was a manager in Belarus!" I tried to explain that, as far as I knew, the sales woman did not mean any harm and had not wanted to humiliate her. Nadya replied that this experience was the reason why it is better to go to the market. "You buy without being judged, while in there, I feel the eyes of the world on me." Yes, I agreed, "but in the market, you cannot find all the beautiful things that you found here. . . . Remember that I saw you buying the shoes and the belt?" She nodded and acknowledged that the place was much better than the market because of its wide variety and reasonable prices. "Yes, it is a great place to go . . . but I tell you, if I come across that *puttana* (bitch) again, I will not be as polite as I was today."[23]

Defensive reactions to what the women perceived as judgmental stares were also common when we were in bars or cafés. One day, Iryna and Vlada, the former director of a training center, invited me to have coffee with them. They loved the small café close to the main square but often remarked that waiters and customers there never treated them properly.

When we sat down, Iryna showed Vlada a new catalogue of her wares, hoping to interest her in buying some lingerie. When the waiter came to take the order, Vlada suddenly asked him provocatively, "What bra would you like for me?" Having made him uneasy, she partly opened her blouse and added, "Any of those might not be enough to contain all I have." Iryna laughed, and the waiter slowly retreated without even taking the order. Vlada concluded her performance by remarking, "All Italians are the same: they get scared when they see that I am proud of my attributes." I had witnessed similarly provocative performances on several occasions, and the women involved often commented that no Italian woman would ever be able to "set the record straight" so easily.

Some women, including Nadya, kept going to Pittarello, although they sometimes complained they were mistreated there. Others went on to experiment with new Italian shops. Iryna and Olga maintained that if Nadya had been mistreated in Pittarello, it must have been her fault because, being naïve and inexperienced, she had behaved inappropriately. The issue generated serious conflicts within the group.

Women who did not like the Italian shops perceived those who were thrilled to enter them as pretending to be *signore*. Those who frequented Italian shops criticized those who resisted as naïve and unsophisticated. Over time, their shopping experiences diverged. All these women, including those who had started shopping mostly in Italian shops and broken what they had perceived as an ethnic barrier, continued to be respectful of the class distinctions among shops.

Women who were knowledgeable about stores selling low-priced goods regarded it as inappropriate to enter those selling high-priced goods. Those are "places for rich people and not for me," as Jena put it one afternoon. Jena was a fortysomething Moldovan woman who had found an original way of enjoying the pleasures of shopping with her adamant focus on her family in Moldova: she bought nearly exclusively clothes for her two teenaged daughters, "who deserve to make men's heads turn when they walk."

We were walking in the city center when I noticed a poster in a Benetton store advertising that sweaters were on sale.[24] I needed one, so I asked Jena if she minded stopping briefly inside. She responded by asking how I dared to suggest such a silly thing.

Why on earth was I inviting her to a place where rich people buy, knowing perfectly well she was "a simple *sidelka*"? I explained about the sale and added that I just wanted company while doing my shopping, but she refused even to enter the shop and waited outside. Her reaction puzzled me.

Whenever I was strolling with women who were more comfortable with Italian shops, I invited them into the Benetton store. I always failed. They considered the store a purveyor of luxury goods from which they were by definition excluded: "Do you think that I am stupid and that I do not see that this is no place for me?"

Once I tried the same trick with Iryna and Sofia, who regarded themselves as expert shoppers in Alpinetown. When I suggested we visit Benetton, they looked at the window and declared that it was not a place for them. I teasingly pointed out that during sales the prices were close to what they encountered in the open-air market. "Come on, it's not as expensive as you believe. In the end, you spend the same amount of money every Thursday."

They did not appreciate my comment, as Iryna felt accused of being stingy. She had always taken a very patronizing attitude with me, but this time she exploded with an accusation: "This is not a place for us . . . But this is a good place for you; you are an Italian."[25] She felt betrayed by my insistence, which she felt was humiliating. Once you enter the shop, Sofia argued, the salespeople will expect you to buy something and, if you do not, "they will think that we have no money or, even worse, will look at us to see if we steal something."

Even the women who considered themselves well-informed consumers assumed that there was a clear boundary between good and bad places to shop, although the boundary they managed had now become more economic than ethnic.

In their explorations of Italian shops and restaurants, women often found themselves in a paradoxical situation: they could either enjoy consumption individually without fear of humiliation, or they could consume in a social setting with their peer group—but they could never do both at the same time. From their point of view, to feel safe required being able to consume appropriately, so that nobody would ever think of them as destitute care workers. It required enough resources, which were hardly ever available to all the women in the group.

Strong norms of reciprocity, however, prevented women from consuming more than their peers could afford. As a result, when going around in groups, they could not shop as much as they thought was necessary, even if they could theoretically afford to do so. The women started to carefully choose the others with whom they shopped, giving priority to those who enjoyed the same kind of outlets. As shopping was a main event, moreover, the norm of reciprocity ended up favoring the birth of separated cliques, defined by similar levels of acceptable expenditure.

When they were with an Italian man, by contrast, they expected him to pay what was necessary for them to behave like decent customers. The women assumed it was the Italian man's duty to make them feel at ease. It was his duty to make sure waiters or salespeople treated them properly. Any sign of stinginess was considered a personal offense.

When I had two occasions worth celebrating, I thought it would be a good idea to invite some of the women for a beer in a local café. I stressed before entering the bar that I was inviting them to be my guests and that I was happy to foot the bill. The women enjoyed celebrations and appreciated spending time together in the café.

Still, on both occasions I noticed that as soon as we sat down, they changed their minds and asked not for a beer but for a cappuccino. I found myself the only beer drinker at the table, surrounded by women who had switched from the vodka we had drunk outside to a sober coffee.

A few months later, Iryna rushed into my office and announced that we were going to have lunch with Paolo, the regional representative for Alpinetown of the direct marketing company she worked for. We met Paolo at a pizza place in the city center, where to my surprise Iryna ordered a beer instead of coffee. I teased her by saying that "when you are with me, you never have a beer, so probably I am not good company for you." She smiled and replied that it would be impolite to let Paolo drink alone.

After lunch, when we were returning to my office, Iryna wondered aloud about how stupid I was. I was accustomed to her frequent scolding, but I could not understand the issue in this instance. She attacked me angrily for thinking that she did not know how to behave in a restaurant. It took me a while to understand she was still angry for my little remark about her having a beer. I defended myself by saying that she had never accepted a beer at a café when I had offered one to her, so I had just been surprised. She perceived my lack of guile, concluded that I was a hopeless case, and shifted back into her patronizing mode. Talking as if she were instructing a child, Iryna explained that she had always accepted my beers at the parking lot, while she had asked for coffee when I invited her in a bar.

The reason appeared self-evident to her: in our drinking clique in the parking lot, she was always able to reciprocate, while she would have found it difficult to do so in the café because the price for a beer is much higher. At lunch, on the contrary, we were two Slavic women invited by an Italian male, and we were exempted from any obligation to reciprocate. He was a man and an Italian, and he had to pay for whatever we fancied.

On another occasion, Olga claimed a similar attitude. Although she usually restricted the amount of money we spent during our nights out, she remarked that two days before she had been in the same place with her lover. On that occasion, she had sampled the most expensive items on the menu, accompanied by a good bottle of wine. "I never refuse a nice glass of wine when Mario takes me out. Why should I?" She went on and added that it was he who was taking her out and, therefore, was expected to pay. He has a good job and, she exclaimed, "If he can maintain that *puttana* [his wife] he can also take me out as I deserve. I am not his wife and I do not need to cook for him. We have sex and have fun. I am responsible for the sex part; the fun part is his job. Learn, Martushka, learn."

# THREE

# Strong Mothers, Great Lovers: Sexuality in Emigration

Fieldwork is always a cultural shock. Doing ethnography involves breaking the strongest and most pervasive rule of social life: birds of a feather flock together.[1]

Academics, like all educated members of modern society, usually take for granted and embody respect for diversity and the virtues of dialogue. Still, like any other group, clique, or subculture, we live largely among ourselves, spending our free time with people who have similar priorities and evaluative standards, and taking for granted that *our* ways are *the* ways. Ethnographic fieldwork implies facing the practical, embodied fact that you will participate in activities you would never do with your own friends, that you will discuss issues framed in ways that you would dispute in any other setting, and befriend people whose names you would never remember otherwise.

During my years of fieldwork, I was often puzzled, and sometimes scandalized, by what the women said or did. It took me quite a long time to understand their reasons, which were valid on their own terms, and to accept the fact that they were equally puzzled, and equally often scandalized, by my own attitudes and lifestyle.

As I wrote in the previous chapter, a main obstacle in our activities together was the way in which the women despised frugality and considered conspicuous consumption an indicator of moral worth. The way in which they considered racial and ethnic hierarchies as natural, self-evident, and pervasive often drove me mad. The most important stumbling block was the fact that I was in my late twenties, had no children, and lived alone, having only a boyfriend living in another country.

I quickly realized that such a condition, which was common and accepted in my own environment, was perceived by nearly all of them as suspicious. Every time I was introduced to a woman who had recently arrived in Alpinetown, the very first questions she asked concerned my children and my partner. Every time, their glance after my answer was revealing. Many thought that my far-away boyfriend was a lousy cover-up: why was I in Italy working, if I really had a financially secure partner in my hometown? If we had been together for years, why I did not yet have a child?

My private life was deemed strange enough that some women felt the only reasonable explanation was that I carried what they regarded as the unspeakable secret of all: I did not like men. Others suspected I was a lesbian, which they regarded as a malady.[2] In any case, I was initially an object of suspicion strong enough to require special caution.

Women who had recently arrived and who were irregularly employed in unstable jobs often needed a place to stay for a night or two between live-in jobs. The sofa in my living room was one of the very few options available to many of them in emergencies. Only many years later, after I had broken up with my boyfriend and started dating an Italian man I duly introduced to Iryna, did she reveal that many of those who had slept on my sofa had done so only after being assured by her that, although I was weird, I was nevertheless heterosexual.

After a while, once they considered me a regular member of the group, they started framing my condition in pedagogic terms. Whenever I was sick, exhausted, or uneasy, the women would emphasize that my maladies were the expected result of not having a man and not having given birth. They treated me as an unfortunate and naïve young woman who needed advice, help, and instruction.

As it provided endless opportunities for telling stories, making jokes, and having squabbles, my reeducation as a woman become a popular pastime. The women addressed what they thought was the root of the problem: my having lost any proper sense of what Slavic womanhood meant. Their concerns ranged from the proper way of displaying oneself in public to private tricks to play on a prospective partner.

One of these pedagogic exercises occurred spontaneously one Saturday afternoon, while we were strolling in the old center of town. Myroslava, a fiftyish woman who had always been particularly motherly with me, decided it was time to initiate some other women into the recently discovered pleasures of the *shyk shyk* shops. Our boisterous group of five entered the tiniest and longest established Chinese-owned shop, which was loaded with cheap, shiny goods.

While the shop assistant watched us worriedly, the women deliberated on how to turn me into the "real woman" they imagined. They quickly chose a white fake fur coat with a golden metal belt similar to the one encircling a pair of white, high-heeled, thigh-high boots. Underneath the fake fur, a diaphanous, purple and green, short dress left little to the imagination.

I felt embarrassed, but they were legitimately happy and proud. They were generously sharing their knowledge and experience with a pathetically ignorant young woman who badly needed their advice. Without asking the shopkeeper, they pushed me into the back room so I could try on the clothes they had selected. I struggled to dress as quickly as possible, while the women kept the door open so that all of them could monitor my progress.

Myroslava stood in the center of the small shop and declared that I should wear this outfit whenever I appeared in public, including the workplace: "Martushka, how can you imagine that a professor wants to talk to you if he does not even understand whether you are a man or a woman? That is why you are alone and you have no kids! Who wants a woman who is not a woman?!"[3]

The Chinese shopkeeper seemed rather impressed by what they had achieved, while I desperately hoped that none of my Italian friends would pass by. I finally persuaded them to leave the shop. My refusal to buy any of the clothes they had selected was held against me for quite a long time.

Fortunately, most of my reeducation sessions were only theoretical lectures delivered while sitting in the waiting room of the bus station or, if the sun was shining, on a park bench. The contents of the lectures the women imparted often puzzled me, as they combined many elements that in my mind did not go together.

On one hand, they expressed a model of Slavic femininity that seemed to me quite conservative. They were anxious to present themselves as decent women and committed mothers, willing to endure the suffering and degradation that emigration entailed in order to guarantee their children a better future.

They constantly stressed that being a woman meant being a loyal wife and a devoted mother.[4] Besides these roles, little mattered in the life of a woman. According to them, a good wife lived to care for, serve, and support her husband.[5]

Their preaching reminded me of the Slavic ideology that I had been taught as a Yugoslav child to regard as archaic and antisocialist. Although Yugoslavia was an unaligned country and had an uneasy relationship with the USSR, most educated Yugoslav families contrasted the backwardness of our Balkan mores with the advanced gender egalitarianism of the Soviet Union.

While my socialization had been fairly conservative and had openly embraced a double standard for boys and girls, nobody had ever tried to persuade me that the roles of wife and mother were the only ones that mattered. These women seemed to be articulating a set of ideas that could have been found in the pages of a forgotten nineteenth-century textbook on Eastern European folklore.

On the other hand, their advice was all but conservative. The very same women who loved to instruct me in the duty of devotion and self-sacrifice were equally engaged in persuading me to welcome any opportunity for sexual activity. They were quite outspoken about sex, boasting about their achievements in seducing men and praising each other for their skills in satisfying men's wildest desires.

Our strolls had become, as I explain later, a rather flashy ritual, during which any instance of a male gaze was noted and enjoyed. They seemed tolerant of casual sex and regarded it as a relatively trivial affair. In their opinion, I was definitely too choosy in my dealings with the opposite sex. Foul talk and luscious jokes were endemic in our conversations. I could not understand how their conservative canon did not include modesty and chastity among the traditional feminine virtues.

A large part of my fieldwork ended up being dedicated to understanding how such apparent contradiction and moral tension were actually part of a complex discourse trying to make sense of the difference between what they regarded as valuable and what they considered necessary, what they took for granted a woman should aspire to and what was attainable in their emigration condition.

## Lustful Decembrists

Very early in my project, I witnessed an event that epitomized the problem I was struggling with. One afternoon, while sitting on some park benches sunbathing, the women started complaining about their employers, Italian women whom they regarded as spoiled, obsessed with their careers, and unable to pay their men the devotion they deserved. I pointed out that actually Italian women do not have a high rate of labor force participation and that most Italian men do not share in the household chores; indeed, Italian women are usually criticized for being too submissive.

Although I tried to say this as softly as possible, I knew that my words would be taken as a provocation. The women's reaction was different from what I expected, however. Instead of criticizing my assimilated way of thinking, they decided that I simply did not understand what they were talking about.

Alina, a fiftyish, Russian-speaking Moldovan who had formerly been a high school teacher, decided to explain Slavic womanhood to me through a history lesson. Standing up, she checked that her hair and clothes were in good order and in a very theatrical way started talking about the wives of the Decembrists, the young officers who attempted to stage a revolution in Saint Petersburg in December 1825. After it failed, their men were given life sentences of manual labor in the Siberian mines. The Tsar made it possible for the wives to dissolve their marriages, so that they would not have to share their husbands' punishment and could keep their titles and properties.

Yet many wives, nearly always against the wishes of their parents and often against the orders of their own husbands, joined them in Siberia, giving up their coveted upper-class lives for menial work and isolation in a forbidding climate. The story was dear to Alina.[6]

She lovingly introduced the main characters: the young and beautiful Maria, who, upon arrival in Siberia, kneeled and kissed her husband's chains; Ekaterina, who followed her husband even though he had humiliated her and betrayed his friends; Polina, who had been the lover of a married man but had joined him in Siberia as soon as his wife divorced him; and the aristocratic Catherine, who traveled for 5,000 miles in a carriage full of criminals.

Alina was usually silent and shy, and nobody expected her to be such a commanding storyteller. The women were uncharacteristically silent, and they seemed to be projecting their own lives onto this model of tragic Slavic womanhood. I could not help wondering if they were finding similarities between these women traveling to Siberia and their own sacrifices as emigrant mothers working in a foreign land to help their children.

I was absorbed in the story, which was completely new to me, when I realized that Alina had suddenly shifted her topic to the sexual virtues of somebody she claimed was a must-have. Exalting his strength and endurance, she provided a detailed description of the quick encounter she had had with him in a less well-lit corner of the park. To the laughter of the other women, she recommended him because he did not waste time in useless foreplay "like the Italians" but was instead strictly focused on penetrative sex.[7]

I was taken aback and astonished until I realized that the nearby bench was occupied now by three young North African drug dealers who customarily worked in that section of the park. One of them was particularly handsome and dressed in designer clothes meant to imitate a hip-hop style.

Quite conscious of being observed by the women, he was nonchalantly engaged in looking cool. The women were interested both in having fun among themselves and in hearing a detailed review of his sexual prowess. When business called the man away to another section of the park, Alina returned to her previous topic, drawing the women back to the ascetic and self-sacrificing femininity of the Decembrists' wives. Nobody else seemed to notice any discontinuity between these two narratives.

## When Men Are "Public Goods"

When I considered how it was possible to preach the virtues of self-sacrificing wifehood and promiscuous hyperfemininity simultaneously, my first idea was that the second dimension represented a fantasy, something the women merely boasted about among themselves. I thought of Alina's tales, and many others I subsequently heard, in the same way I would have about the conversations of a crowd of adolescent males in the locker room of a gym. I also needed to acknowledge my own prejudices: many of the women were in their forties or fifties, overweight and poorly dressed, and constantly stressed by material scarcity and social insecurity. I simply could not visualize them as the Eastern European equivalent of a *Cosmo* girl. How did they find the time and energy to pursue such an exuberant sexual life?

A few weeks after our history lesson in the park, I was chatting with three women at the bus station. Gabriela was showing the others a V-neck shirt she had recently bought, while Nyura and Aleksandra looked for the best ways to criticize it.

Gabriela retorted that Marco, her new Italian fiancé, liked the way it looked on her. Being one of the very first to have established a relationship with an Italian man, a widower who owned a flat, she confidently anticipated becoming a *signora* and refused to accept any aspersions cast by her friends. Defeated, Nyura and Aleksandra switched to a critique of my unfeminine clothes.

They thought my usual graduate student uniform—jeans and a hoodie—was among the causes of my being single. I tried to explain that I was actually in a relationship, but the existence of a boyfriend in Croatia was, as usual, dismissed as irrelevant. Nyura mentioned what she claimed was an old Ukrainian saying: "far away from the penis, far away from the heart." Until this point, our conversation had followed the usual joking pattern.

Our repartee was disrupted by two young Moldovan men who greeted Nyura and Aleksandra. Both the Ukrainian and Moldovan communities in Alpinetown were overwhelmingly female; there were almost no Ukrainian men in town, and just a handful of Moldovan men. Their arrival changed the atmosphere. The women greeted them, and they sat down with us.

Introducing them to me as Mykhayl and Alexey, Aleksandra explained that they had arrived in Italy just a few days before, after crossing the border hidden in a truck. They appeared much younger than the women, perhaps in their late twenties. The women acted motherly with the two men, scolding them for not having yet found steady jobs and warning about their excessive drinking.

After a while, Mykhayl and Alexey stood up and invited Aleksandra and Nyura to go out with them. As drinking alcohol in the waiting room was forbidden, it was common to be invited to leave the hall with some-one and drink some cheap wine or vodka on the benches of the nearby park. Aleksandra, however, stopped and whispered something in their ears, and they nodded.

She grabbed my hand and said I was her friend and she wanted me to go to her place. I could sense there was something slightly naughtier involved here, but all the other women were smiling approvingly. While I feared the consequences of a drinking marathon at 2 p.m., I did not want to disappoint Aleksandra, who was clearly acting as a friend. In order to avoid drinking too much, I explained that I was supposed to go back to work in the late afternoon. Both Mykhayl and Nyura laughed and promised me that I would work much better afterward.

When we left the hall, we did not turn toward the park, as I had ex-pected, but walked to a nearby deserted shopping place and went down a corridor to a well-hidden restroom. The guys entered the ladies' restroom, and Nyura and I followed. I tried to say that they were in the wrong place, that we were all in the wrong place, and that I could not understand what

I was doing there. Mykhayl grabbed Nyura, who smiled at me and wished me a good time with Alexey.

When I saw Alexey coming close, I lost my temper, as I felt betrayed by women I had come to regard as friends. Rushing away, I shouted that I loved my boyfriend and I would never betray him in a public bathroom with somebody I had never seen before. My shouts brought Nyura, already in her bra, out of the toilet. She was pissed off, and she accused me of being a silly spoiled brat. I replied she was free to do whatever she wanted, but I did not want to have sex with Alexey, or with Mykhayl for that matter. Nyura looked at me as if I were just being difficult. But, quick to see an opportunity in my foolishness—or maybe fearing to disappoint them—she claimed that she could have both of them. At least, she added, I could be of some use by keeping the main door of the restroom closed.

Standing against the door, I counted the minutes, fearful that someone might arrive. I was listening to the noises coming from the toilet stall and trying to imagine what was happening there. This moment was among the most stressful events in my research; I was scared somebody would arrive at any time, I was feeling completely alienated, and I had never imagined finding myself in such a situation. I was not sure I loved sociology enough to endure such experiences for the sake of fieldwork. It did not last long, but it seemed an eternity to me.

Eventually, the whimpers of pleasure attenuated, and Nyura, Alexey, and Mykhayl came out, red-faced and sweaty, telling me they had had a fully satisfying shag. Nyura walked proudly to the washbasin in front of the mirror and straightened her shirt and bra, brushed her platinum blonde hair, and refreshed her makeup. The two men headed for the door as if nothing had happened, and Nyura did not even bother to say goodbye to them.

I was blown away by what had happened and did not know what to say to Nyura. I tried to behave naturally, suggesting that she fix her eye makeup, as a friend would have done. She was relaxed and happy as we walked back into the bus station. The other women welcomed us warmly, asking if we had had a good time. Nyura proudly said we had and wished the same to these women, who would have the opportunity the next time.

Beyond that, our adventure did not interest them; they seemed much more interested in the new catalogue that Iryna, who had just arrived, was circulating. When we left the station, I walked with Iryna and told her what had happened. She laughed heartily. I asked why she was not shocked by Nyura's behavior, but she just replied that I had still a lot to learn. "In the end," she told me, "everybody needs to get laid. Sex is something a woman needs to stay healthy."

Nyura had done what any woman had the right to do: seize the opportunity to satisfy her needs. She had done nothing wrong, and—unlike me—she was now filled with some human warmth that would help her to cope with her life as a care worker. Iryna concluded her analysis with a very simple statement I subsequently came to regard as the crux of the issue: "Nyura has just arrived and does not know many people. She will find something better in due course."

Over the years, I have witnessed numerous instances of this collective acceptance of promiscuous hypersexuality. I quickly discovered it was not restricted to informal settings, nor was it deviant behavior engaged in only by the most marginal members of the group. About five years after my adventure in the restroom, I was invited to a barbecue in one of the Alpine parks a few miles from the city.

At the time, barbecues were a very new form of recreation and signaled a great achievement. Organizing a barbecue required having access to cars, which had been unthinkable just a few years before, and having some money to spend, as a barbecue was more expensive than any other kind of party. Moreover, as a barbecue was felt to be a family event, organizing one implied that a woman had men and relatives. This barbecue was held by Natalya, Maria, and Olga, three women who had arrived earlier than most, had started relationships with some of the very few Eastern European men available, had brought some of their adolescent children to Italy, and had recently left live-in care work to become hourly maids for a pool of employers.

From the point of view of Alpinetown natives, visiting a park meant investing physical effort in order to enjoy the severe beauty of an unspoiled environment. Mountain parks were cherished for their peaceful silence, and families relaxing along the shores of the lake avoided any conspicuous behavior. Our barbecue was clearly premised on a completely different definition of the situation. The music was loud, alcohol was plentiful, all the women were wearing high heels and flashy miniskirts, and a multitude of colored strings had been attached to the branches of the trees. It was a celebration of family life, and the women behaved as proud, full-fledged women taking care of their men. Among the participants were some women who had arrived more recently and a handful of other men.

One of them, Boris, was known for his relative wealth, as he was practically the only Ukrainian in Alpinetown to have a brand new, rather than secondhand, car. The night before, Natalya and Olga had called to inform me he would be coming and to try to convince me to have a date with him, adding that he did not drink too much or waste his money gambling. A few minutes after my arrival, Boris introduced himself and invited me to go for a ride in his car. When I turned him down, Boris appeared surprised; perhaps he had also received calls from Natalya and Olga. But he was not necessarily offended, just puzzled, and quickly joined the other men clustered around the fire. A few minutes later, I noticed him chatting with Maria's sister, Ana, a pretty girl in her late twenties. Ana had arrived in Italy some months before, but because she was working as a live-in helper for an elderly couple in a remote village, she did not participate regularly in our social life.

Right away, Boris and Ana went off for a ride. The women started laughing and telling Maria that her sister was going to get what she had missed while spending all those months in the middle of nowhere. Maria did not seem particularly shocked, and just said philosophically, "Anybody needs a piece of meat." I took the occasion to ask them if they thought it was a good idea to have sex with someone they had just met. Of course, Maria said, "What a woman needs is a husband. But if you do not have one, you have to manage anyway, don't you?" Natalya kept asking in disbelief if I really had never had sex with someone I had just met. After having been considered an emancipated woman for most of my adult life, I was now being treated as a ridiculous prude.

The ensuing dialogue helped me to understand the conceptual frame that kept these two, opposite, visions of womanhood together. From their point of view, sexual promiscuity was not equivalent with full womanhood. What a woman needs is a real husband, somebody she can live for. As Maria made clear, a "real" woman needs a monogamous relationship in which she can freely provide love and devotion to a "real"—that is, responsible, strong-willed, and reliable—man who pays her back in passion, protection, and support. That was how things should be and how they used to be. Such a natural exchange, however, could not be taken for granted anymore.

During the transition from state socialism to free-market capitalism, the women had discovered that their men were unable to provide for their families financially and failed to offer adequate guidance to their children. The women had been forced to take responsibility for family survival, while their husbands wasted their time on alcohol and other women. In the new economic order, the women's educational credentials and employment seniority did not gain them access to the few available career opportunities. Natalya claimed cheekily that post-Soviet women had been forced to rely on seduction, feminine tricks, and "our treasure, of course." While they were adamant that less structured forms of sexual liaisons could never attain the splendor and moral stature of the original, they were equally adamant that casual sex was better than investing emotions and long-term commitment in men who, like their former husbands, were unable to take care of their wives.

Olga added another line of argument: life in emigration was difficult, they were isolated, nearly all the other emigrants they knew were women, and their employers expected them to behave like old babushkas, looking at them suspiciously every time they dressed like women. Although the women were eager to meet and experiment with suitable partners, it was often very difficult to do so.

Deciding to put some spice in the conversation, I practiced my newly acquired role of moronic prude and asked bluntly why a woman should not wait for a worthy partner instead of giving herself away to the first guy she met. What was wrong with abstinence? After all, I argued, you always preached that a real Slavic woman would be like a Decembrist, remaining faithful to her man even if they are far apart.

These remarks caused an amazing stir. Even Iryna, who enjoyed acting as my life coach, looked at me as if I were a nutcase. "The simple fact is that there is nobody to be faithful to," she argued. Most women were divorced. Others were only nominally married to men they seldom saw. Their only obligations were to their children and to their parents. They satisfied those obligations by washing old asses for undeserving families in an alien country. They did not feel there was anything wrong in getting satisfaction through whatever means were available.

A key element to their stance was that they framed these sexual activities mostly as a health issue. It was a self-evident truth for them that a woman needed to experience penetrative sex with a certain frequency. Sexual deprivation was considered the cause of several pathologies from which these women suffered, such as insomnia, weight loss, and frequent migraines, not to mention wrinkles. No other form of sexual stimulation was considered by the women to be adequate, both medically and morally. If sex could not be provided by a stable partner, then women should get it from whoever was available. As Natalya was keen to highlight, the fact that I had become a frigid Italian woman did not authorize me to criticize those who, like Ana, were still full-fledged women and needed "more than a finger."[8] The women did recognize the difference between Maria's situation and that of her sister. But that difference had nothing to do with morality or decency; it simply was a matter of time and luck.

Then, their line of argument shifted toward a more political under-standing of sexuality in emigration. They perceived emigration and care work as forms of degradation that tried to "dewomanize" them, turning them into pliant, sexless babushkas.

The women considered sex, even casual sex, as an empowering re-source that helped them feel both satisfied and dignified. It reminded them that, although they were care workers, they were still women, ob-jects of desire and appreciation. They insisted that male appreciation was a key resource to remember that they were real women, only tem-porarily forced by circumstances to work as slaves in foreign households. Their notion of femininity as sexual prowess was not merely a matter of bragging among friends but also an important resource for their survival in emigration.

The conversation was interrupted by Boris and Ana's return. While he went straight to the cluster of boys tending the fire, she joined us at our table. The women asked her simply if she had had a good time, and she happily replied with a self-conscious smile.

## Achieving Beauty, Eliciting Desire

Through many conversations, I realized that questions of sexual behav-ior and morality were enmeshed in a wider symbolic framework linking sexuality with broader issues of womanhood and physical beauty.

As I explore more deeply in the conclusion, migrating to Alpinetown had changed the women's sexual self-definition. Emigration was like "returning to girlhood," Aneta, a fortyish Moldovan brunette, told me. Before migrating, most women had quietly accepted their status as ma-ture women whose legitimate femininity was largely restricted to caring for their children and grandchildren. Once divorced, or after their hus-bands had left them, they had regarded themselves as too old to actively look for a new partner.

As I have had many occasions to observe directly during our trips home, when in their hometowns, the women behaved, and were ex-pected to behave, as mothers, consumers, and respectable members of their households, those dimensions being closely intertwined. During several trips with them in Ukraine and Moldova, I never witnessed the slightest sign of gallantry, let alone courtship, exhibited toward any of them. Although they were economically independent and socially en-vied, none was ever asked out on a date. Even when they showed off their flashiest clothes and their hyperfeminine, curly, Dolly Parton-like hairdos, they did so for an audience of family and friends, as a demonstration of the social standing of the household, rather than as proof of their sexual desirability to men.

In Italy, by contrast, the women had quickly discovered that, despite being employed in a low-status job, they could find themselves the objects of gallantry and courtship, even of naked desire. They had witnessed how even women in their fifties could be actively sought after. They thought some Italian men regarded them as potential sexual mates or even as potential life partners. They believed that many little things, such as receiving compliments in the street, certified this new status.

On the benches where we usually met in the bus station, we once found photographs of an old man in his best attire, with his name and telephone number on the back. The women were thrilled, rather than offended, by the discovery.

Paradoxically, this discovery also confirmed the stereotype they were victimized by: many Italians thought that they were loose, amoral, and cheap women who had migrated to Italy in order to seduce simpleminded elderly men or to steal someone else's husband. This view meant fewer job opportunities and more suspicious attitudes among the families they worked for, but it also confirmed that they could be feared, successful competitors in the sexual arena.

The male gaze was a very important source of recognition and self-esteem, and the women responded with an intensity I found surprising. Their delight in attracting male attention was particularly conspicuous when our urban strolls, originally born out of the dire necessity of doing something in our free time without spending any money, had quickly started to become elaborate performances.

Wearing heavy makeup and stiletto heels, they formed a group of mature platinum blondes scantily clad in overly bright colors. They would stroll down the middle of the pedestrian street, moving defiantly and loudly among the whispers and stares of the onlookers sitting in the cafés. Their demeanor seemed deliberately and radically at odds with the traditional values, modesty, and humility prescribed by the more accepted image of the foreign care worker. The performance was designed to be noticed and to impress, and it assuredly did. The few times I observed them while sitting among the locals in a café, I overheard the reactions generated by my friends' promenade. They were definitely talked about.

The women enjoyed feeling provocative. They emphasized that "it was great not to be a foreign care worker for a while." Comparing their flamboyant attire with that of the Italian women who crossed their path, they insisted that men admired and desired them rather than the drab Italian women. Such street parades, like many other hyperfeminine performances we were involved in, were ways of both exploring and advertising their new status as resurrected sexual beings. As a very distinctive way of claiming respect and recognition, they were a key ritual for the establishment of our group.

At the core of these strolls, as well as many other activities we were involved in, was the notion that being a woman is not a natural gift but rather an achievement that requires considerable effort. Understanding this point took me a great deal of time and several puzzling experiences. I was often struck by the clash between the women's physical characteristics—looking older than their chronological age, heavily overweight, tired, and worn out—and their proclivity for using whatever little was left of their earnings, after paying their bills and sending remittances, to buy cosmetics and underwear.

Similarly, some women favored flashy clothes that struck me not only as inappropriate but also as unflattering. Most Italians I overheard noticed the same contrast between these women's bodies and their adornment and considered their mode of dress vulgar and exhibitionistic. The women appeared indifferent to the setting: it seemed that they dressed inappropriately and behaved as if they did not care what others thought.

To understand their behavior, I had to abandon taken-for-granted assumptions about what it meant for a woman to take care of her body and public appearance.[9] Previously, I had thought that involved eating healthy food, exercising in the gym, dressing comfortably, and adopting a style that made me feel at ease. The migrant women's self-presentation provoked a radical revision of my view of self-appreciation.

Their approach to taking care of the body was the consequence of a symbolic logic that identifies being a woman not with her physical appearance per se but rather with the effort it requires. For my informants, enhancing their appearance did not mean developing their natural physical beauty. Rather, beauty was something to be constructed *on* the body. Being an attractive woman was largely the result of will and competence in painting a surface on the self, a highly elaborate mask.[10] Every woman should aspire to "look nice"; such a status cannot be denied to anybody. All women could be beautiful if we committed ourselves to creating our own beauty, or so they thought. These women endured tremendous sacrifices, ranging from wearing tight girdles to fasting, in order to uphold and reproduce these ideals under extremely difficult conditions.

Beauty-as-effort was largely independent from the physical features of each body and personal aesthetic preferences or social suitability. One day I was invited to a direct sale of cosmetics held in the rooms of an association somewhat connected to the Russian Orthodox Church. These women, given their stronger religious identification, were often critical of the "looseness" of their compatriots' sexual morals, so I expected them to exhibit a different way of understanding and practicing womanhood. What transpired there, however, attested to the cross-cutting, shared nature of the hyperfeminine ideal.

The gathering celebrated the visit of Lyuba, a Ukrainian care worker and salesperson who, after a spell in Alpinetown, was now living and working in another Mediterranean country. Diana, a pillar of the local church, praised her: she was high up in the pyramid system; she "knew her job well and was a beautiful woman." She was greeted with reverence and, in a firm tone of voice, she then ordered us to sit around the table and take notes.

Lyuba gave a testimonial contrasting her life before and after she had been rescued, physically and psychologically, by the products she now sold. Before starting to use them, she was fat and ugly. She disliked her body and felt like "half a woman." The discovery of her products had saved her life. A huge woman wearing a pink shirt tied up in front and tight jeans, she proudly exhibited her generous form. She wore red blush, pink lipstick, and blue eyelashes, and her eyebrows were thin and penciled. Her haircut was reminiscent of the 1980s. She acted in a professional and authoritative way: her goal was to teach the women how to appear their best.

Looking for a woman who needed a physical makeover, she chose me. Before starting the work, she asked all the women to touch my skin and feel how old it felt, although I was the youngest of the group. Then, remarking that my skin was "really dirty," she applied a purifying mask. I was ordered to wash my face before makeup was applied.

When I tried to explain that makeup did not work on me, she replied that I did not know how to use it properly. Since my skin was too pale, she would apply a darker foundation to make it copper-like. I retorted that, since my neck was light, the contrast would be quite jarring.

My opinion did not matter: she applied olive foundation, red blush, greenish eyeliner with eye shadow, a lot of mascara for what she called a cattish look, and bright red lipstick. I looked absolutely awful, but how I felt did not matter. The other women adored it, pronouncing it as the way a woman should look regardless of her natural complexion.

For the participants, the seminar was not just a lesson about the goods they were hoping to sell in the future, but, rather, understanding how a woman should appear. The tricks Lyuba taught emphasized femininity, covering the skin with a layer that called attention to its artificiality.[11]

For the women, beauty-as-effort had a broad range of relational meanings beyond sexuality. Beauty certified a woman's strength of character and trustworthiness. The women interpreted the perceived sloppiness of their Italian female employers as proof of their lack of moral character, so they were constantly policing themselves—and me in particular—for any sign of assimilation to Italian ways. When conflict arose within the group, the battle cry was always the accusation that the enemy was becoming too relaxed and, implicitly, "Italian."

I eventually understood why the women resented the fact that Italian employers regarded certain ways of dressing as signaling that a woman was not a reliable care worker. While congregating in the park, women were commonly approached by newly arrived migrants who wanted to know how to behave in their initial contacts with Italian families. They were instructed to use props and tell stories to suggest that they were bona fide care workers.

For instance, they were advised to wear wedding rings, so that the prospective employer would think they were married women accustomed to domestic chores. Talking about their children was another way to suggest their reliability.

In contrast, flashy clothes and heavy makeup, which these women cherished as a sign of femininity, were to be avoided at all costs. They felt that Italian employers forced them to appear not as what they authentically were—strong, independent, well-educated, urban women—but rather as what they despised, docile and ignorant babushkas, old peasant women. One night Anja, a former store manager, stated her advice to a novice concisely: "They want you to dress as if you were still in Soviet times!" All the women laughed, and her declaration became a maxim that others repeated.

This notion was flexible enough to include new understandings of beauty. The more they were experiencing life in Alpinetown, the more many women started integrating new dimensions and goals into their normative stance on beauty. They initially considered being slim unimportant. The women claimed that their being overweight was related to the strength of their sexual appetites: being slim connoted frigidity. In Italy, however, slimness was a dominant criterion for feminine attractiveness. After spending some time in Italy, many women started complaining about being heavy, and Iryna responded by offering slimming creams and girdles. Criticizing others for "eating too much" was another way in which weight become slowly incorporated into their ideal of womanhood as effort.

## In Emigration, Not All Males Are the Same

From the point of view of the women, there were no real differences between what it meant to be a decent woman in their homelands and in Italy. They made a strictly functional distinction between a stable partnership and casual sex.[12] In contrast, blurring the boundary, mixing partnership and casual sex, meant being a *"blyat."* Using this term, the women did not refer to a concrete exchange between sexual services and monetary payment as much as an unrestrained, indecent lifestyle that blurred the boundaries between the two worlds.

To move willingly from the first to the second was inconceivable, a mark of infamy. To accept the benefits of casual sex was acceptable as long as it did not imply making it a way of life. A healthy woman, capable of devotion and deserving respect, was able to engage in casual sex as a necessity under her current circumstances and still regard herself as decent if she kept long-term commitment as the only worthy goal.

When in the mode of giving me motherly advice, many women presented a script in which a relationship evolved from more transient encounters. Being able to attract the gaze of sufficiently worthy men was proof of female worth. Recognizing the value of my feminine qualities, such men would realize that they should commit themselves to a stable partnership.

This script explained why the women did not see any contradiction in trying to push me, like other young single women in the group, toward freely experimenting with those men who were considered, like Boris, acceptable candidates and, at the same time, toward prescriptive traditional womanhood. The first was regarded as a step toward the second. This way of thinking was particularly important in emigration, a situation in which casual sex carried the additional function of protecting women from defeminization. It was considered as a training ground for searching for a stable partner in an alien environment.

Following such a script in Alpinetown was much easier said than done. The women quickly discovered that the set of prospective partners was much more heterogeneous than in their past. Older women could be active participants in that environment, but they had to deal with men who were much younger, as many migrant men were, or much older, especially Italian widowers, who were the most sought-after partners.

The main difference had to do with ethnic and racial heterogeneity. Their script implied that all potential mates could, in principle, become partners. Their life in Alpinetown, however, was defined by the abundance of desirable short-term mates who could not be considered prospective partners owing to ethno-racial reasons.

They classified men in Alpinetown into two separate groups. First came what Kateryna, a Ukrainian grandmother working as a cleaner in a shopping mall, called "just meat," who were acceptable only as sexual partners. From their point of view, these males were what an economist would call a public good: no woman could claim exclusive access to them and no woman should be excluded from enjoying them.[13]

This category included males from many different ethnic, racial, and age groups, as long as interaction with them was transient and strictly restricted to the satisfaction of sexual needs. Then there were the "real men" with whom a sexual partnership could and should evolve into a stable, caring relationship. To be in this group, as I explore in detail in the next chapter, implied having a certain degree of economic security, being older, showing some potential reliability as a long-term partner, and, implicitly but inexorably, being classifiable as Caucasian.

While it was perfectly acceptable to meet men in the first category for sex and small talk, regularly dating one of them was frowned upon by the other women. The women also firmly discouraged any attempt to develop a serious relationship with men like Alexey, Boris, and Mykhayl—indeed, with nearly all single Eastern European men in Alpinetown. Few of them had attained the economic security that the women regarded as necessary.

Fundamentally, the women were openly biased against their compatriots. They attributed their previous conjugal failure to the poor quality of post-Soviet males, and they usually assumed that their male compatriots were inevitably prone to alcoholism and unreliability.

As I will detail further in the next chapter, when Iryna met and subsequently married Avel, a Russian construction worker a few years younger than she, most of the women lamented the news as spelling certain doom. It took years for them to accept the fact that Iryna had been lucky, admitting, begrudgingly, "Avel is not like the others."

The least eligible men for serious dating were immigrants from North Africa and South Asia. In the park, as elsewhere in the city, the spaces used by North African immigrants were nearly always contiguous to the spaces used by Eastern European women. They were mostly male, and although many of them were married, very few had brought their wives to Alpinetown. They also had higher incomes than the women and found it natural to pay when they did something together.

The women appreciated this as a sign of respect, particularly the new-comers, who had to count every cent. In the group, I never heard anyone speak against having one of these immigrants as a sexual mate. On the contrary, they were the focus of endless jokes and stories centered on their strength, prowess, and endurance. It was, however, taken for granted that they, as Muslims and *"chórnenky"*—a blanket term the women used for all people with dark skin, including North Africans and South Asians—could never become "real" partners or husbands. A long-term commitment to a *chórnenky* was simply inconceivable.[14]

Policing the boundary between the two categories of prospective partners was crucial to the women's sense of decency and self-respect. The women were quite strict in their functional differentiation between different kinds of men and different kinds of needs. To mix them up was a cause of social doom as well as moral degradation. Still, policing these boundaries in Alpinetown was fraught with difficulties, and efforts to uphold this distinction often created severe strains within the group.

The main problem was that some of the women's affairs with their casual partners slowly turned into stable relationships. This situation was very uneasy: they were emotionally attached to men who they knew could never become legitimate public partners. The case of Natasha was particularly striking. I met her when she was thirty-seven years old and had recently moved to Alpinetown after spending four years in Naples. A very talkative person, she soon briefed me on her affairs with North African immigrants and married southern Italian men. She regarded her intimate life as a crucial resource in her emigration career. She did not mind "working hard washing Italian asses for little money" as long as it was necessary to keep her children happy. She insisted that she also needed to have some fun. She needed to feel desired and loved. And only the love of a man could provide such self-assurance.

A few weeks after her arrival, Natasha had met a young Moroccan, Adel, who was working in the open-air market as a sales assistant. Even if he lived with other North Africans in a crowded flat, she had snuck into his room to passionately have sex while his flatmates were asleep. She cheekily retold this story several times as the epitome of a casual affair. She never told me anything more about Adel, and I took for granted that it had been a pleasant one-night stand.

A year later, I met Natasha alone and in distress while strolling in the open-air market. As I pleaded with her to tell me what was the matter, she circled around a cluster of stands and stopped several times in front of a stand that was managed by a handsome North African man in his late twenties, who pretended not to notice us, and by an Italian woman, who was clearly annoyed.

Drawing Natasha away, I asked who the man was and why the woman was staring at us with disgust. She tearfully told me the man was Adel, whom she had been dating regularly in secret. The woman was his fiancée. Some days before, as the date of the wedding approached, Adel had told Natasha he wanted to stop seeing her. She had taken the day off to see him and was offended by the fact that Adel pretended not to know her. She claimed she was not jealous of him getting married. "In the end," she admitted, "I am married too." She claimed she was happy that he would live in a family and have children. Still, she explained, she did not accept that he had decided to leave her "as an old shoe" to be faithful to that "fatty woman." She was depressed and humiliated, in sharp contrast to the cheerfully authoritative woman I had known.

She had apparently never conceived, even in that excruciatingly sad moment, that she and Adel could ever be a couple. When I asked her, she said that would have been impossible because he was a Muslim. I replied that religious difference did not seem to be a problem for him; after all, he was marrying an Italian woman. Natasha was, however, unwilling even to contemplate the idea. After taking her into a bar, I asked why she had never told me anything about Adel in all these months. She said, quite simply, that people talk too much, and she was not sure I would have kept my mouth shut about Adel. "Some affairs make more sense when lived below the radar." Adel was "her little secret." I had the clear impression that her love for Adel had exceeded what was admissible with a *chórnenky*, and Natasha was struggling with a pain she could not even admit she was feeling. After a few weeks, I heard that Natasha had abruptly returned to Naples.

Some time before, I had met the only slightly luckier Nastenka. She originally arrived in Alpinetown with a scholarship to study at the university, but she had overstayed her visa and started working as a housekeeper. She became friends with the South Asian manager of a small shop where she bought groceries. At first, their affair was an easy game to play. The other women considered it a youthful indiscretion, and his friends regarded her as an exotic but temporary presence.

After a while, both groups grew increasingly alarmed. His friends started worrying that their love could ruin his long-awaited marriage with a girl in Pakistan. The women regarded it as improper that she spent so much time in his shop, the only white woman among a large number of Asian men. They started criticizing her and spreading rumors that she was working as a prostitute servicing Asian customers. One afternoon in the waiting room, the women seriously discussed whether they should contact her parents and inform them. As they had always claimed nobody should say anything about what the other women did to those left behind, I was quite surprised they could even consider such an option. Both partners were in obvious distress, and after a while, Nastenka announced that she had left him. Only a few trusted friends were aware the crisis had actually been carefully staged and Nastenka kept meeting her lover more discreetly.

In subsequent months, I realized that Natasha and Nastenka were not isolated cases. Several women, especially the younger ones, had moved from isolated encounters to more stable relationships with *chórnenky* or with members of other groups perceived as unsuitable. For them, the line between casual sex and emotional bonding had become blurred. When their relationship acquired a certain regularity, their commitment to the group would weaken.

Having only a few hours free from work each week, they had to choose between seeing their lovers and spending their leisure time with the group. In the case of a legitimate relationship, as with an Italian, this shift was not considered a problem: the women took for granted a *signora* would visit them less often and only when it suited her busy schedule. Such special treatment was not extended to women involved in relationships with men who were acceptable as occasional lovers but did not qualify as objects of devotion. This kind of affair did not provide any status, and the women felt uneasy since they could not talk freely about a significant part of their lives without becoming the subject of gossip.

Jealousy also weakened their loyalty to the group. Many of their male lovers had previously been part of the pool of casual sexual mates whom the women regarded as a public good. Now, some women resented the jocular comments made by others, interpreting them either as a manifestation of interest or as a way of degrading them. As many of the women maintained the assumption that *chórnenky* were by definition available to anybody interested, friendships frequently turned sour.

Women who had somewhat stable relationships with problematic partners would try to manage the stigma. Very few of them tried, as Nastenka had done, to enter a public long-term relationship, becoming members of one another's personal networks. They knew such news would easily travel back to their families. And, as Natasha had discovered, they would often run into serious constraints also from the man's side. As these issues became more fraught, some women would congregate in smaller groups of those who had experienced similar situations or were felt to be more open-minded. These attempts at secession seldom became a viable alternative to the usual sites and networks.

The women who were having sustained relationships with men regarded as unsuitable often ended up inhabiting an uncertain space, simultaneously alienated from the group of women who criticized them but also unable to leave it behind completely. While the initial sharing of casual partners had strengthened the group, the emergence of a number of women with stable relationships that did not provide either status or respect implied the development of distinct cliques patterned by very different trajectories.

# FOUR

# Getting Serious: Courtship, Love, and (Maybe) Marriage in Emigration

Early spring has always been the best season in Alpinetown. On Sunday mornings, it was tempting to make a quick stop at the parking lot to buy beers and sunflower seeds, and quickly proceed to the nearby riverside benches. There, I would find some of the women, chatting, enjoying the mild sun, and staring at the water flowing peacefully. Each woman would have something for our Sunday morning feast, and we would spend a couple of hours together.

On one of these occasions, late in my fieldwork, while I was busy chatting with a few old friends, a tall, middle-aged man stopped his bicycle along the path. I was immediately informed he was Amir, a Macedonian quarry worker who had arrived in Alpinetown nearly two decades before. I had never met him, but I had heard a lot about him from Kalyna, a woman I considered one of my best friends. I knew Amir was married to an Italian woman and the proud father of one child. He was fluent in Italian and had a steady income from his work and a new car.

I knew Kalyna had met Amir a certain number of times, and I suspected he was the main reason behind her recent enthusiasm for housesitting my small flat when I was away. I knew Veronika, another of the younger women in the group, had recently had a night out with Amin, one of Amir's Macedonian friends that Kalyna had introduced her to.

Since we shared the same Yugoslav background, and we had left our former country more or less at the same time, I was looking forward to meeting him. Once Iryna introduced him to me, I found it easy to start speaking in Croatian, telling stories and making jokes about the ways we had been received in Alpinetown in the very early 1990s.

It had been a long time since I had spoken in my mother tongue, and I really enjoyed our small talk, thus paying little attention to what was happening around us. After a while, I started feeling that the atmosphere around us was definitely cold. Most women wanted to let us know that they were listening to all that we said. When Amir decided to go, we said goodbye and we exchanged phone numbers.

As soon as he left, Veronika rushed to me deeply disturbed, claiming I was not a real friend, as I had humiliated Kalyna by trying to "steal Amir" in front of all the other women. She warned me aggressively that Kalyna would fight tooth and nail to keep him tight. While talking, she was pressing her body against mine to make me retreat. All the other women approved of her behavior, looking at me and judging me as if I was the worst being ever born on earth. I was actually shocked: my conversation with Amir had been quite innocent, driven purely by the pleasure of speaking Croatian.

I did my best to assure Veronika that I had no intention to steal Amir from anybody, that I had just enjoyed some small talk with a former compatriot. I worked out a precarious truce. It ended abruptly when my phone rang. It was Amir inviting me for a pizza. I replied that I was busy and turned down the offer, but it was of little help. The very same women who had been trying for months to persuade me to participate in their friendly consumption of shared resources, who had often incited me to trespass all obstacles whatsoever to get a man, were now looking at me like a bunch of Furies ready to throw their vengeful weapons of destruction upon me.

Maria, one of the oldest women in the group (and usually a motherly figure), openly insulted me as a sneaky, spoiled brat. She claimed I was willing to take what I wanted without any consideration for the others, without any respect for honest women like them. I kept repeating that I was not interested in Amir, with no success. The climate was so dark I really thought my fieldwork had come to an abrupt and unexpected end, as the women would never accept me again among them. I was heartbroken and I slowly retreated toward the parking lot, mentally saying goodbye to my project and to a bunch a people I had slowly came to regard as friends.

Luckily, my assessment was overly pessimistic. I never had pizza with Amir, and in a few days, the women changed the assessment of my behavior from "guilty" to "silly." I was typecast again as a young woman who did not know how to behave properly. I was naïve, unable to understand men's real purposes.

Still, the incident marked a breakthrough in the life of the group: for the first time, I had seen men who were not publicly available resources, men who were not goods to be shared, but precious private properties to defend. Learning how to deal with this new kind of prospective partner, which had been only dreamed about for a long time, represented quite a challenge for the women, full of long-term consequences.

In some cases, the relationships established would strengthen and fortify the life of the group, helping create a smooth transition from a bunch of single women to a stable network of women *and* families sharing a cherished reference to their origins. In others, on the contrary, the development of stable relationships with Italians would weaken, and ultimately sever, the linkage of the women with the group, progressively detaching the successful *signore* from the rest.

## Migrating Households

During all the years of my fieldwork, I met only a handful of women who still had a partner in their place of origin. Most of the women had divorced before emigration, and a large number of those still legally married regarded such status a mere formality. Those who wished to settle in Alpinetown would go a long way to get visas for their sons and daughters, a process that often required bribing their fathers to grant permission for the children to leave.

The other women regarded as utterly silly the few women who had partners in Ukraine or Moldova and made some effort to keep their relationships alive. The women would joke openly in front of them about what they thought their men were doing *there* while their wives were sacrificing for them *here*. They took for granted their men would surely waste the money so excruciatingly earned by their wives on gambling and alcohol. Any time the wives tried to show the other women some kind of loving message from their husbands, the other women would interpret it as a sign of a looming disaster: if their husbands were affectionate, it meant they wanted to cover some horrible action they had done or intended to ask for more money in the future.

Still, after a few years, some women left Alpinetown to return to their hometown and to their husbands.[1] In very few cases, the women decided to apply for a family reunification visa for their husbands. It was a difficult choice, as sponsoring a relative was not an easy procedure. The economic and bureaucratic requirements, moreover, were matched by equally heroic emotional challenges.

When the women were able to call for their husbands, many years had passed. Sometimes, the woman had not even been able to return home regularly for visits. The job market in Alpinetown provided a large supply of care jobs for the women, while their men had to face much stiffer competition and frequent long spells of unemployment. Some of the (few) reunited couples did not survive the tribulations, thus providing further evidence to the women about the unredeemable nature of their national variety of males.

Svetlana, a middle-aged Crimean Tatar who had worked as a family doctor before emigration, was among the very few Ukrainian women who had dreamed of and actively sought to reunite her family since the very beginning of her emigration. When I first met her, she had just arrived in Alpinetown from southern Italy. She had acquired her papers there, but she had moved to Alpinetown because she thought it would be easier to satisfy the conditions for family reunification.

To get a visa for her husband was her priority, and she always talked about her emigration as part of a family project: they would have left together, if only they could have mustered enough money. She was extremely focused and very tight with her money, thinking that any money spent on herself implied a delay in his arrival. Still, it took more than three years and a large dose of luck to satisfy the appropriate conditions for a family-reunification application.

She was lucky because her employers, Rita and Giuseppe, were extremely sympathetic to her plight and had decided to help her. They found her a job in a bar managed by a nephew of Rita, and Giuseppe guaranteed accommodation for her with the owner of a small flat. They posed only one condition—that Svetlana had to find them a new reliable woman they could trust to replace her.

Svetlana started her new life as a waitress. She was remarkably happy with the change, but she quickly discovered her new wage would not allow her to sustain her new expenses. She tried to work as many extra hours as she could, but the owner did not like the idea of having an overworked waitress dealing with his customers in one of the holiest rituals of Italian life, the espresso. In the end, she had to find a second job cleaning offices at night.

When her husband, Arkadiy, arrived in Alpinetown, Svetlana was over-joyed. All the regular customers of the bar noticed the hard-to-miss change, and she briefed all of them in great detail about the reason for her happiness. Within some weeks, however, the situation soured. Arkadiy did not speak any Italian, he had difficulties navigating the town and finding a job, and Svetlana was continuously busy with her two jobs. He was alone most of the time, and he started spending most of the day with a small group of unemployed Romanian young men in the park, a regular object of scorn for the women. As they congregated a short dis-tance away from the women, they were able to report all the times Arka-diy had been seen with them, smoking weed or drinking cheap wine on the benches.

Maria and Olga, increasingly outspoken in their patronizing, were al-ways keen to stress that Arkadiy's association with those losers spelled doom for Svetlana, who would have been much better off without him. Most women agreed, and she became the symbol of female martyrdom the women identified with the life they had left back *there*. Their sympa-thy was also a critique of Svetlana's naïve hubris: she had lived under the delusion that the males *there* could be somewhat reformed if brought *here*.

Svetlana was heartbroken but kept insisting that she loved her hus-band and that he was just going through an understandably difficult moment. Even her patience came to an end when Arkadiy refused a me-nial job Giuseppe had found for him in a local junkyard.

In the morning, when I went to the bar to have my coffee, I faced a very pale Svetlana, who was quick to tell me she had had a terrible fight with Arkadiy the afternoon before. He had left home, and she did not know where he was. She was totally devastated, and she kept repeating that she had done so much to be with him again. She had only asked him to do what all emigrants must do, to accept the first job she could find for him and be patient while he learned enough of the new place to find some-thing better. She had been particularly offended by his claim that it was not worthwhile to work for 500 euros. She felt such an attitude to be an implicit criticism of her, of her willingness to accept everything she could find to make more money.

Clearly, he did not want the same thing she wanted, to accumulate quickly what was needed to bring their teenaged children to Alpinetown and again be a family. I tried to console her, assuring her that everything would be fine again, but I could not help thinking that the other women had foreseen the future better.

To my surprise, that very same evening, Arkadiy rang the bell of my flat. He was in pretty bad shape, reeking of alcohol and obviously needing to talk. He sat at the table and, while I was cooking some food for him, he erupted. He had never talked much before, and I was surprised by his willingness to ask openly for help. He said he felt lost and useless in Alpinetown. He could not find a job and felt he was not able to help his wife.

Svetlana was so stressed *here*, so focused on making money that she hardly ever talked about anything else. He felt the need to catch up with their lives, after so many years of separation. In his eyes, Svetlana had become a different person, obsessed with the future. Since he had arrived, she had bossed him around, always pretending to know what was best for him. He felt his opinions did not matter, that he was not the husband anymore. The day before, when he had tried to touch her, she had "refused him, saying she was tired." He felt humiliated and unable to handle such a situation.

While he was eating, I argued that if he really wanted to straighten things out, he should accept the job at the junkyard. He seemed to understand how difficult her situation was. I explained how difficult it had been for her to live without him all those years, and how exceptional her commitment to him had been. We had coffee and kept talking about how much Svetlana loved him, and how he could manage to adapt to the new environment. He nodded and said he knew he had been wrong, but he just could not stand her bossy attitude any longer. After he took a nap, I gave him a lift to their flat. He rang the bell and offered her all his love, asking her to welcome him back in her life. Svetlana opened the door, and the two hugged. I left.

After a little more than a year, Arkadiy was able to leave the job in the junkyard and move to a better-paid job in a small construction firm. This allowed Svetlana to get rid of her second job, maintaining her "profession," as she called it, to which she added some cleaning jobs during the weekends, which they could fulfill together. In two years' time, they obtained a mortgage and purchased a run-down flat in a village close to Alpinetown. Arkadiy spent all his free time improving it, and he was quite proud of his achievements. As soon as the town council confirmed that the flat complied with regulations, they were able to call for their children. When they arrived, Svetlana proudly stated that she had achieved what she had dreamed of for nearly a decade.

During the years in which they built their success story, Svetlana slowly decreased her participation in the group of women. Arkadiy did not like to spend too much time with the women, and they preferred spending their (scarce) free time with the few other Eastern European couples in the area. When their children arrived, they were among the first to start the practice of barbecues in the mountain parks, where they could invite the few other couples with children for socializing.

They are now quite well-known figures in the life of the Greek Catholic Church, and they are very proud of their children's participation in a group of traditional Ukrainian folk dancers. While their activity in the network of Ukrainian families in Alpinetown has become more and more pronounced, their relationship with Ukraine has reached a nadir. With their children in Italy and their parents dead, they return to their village very seldom, and only for short visits. Their children prefer to spend their holidays somewhere else, together with their Italian friends. They still have a house in Ukraine, but they have not made any improvements to it, as they think they will need the money to help their children in Alpinetown.

Some other families originated from liaisons with men of the "same group." For the women, such sameness had nothing to do with the nationality inscribed in a passport. It was rather a matter of a common Soviet past and reciprocal linguistic intelligibility. All the men who had a Soviet past and could speak languages the women could reasonably understand were considered to be "ours."[2] As I have described earlier, the women regarded the men of their group a real disgrace. To start dating one of them in emigration was a poor choice, which for the women too often spelled doom.

At the same time, such a boundary was not completely impermeable, an important difference from the women who fell in love with a *chórnenky*. Those who started "serious" relationships with an Eastern European man had rather to face the heavy burden of proof that their men were "different from the others." If they succeeded in doing so, it would mark definitive progress in the women's trajectories in the erotic ethnic stratification of Alpinetown. Their partnerships could be accepted, albeit reluctantly, as bona fide families and they could enjoy the status of successful, respected women. This outcome was deemed plainly impossible in the case of the *chórnenky*.

Iryna's relationship with Avel was one of these cases. When she arrived in Alpinetown, she was one of the very first, leaving her daughter Lena entrusted to her mother, and Iryna was nearly alone. The city park was one of the very few spaces where she could rest, although it was attended by many *chórnenky*, whom she did her best to avoid. One day, however, she met Ahmed, a Moroccan immigrant she started dating secretly nearly immediately. She was happy, but the problem was that their love story had begun precisely when the number of Ukrainian women in town had started to grow.

Iryna did not want to be seen by them with Ahmed, as she feared the news could travel back to Ukraine. When she confided in me the news, she expressly requested that I keep it to myself. She explained, "You never know what they will say . . . a word is enough to become a *blyat* . . . and then the news travels back there and nobody remembers you are actually here washing old asses to provide for your family." The relationship with Ahmed was an important experience for Iryna. Years later, Iryna was fond of telling (to a selected public) plenty of stories about him, which she always presented as her erotic awakening. He was said to be tall, with dark eyes and a great smile, and he never tired of making love.

Iryna described him cheekily as her sex teacher, who had made her a sophisticated woman, making her appreciate many sexual practices she had known before "only from smuggled videos." Ahmed "rented" her a room in his flat and helped her find many cleaning jobs. He also helped her with filing her application for an adjustment of status. Iryna was thus able to leave live-in care work and slowly begin the transition to an hourly paid housekeeper. She subsequently started to build, on the side, the commercial activity in which she recruited me as an unpaid helper. Ahmed even bought a bicycle for Lena that Iryna sent to her with one of the minivans.

According to Iryna, Ahmed was deeply in love with her, and he wanted to marry her. Iryna was unable to overcome the fact that he was a *chórnenky* and her fear that the other women would judge her a *"puttana"* if they discovered she was in love with him. Only a handful of us knew the person she shared the flat with was also her lover, and she hardly ever mentioned him to the other women.

The real crisis started when they decided to cut their expenses by subletting another room of their flat: *"Blyat*, it was the worst idea ever!" Ahmed had met a newly arrived young Eastern European man, Avel, who he thought might be the right person to share the flat. Ahmed felt that Avel treated him in a friendly way, and he explained to Iryna that he could be instrumental in helping Ahmed become accepted among the Eastern European immigrants of Alpinetown.

After a few days, however, Avel and Iryna had become a bit too friendly. One evening, mad with jealousy, Ahmed accused Iryna of fooling around with Avel. A fight ensued, in which Ahmed slapped her. Avel left his room and defended her, knocking Ahmed down. Avel and Iryna kissed.[3] She suddenly found herself without a place to live and with responsibility for a (relatively younger) undocumented immigrant from Transnistria.[4]

Iryna found it difficult to ask for help from her friends, as she faced the double stigma of dating a much younger man from the former Soviet Union. She insisted with her closest friends that Avel was a responsible man and even a good father, as he worked hard to send remittances to the mother of his five-year-old child. That very commitment was a problem for Iryna, who was increasingly worried about her daughter. She wanted to bring Lena to Alpinetown, but she could not satisfy the requirements for applying for family reunification. She wanted to improve the house in which her parents lived, which was in dire condition.

Ahmed had a steady income and permanent residency papers, and he had always been willing to take responsibility for her, her daughter, and her parents. "If only he had not been a *chórnenky*," Iryna once confessed wistfully. Avel was not only a risk, as any Eastern European male would have been. He was also unable to help her financially, and he had his own child in Transnistria. When he broke the news to the women, none of them had any doubts that he was a bad choice.

Iryna continued her relationship with Avel, disregarding the other women's advice. From being one of the most authoritative members of the group, Iryna moved to a much more dubious status. She was, moreover, increasingly frustrated with her inability to call for Lena; she had been able to find a flat, but her legal income was just under the required minimum. Visiting Ukraine only once a year, she was always afraid that Lena would not recognize her or would treat her coldly.

Then, Avel suggested an ingenious solution. He and Iryna should marry, enabling him to get his residency papers as the husband of a resident foreigner. With the papers, he would be able to get a regular work contract, significantly increasing the family's—legal—income. Consequently, Iryna would be able to obtain a family reunification visa for Lena.

This strategy ultimately worked, although it was far from easy. The fact that Avel's nationality was uncertain further complicated the process. Over the two years it took to complete the plan, I often accompanied Iryna on her odysseys to a multitude of offices and listened to her anxieties while waiting for documents from three states—Ukraine, Moldova, and Russia—that often turned out to be incorrect. While fighting for her family inch by inch, Iryna could not rely on the support of the other women. They openly accused her of being more concerned with her man than with her daughter. They were equally sure, and equally outspoken, about the fact that Avel would dump her as soon as he got his papers. She was considered a mature woman who had lost her mind for a young man and pursued a futile project in order to keep him with her. Iryna, previously a pillar of the group, deeply resented their change of attitude.

Finally, everything worked out and Lena arrived. The three now faced the task of living together in a cramped flat. Lena used the only sleeping room, while Iryna and Avel slept on a sofa in the kitchen. Despite ups and downs, their marriage endured. Iryna kept visiting the women for a while, mostly because she needed to continue her sales business. Her participation in the group was increasingly instrumental and ceased altogether when she decided that the returns on her commerce were not worthwhile. Avel has maintained a steady job as plumber. After completing high school, Lena found a job as clerk for an insurance company. They have recently moved into a larger flat in a working-class neighborhood of Alpinetown, where they plan to settle.

I observed in Iryna's life the very same process that I did in Svetlana's: involvement with their coethnic family *here* made the place of origin a very important symbolic reference but greatly diminished their direct contact both with their hometown and with the group of women. At first, Iryna and Avel spent all their holidays there, with Avel working full time to improve the house there and Iryna visiting relatives and managing bureaucratic hurdles. Iryna, as she claimed in the prologue, had as her point of honor that Lena would spend as much time as possible among her own, in her hometown.

After a few years, however, Lena increasingly complained that she wanted to see other places. Iryna became annoyed with the rituals of return, with both her and Avel's relatives always expecting to receive presents or becoming offended by whatever she did. And when they returned to her hometown, she complained that the Ukrainian shopkeepers overcharged her as a matter of course. Just shortly after having proudly claimed at my ill-fated party the axiological moral value of spending their holidays in their hometowns, Iryna and Avel decided to behave precisely like the women she had criticized at the party: they spent their holidays on the Adriatic coast, "like real tourists do," rather than returning to Moldova and Ukraine.

## Lovers, Mistresses, Wives: The Building of a Cross-ethnic Immigrant Community

The women frowned upon relationships with Ukrainian or Moldovan men, and both Svetlana and Iryna were regularly subjected to prophecies of impending doom. Moreover, Moldovan and Ukrainian men were quite scarce in Alpinetown. Their negative judgment did not extend to the entire population of male "Slavs"; it covered only males from the former USSR. The women, on the contrary, thought quite highly of those whom they called "Makedonac"—men who, like Amir and Armin, had arrived in Alpinetown from the Balkans a decade before to work in the local quarries.[5]

They perceived them as the embodiment of a superior model of Slavic masculinity, exempt from the alcoholism and general unreliability of former USSR men. They were talked about as strong-willed, responsible for their women, and good potential fathers but, at the same time, as tinged with a Mediterranean aura of romantic passion. Most importantly, they were abundant and available. Since the Balkan wars of the early 1990s, Alpinetown has had a sizable group of (predominantly male) immigrants from the region. Some of them frequented the places where the women congregated.

A few weeks after I was criticized for trying to steal Kalyna's lover, she and Veronika proudly announced to the group that they had entered into stable relationships with Amir and Armin. The two men would soon rent a flat to share with the two women, where they would start a new and decent life. They would support them in leaving care work and looking for different jobs. The other women were thrilled; no one said, despite the fact that both men were married, that these relationships were bound to end badly. The next day, Kalyna graciously invited me out, to share her joy and to show that she was not angry with me any longer. We spent the evening drinking and talking, as if we were close friends meeting just a few days before one of us married.

Kalyna told me the story of her life as she now saw it. I had heard about most of the incidents before, but she placed them in a wholly new frame. It was now the story of a woman who had lost her way in the wilderness before being rescued by a worthy man. She described her previous life in Alpinetown as marred by chaos and inexperience. She had never forgotten to work hard and sacrifice her own pleasures for the welfare of her daughter. But she had also felt lonely and destitute, and she had been weak willed. On and off, she had dated several men who could not give her what she really needed.

Luckily, one day when she was in the parking lot drinking some beers with her friends, an unknown man had abruptly declared that a woman like her should not be drinking beer. She had blushed, feeling rebuked by but also attracted to his direct, strong, willful style. Quickly adding that nice ladies should drink only good Moldovan wine, the mysterious stranger handed her a bottle of red wine before suddenly disappearing.

A few days later, a friend told her that a man had asked her for Kalyna's telephone number and she had given it to him. Kalyna was not pleased: as an irregular migrant, she did not like people asking around about her, let alone collecting her telephone number. But the man was Amir, and he had flowers in his hands when she met him for their first date. The last time anyone had given her flowers was when she had given birth to her daughter. She felt alive again, and she felt that Amir was special.

They met several times, including in my flat, and he always presented her with a gift: candy, wine, flowers, lingerie, a cell phone, and even a doll for her daughter. She claimed that he had never treated her as a casual partner, but always as a middle-class, well-educated woman who deserved to be courted properly. On one occasion, when she had not worked for two weeks, Amir had been willing to give her the money her mother was waiting for. Amir was definitely not like the others.

Still, Kalyna had no idea what she could expect from Amir, since he had previously dated other women in the group. Just a week before the incident involving Amir and me, Amir, Kalyna, and another woman had gone to a lake in the countryside. They were quietly strolling along a path by the shore when they met another Macedonian man cycling in the opposite direction. The man had asked Amir for a cigarette and started making jokes about how lucky he was to have two women all for himself. He seemed to be interested in Kalyna; "his glances were undressing me all the time," she said. Amir had taken it jokingly at first, saying that he was the king of the Balkans. But the guy had become pushy, asking Amir to share his kingdom. Amir replied bluntly that he would never share his kingdom with anybody—a declaration that was full of meaning for her. When the man kept insisting, Amir told Kalyna and the other woman to go away, and a short fight ensued. The two men insulted and pushed each other around, until Amir defeated the other man and threw his bicycle in the lake.

This fight was the turning point; from then on, Kalyna felt protected, respected, and supported. Since that day, however, she began to worry when Amir met with the other women in her absence. She did not like the idea that he had had affairs with some of them, and she thought all of them would have gone a long way to take her place. She spent all her time alone with Amir, in the secluded places he selected in order to avoid being spotted by his wife's relatives or friends. When Amir and Armin had invited her and Veronika out to discuss their idea of sharing a flat, she was elated: "Now it's my turn to live the good life, to be a *signora*." Amir had given her a ring she proudly showed me, certifying to the world that they were a real couple.

I asked Kalyna what she thought would happen with his wife. I knew that she worked in the city center, and that Amir was always frightened that she would catch him with other women. Kalyna replied that Amir could not leave the "old fat cow," as he had started to call her. His wife's family was backing a small construction business he had started in addition to his work in the quarries, and he could not afford to lose their support at this stage. Kalyna presented Amir's reluctance to get a divorce as proof of his masculine seriousness: he was willing to suffer the pains of staying with his wife in order to protect his new business venture.

The ring was meant as a promise that, as soon as it was convenient, he would divorce the "old fat cow" and marry Kalyna. He was married, but she was not his mistress: they would have their own flat, and she would invite friends to their house whenever she liked. He agreed that she should make their relationship public among the women, as she was fed up with feeling "like a *puttana*." All the women, including his former lovers, had to know that he belonged only to her.

A few days later, Veronika explained to me that she had entered into a similar arrangement. The only difference was that Armin could not leave his wife because he had a very young son and did not trust his wife to be reasonable with his custody in case of divorce. Veronika, too, presented this commitment as evidence that he was a real man, willing to endure a difficult life in order to protect his son. She also insisted that she did not care that he was married; she only wanted to be recognized by Armin, his friends, and the other women as his bona fide partner, the woman he really wanted to share his life with.

Once Kalyna and Veronika moved into the flat with Amir and Armin, the place quickly became one of the centers of the migrant women's life in Alpinetown. It was organized as a flat shared by two couples, although Armin and Amir hardly ever slept there for the whole night. There was a silent agreement that we could come and visit whenever we wished and even use the flat to take a shower or rest while Kalyna and Veronika were out working. But it was tacitly agreed that we would leave immediately when Armin or Amir called to say they were arriving, to respect the two couples' privacy. After a while, the two women left live-in care work and found jobs for cleaning companies. Their wages were lower, and they could not have afforded to make this change without some financial help from their men.

They organized small parties, in which Amir and Armin proudly starred as masters of their own house. They opened the bottles, proposed toasts, and criticized those who did not drink enough. Moreover, they invited some of their friends, usually other Macedonian men working in the quarries. The parties were consequently very popular among the migrant women: at last, they could encounter respectable men in a dignified setting. Several additional couples formed at these parties. After a year, Kalyna and Amir moved to a separate flat in the same building so that Kalyna could apply for a visa for her daughter. When she arrived in Alpinetown and was enrolled in a local school, Kalyna felt her family was complete. Armin and Amir still continued their double lives for some time, but finally decided to leave their wives and move in with Kalyna and Veronika.[6]

By then, a tight network of Ukrainian women and Macedonian men had developed, and these couples had their own meeting places and social rituals. This shift quickly created a cleavage among the women. While the (now called "Macedonian") women would have liked to show off their men to the other migrant women, many Macedonian men looked down on them. Many of the men had previously dealt with the group as a reservoir of easy sexual contacts, being able to simultaneously criticize them as morally loose. Once entered in steadier relationships with some of them, they regarded their partners' desire to keep going to the waiting room or to the park to spend time with their friends as suspicious.

When the Macedonian women needed to go to the parking lot to send parcels or to buy something, their men would drive them there but wait conspicuously in the driveway without entering it. At their flats, they only welcomed other women who were in stable relationships or whom they considered respectable.

Their women were held responsible for the morality of their acquaintances. Kalyna had a protracted conflict with Amir when one of the women she had invited to a party started dating another Macedonian without telling him that she was also seeing a *chórnenky*. Amir felt she had not chosen her friends properly and that she had made him lose face with his friend. Women who were able to bring their daughters commonly complained that the Macedonian partners criticized the ways they were bringing up the young women, especially the clothes they allowed them to wear.

The partners supported one another in their assessment that the women were potentially sexually loose, and they took for granted that they could prove the contrary only by strictly policing them (and their daughters) and severing any contact with those women whose love lives were not adequately disciplined. This attitude created a good deal of ambiguity for the women. Sometimes they justified their men, seeing in their jealousy proof of attachment and manly discipline. Sometimes, on the contrary, they felt distrusted and despised. In both cases, the strain with many other women in the group became increasingly visible.

The growing network of Macedonian-Eastern European couples also had to deal with the fact that they had two different locations of *there* to take into account. Although the men were well rooted in Alpinetown, they were still working-class immigrants with remittances to send and relatives to handle. Being in love with them entailed the promise of a respectable family life. Their family life would, however, necessarily develop within the constraints of their social class: struggling with money, having to cope with unappealing jobs, living in small suburban flats, and making ends meet on a limited income.

The women who entered these relationships were expected to invest most of their energies *here*, in caring for their men. But they remained responsible for their relatives and projects *there*, while their partners remained responsible for their own—in addition to the child support payments they often owed to their former partners in Alpinetown.

These competing pressures were frequently difficult to reconcile. The women were regularly criticized—by their left-behind relatives as well as by the other women—for placing their new intimate relationships ahead of their preexisting obligations to their kin; the men were attacked by the women for failing to help them in their family obligations; and the men in turn complained about their overdemanding in-laws. As the couples had formed without a previous tradition of interethnic mating, there was simply no accepted reference norm to invoke that would regulate the strains that often escalated.

## Men Who Really Make You a *Signora*

When the news of a newly formed couple reached the group, Aksana would invariably comment that she was happy the woman had found her "Makedonac." Looking older in years than her late fifties, and busy caring for a very difficult old couple, Aksana knew that she could not participate in the race to find a man, but she felt fully entitled to comment upon it. After expressing her joy for the woman, she would inevitably add, even in the woman's presence, that "he is still an immigrant, just a little better." The same assessment was sometimes articulated by women who had themselves entered into relationships with Macedonian men.

One evening, Veronika visited us in the waiting room. We were surprised, because she had nearly stopped visiting us since Armin had left his wife. This rare act of defiance was unexpected and we were all very interested in learning what happened. She had just had a fight with Armin, and she was furious. She was not looking for a friendly word, but rather for an audience in front of which to air her indictment of his faults.

Sitting on a chair and looking directly at us, she began by saying that he was just an immigrant "like us"; he was a pretentious fool who claimed that he would treat her as a *signora* but was unable to do so. He criticized her way of living; he claimed he had saved her from poverty and depravity, but, in fact, he had the same economic problems, the same crappy jobs, the same fights with his family in Macedonia, who always wanted more, and the same immigrant friends full of problems needing a sofa to sleep on. Since they had started living together, "There has never been money for us. I cannot remember the last time he asked me out."

There was always some emergency *there* to deal with, and he was unwilling to acknowledge the needs of her parents in the same way that he recognized those of his relatives. I had the impression that Veronika felt genuinely betrayed by what she had previously regarded as an immense stroke of luck.

Veronika then expressed regret, saying, "I should have been smarter. I should have seen better. I should have dated an old prick who simply pays and does not complain if the money is not enough for the parents, the kids, the house. I should have chosen someone who could really make me a *signora*." Once she uttered these words, Veronika left hurriedly and never returned. She seemed to me to play the role of a ghost in a classical drama, warning the characters of the hidden truth behind their desires.

The disappointment Veronika voiced was very similar to what Aksana had always stressed: Immigrant men could make your life better, but they could never enable you to escape the immigrant life. A real life as a *signora*—an economically secure and socially respected life—required a nonimmigrant man, an Italian. The women thought Italian men possessed an appropriate combination of attractive qualities: passionate and romantic but family-minded, with some income and property but not stingy, willing to take responsibility for the woman but in need of support and love, moderate drinkers but hardly ever completely drunk. They held as a self-evident truth that dating an Italian would immediately give meaning to all their tribulations and hold the promise of a rosy future.

Very few women were actually able to meet Italians who could become prospective partners. Most of the women spent nearly all their time taking care of an elderly person. During their working hours, they went outside only to accompany their "grandpa" or "grandma" somewhere or to do hurried errands for the household. During the few hours when they were free and alone, they had very few alternatives to spending their time with other women like them. Despite their shared fantasy about Italian men falling for them and paying for them to become their *signore*, they had very few opportunities to meet Italians.

In the first, long phase of their settlement, the women had contact nearly only with two categories of Italians: the relatives of the elderly person they were taking care of and the men they could meet in the streets or the park. In both cases, it was highly likely the men were already married and disinclined to change their status. When the women first arrived in Alpinetown, they had been thrilled to discover that many men looked at them "as women"—potentially sexually desirable. Over time, however, they discovered that this abundance of males was accompanied by a severe scarcity of prospective husbands. The choice was simply between married men who might want a mistress and elderly widowers in search of someone to take care of them.

Within this context, becoming the lover of a married man or dating a much older widower were both considered acceptable options. Those women who had any kind of romantic liaison with an Italian man, regardless of his conjugal condition, were the object of tremendous admiration. They could mesmerize the others with tales of dinners in restaurants, well-chosen gifts, and smoothly running cars. The men were willing to support the women in many little ways, particularly by giving them money when they were unable to save enough for their remittances. This financial assistance gave them a measure of security in their new environment.

Many women found it reassuring to have a chaperone for their first date with their Italian "friend." It was not, usually, out of concern for their safety, or for fear that the situation could get out of hand. It was more because they wanted to show they were decent women, with an established and reputable social life, who had to be courted properly. As an Italianized Slav, I was often asked to play such a role, engaging in an adequate amount of small talk, and then, if the climate was right, tactfully leaving owing to an unexpected emergency. I thus met many of these men and became an acquaintance of many couples. I soon discovered the men felt reassured by my in-between status: I was "Slav" enough to be considered low risk from the point of view of their privacy, but I was also Italian enough, meaning I was able, in their opinion, to understand their point of view. When tensions or conflicts arose, I would often listen to both parties.

I soon realized that the main problem in these relationships was rooted in the fact that the women framed issues very differently from their Italian partners. The women expected their role as mistresses to be of limited duration. They sympathized with the men's reluctance to leave their families, interpreting it as proof of the importance they placed on family obligations. They even accepted the idea that the men needed to be sure that they were adequate partners. They regarded, however, their affair as a trial period, as a phase in which they had to demonstrate their moral and practical competencies as women and potential wives, thus proving their superiority to the men's current wives.

For the Italian men I talked with, what they had negotiated with their lovers was a stable arrangement that would never lead to cohabitation or marriage, as they did not really want to leave their wives. Most were middle-aged, working-class men, often with teenaged children, and they feared the economic and social consequences of a divorce. Many felt that marriages, no matter how cold the relationships with their wives had grown, was an important institution that had to be preserved at all costs.[7] In many ways, dating foreign women whose relatives were far away, and who had limited free time and few local connections, was seen by them as an unexpected opportunity to enjoy a romance without feeling like they were endangering the stability of their own families. They felt empowered by these relationships and thought they did their best to make the women happy.

These divergent frameworks inevitably came into conflict, and when the migrant women realized that the Italian men were unwilling to leave their wives, they often experienced it as a personal failure, interpreting it as a mark of second-class womanhood, a condition of not being womanly enough to have men entirely to themselves.

Olga, one of the women who attended the party narrated in the prologue, and one of my closest friends in the group, was one of the first women to become the stable mistress of a married Italian man. Although she enjoyed such status for a long period, she felt subsequently that she had paid a disproportionate price. At the time, she worked as a live-in care worker in a small village close to Alpinetown. When I met her the first few times, I was impressed by how well groomed she always was. She always had makeup, tight jeans, and shirts that accentuated her generous curves.

Already remarkably tall, she made quite an impression, especially when wearing the stiletto heels she favored. She seemed happy and proud of her life. The first thing she told me after we were introduced was that she was ecstatic because she had just found her prince. Despite her insistence that she did not want me to tell the others her secret, it was evident that she was yearning to recount her story to anybody who would listen.

Her prince was Mario, the son of the woman she cared for, who lived with his wife and children on a different floor of the same building. He used to visit his mother every evening after dinner. Slowly, his daily visits had become longer, and when his elderly mother had fallen asleep, he would sit in the kitchen with Olga, drinking a glass of wine and talking. A couple of weeks prior, they had started kissing each other goodnight, and their kisses had become passionate. They had made love on the kitchen table while his mother was sleeping peacefully in the living room, and since then, Olga had been in a state of physical and emotional bliss. He would often visit her, and he called and sent short messages almost every hour.

Whenever I met Olga, I was always briefed on her affair. Soon Mario would leave his wife, and they would move in together. She would keep taking care of his mother, but this time as a labor of love. Mario would provide what was needed to obtain a visa for her children, who would surely get along well with Mario's sons. She wittily recounted the little discoveries produced by her intercultural liaison: the strange fondness of Italian males for performing oral sex, her success in introducing Mario to the deliciousness of *bliny* (thin crepe-like pancakes), and the peculiar ways in which his mother treated her grown-up son as if he were a child.

One day, Iryna called me hurriedly to ask if I had heard anything from Olga, who had called her briefly and seemed in distress. Olga had said she had to leave her job immediately and asked Iryna if I could let her sleep on my sofa temporarily while she worked out another living situation. I called her several times to no avail, until she called to say she was close to my office and needed to see me. She looked tired, and her eyes were red from crying. As soon as we hugged, she burst into tears.

Mario's wife had discovered their affair. Becoming suspicious of Mario's sudden devotion to his filial duties, she had checked his telephone and found some of the messages he had sent to Olga. Sobbing, Olga said she was afraid that everything was over. He had come to his mother's flat in the morning, before going to work, to tell her that she should invent an excuse for an urgent trip. His wife had just announced her intentions to go visiting her mother-in-law in order to settle a few scores with *"la puttana slava."* He looked tired and scared, and he said he would call when the crisis passed.

I hosted Olga in my flat, while Iryna took her job with Mario's mother. This arrangement helped Olga, but it also gave Iryna access to information about what had happened. She reported that the two flats were one above the other and she could hear Mario's TV from his mother's living room. She was surprised his wife had not discovered their relationship earlier. While Olga was staying at my flat, Mario called several times, asking her how she was and if she needed anything. She was so happy to hear his voice that she never asked for anything apart from seeing him. "Soon," he always answered.

Within a few days, Mario found Olga a job at a hotel in a nearby village. With the job came a basement room where she could live free of surveillance. Mario would visit her almost every day on his way to or from work. Olga appreciated his help. After a few weeks, she started complaining. What she had thought was a step toward a life together had obviously become a stable secondary arrangement. She said they would "spend an hour together. I wake up, work, and wait, hoping he will visit me at night." She felt his love only "because he helps pay my bills and he found me a room where he can come over when he has time to screw me."

Olga increasingly resented the secrecy Mario insisted on. She often complained that he would take her out only to remote places where he would not run the risk of being recognized by anyone who knew him or his family; he would not even have a pizza with her in the village. He expected her to be nearly invisible, and he always complained about her conspicuous way of dressing, not out of jealousy (which she considered acceptable) but out of fear that it might attract attention.

One day, Mario called me and said they had just had a row. They were in the car, at an isolated mountain spot where he had hoped to have "some time for tenderness," when the half-undressed Olga had suddenly confronted him with his unwillingness to leave his family. He had tried to explain that his wife was very fragile, and he did not want to make her suffer. He did not feel able to shock his son, who was approaching adolescence. He had often advanced these explanations before, and they mattered a great deal to him.

This time, Olga had reacted furiously, emphasizing that when she had left her young children to come to Alpinetown to work, they had managed. She shouted that he cared only for his wife, while he felt free to treat her "like a *puttana*" who was entitled to nothing, not even to a "stroll hand in hand." She had slammed the door of the car and disappeared along a path, briskly dressing herself as she fled. Since then, she had not returned his calls.

Regardless of what I thought about his choices and behavior, I had no doubt he was genuinely heartbroken. Not only had he failed to anticipate this crisis, but he had always thought his position was righteous. He kept insisting that he had never promised Olga he would leave his wife and that he had never treated her as a *puttana*. He was in love with her, and he had done everything he could to support and protect her. He hoped that I could convince Olga that he loved her and wanted to make her happy. It was clear, however, that leaving his wife was out of the question.

I was puzzled by Olga's sudden decision to confront Mario. Although I knew she had become increasingly disillusioned, she had always told me she could not imagine leaving him. I often wondered what had been the precipitating factor in her sudden change of heart. A few days later, I received a call from Dasha, the future host of the prologue party, who at the time lived in the same valley as Olga. She asked me to come to the Moldovan parking lot the following Sunday because she needed to tell me something.

When we met, I could not help thinking that meeting Dasha, and comparing her situation with her own, might well have been the precipitating factor in Olga's sudden decision to demand that Mario leave his wife and live with her. Dasha's life exemplified everything Olga hoped for in her relationship with an Italian man but had failed to achieve.

I had met Dasha a few years before, a few hours after she had arrived in Alpinetown. She had left her city without much preparation after divorcing her alcoholic husband and entrusting her two daughters to her father's care. A few months later, her tourist visa expired and she became an irregular immigrant. Dasha found quickly work as a *sidelka*. Like Olga, at first she had been obsessed by the need to repay the money she had borrowed for the trip and the need to take care of her daughters.

She could not afford much, and the few times she had been able to visit Alpinetown she had hung out with the women in the waiting room. She had felt very lonely, she confessed to me later, and she had occasionally gone out with some of the *chórnenky* who frequented the nearby park. They were nice, but they could never be a substitute for "the real thing."

After a little more than a year, she found a new job for a well-known local family that owned a small manufacturing company. The family was located in a village on the outskirts of the area, and I had seldom heard of her since she had moved to her new job. I only vaguely heard from other women that she, like Olga, had started dating one of the sons of the couple she was caring for.

On Sunday morning, I was waiting for Dasha and chatting with some van drivers when a brand-new car entered the parking lot. The conversation stopped when the car door opened and Dasha got out, sporting a new haircut. She waved regally, walked past us, handed a package to one driver, paid the fare, and stopped briefly to tell me that we would meet in the evening "for an aperitif." She quickly returned to the idling car and waved goodbye as it drove away.

I was puzzled—and became even more perplexed when I received a telephone call from her just a few minutes later. She wanted to know how the women and the drivers had received her arrival. I told her that I did not understand why she had asked me to be there if she was going to run away immediately without even introducing me to her companion, but she disregarded my complaints as irrelevant.

When we met, the very same evening, she explained that the driver had been Gianfranco, her employer and one of the sons of the elderly couple she was taking care of. He was now her partner; he was leaving his wife, and they would soon be living together. They could not marry yet, as Italian law at the time required a separation of several years before a divorce was granted, but they would surely marry as soon as he had a divorce. They had met while he was visiting his mother.

He soon began courting her, and they fell in love. She had told him that she was not a plaything but a mother of two and a former physician who had already suffered more than enough from undeserving men. She was not interested in anything less than marriage. Yes, she later admitted, they had made love "a couple of times"; well, maybe "a few more times," as they could "not help being fatally attracted to one another."

As Gianfranco had never found a woman who could "satisfy him so deeply," he realized he could not live without her. He left his wife and found another care worker for his mother. She would soon move to his chalet, where she would take care of only him. He later offered to sponsor the arrival of her daughters, but since they did not want to leave Ukraine, he agreed to pay for their studies instead.

Dasha had definitely become a *signora*, and her performance in the parking lot was meant to notify the other women and, through the drivers, those in her homeland of her new status. Her new life as a *signora* implied a progressive withdrawal from the group. She did not have time for casual meetings in the streets or parks, and she went to the parking lot only when she had a package to send or to receive. She acknowledged that Gianfranco preferred to maintain his routines. He was not comfortable in the presence of foreign women speaking a different language and behaving in ways that he found strange.[8]

For a while, Dasha kept up her connections with some of us on individual basis. But even these connections slowly faded away: many women could not afford the kind of places Dasha had started inviting them to, and they did not want to depend on her footing the bill. Even

Olga and Iryna, who had been closer to Dasha than most, complained that they met each other rarely.

After some years, the divorce papers were finally ready and Dasha and Gianfranco were married in a ceremony to which very few of her former friends were even invited. When the news that she had married circulated among the women, they said it was what they had expected from the very beginning.

A few months later, Dasha invited me to a pre-Christmas dinner at their new place. With a bottle of wine in my hand, I rang the bell of the gate of the chalet. To my surprise, the dinner featured several Eastern European dishes, including borscht, *bliny*, and kielbasa. Dasha stressed that it was difficult to find the necessary ingredients of the required quality; only the cheapest brands were available in Alpinetown, and the minivans were unreliable. She had found a satisfactory solution only when she discovered a German website where she could buy what she needed and have it shipped directly to her.

Gianfranco had learned to enjoy Eastern European foods, and he was proud to offer his guests something different. Dasha announced that they were also buying a flat in a nice neighborhood of her hometown. While accompanying her during her trips home, Gianfranco had reckoned that he could find a new market for his company's products in Ukraine, and one of Dasha's daughters, now studying business administration, could help open many doors.

The newlyweds planned to spend part of the year there and part *here*.[9] While they were talking, I noticed that nearly all the other guests were Italians. Besides me, the only guest who had any connection with Dasha's past was Mario, Olga's former lover, who was attending the dinner with his wife.

## When Age Is the Solution, Not the Problem

The stories of Olga and Dasha reveal two different scenarios for liaisons with married Italian men. In both cases, the women were comparatively younger, and the men were the older sons of the elderly people the women were taking care of. In other cases, some women, usually those who were older, were able to find a suitable partner in the elderly person himself, usually a widower who was still in good health.

Italians usually malign intimate relationships between middle-aged Eastern European women and much older Italian men, particularly when they lead to marriage.[10] They reinforce the stereotype of Eastern European women as cynical predators, as gold diggers who are willing to do whatever it takes to dupe a naïve older man and take control of his pension and assets.[11] The fact that these weddings allow migrant women to obtain Italian citizenship and survivor's pensions has triggered not only waves of moral panic but also rounds of restrictive legislation.[12]

During my fieldwork, I encountered some instances of what might technically be called "fraudulent marriages." I also met women who pursued the opportunity to marry an older Italian man as a way to climb out of poverty or to satisfy the requirements for bringing their children to Italy. In fact, older widowers had a definitive advantage over married men because they were able to provide the resources needed to apply for a family reunification visa. Nor were cases lacking in which the predators were actually the older men. Sometimes, a man would refuse to marry the woman but would guarantee her that she would be taken care of in his will. I encountered several instances in which a woman discovered only after the death of her partner that he had shown her a false will, while the legally binding document left her nothing.

Despite the potential for reciprocal cheating, during my fieldwork, I discovered that marriages between older Italian men and Eastern European women couldn't be explained away as a purely instrumental way of obtaining legal or financial advantages. Most women I encountered regarded the elderly widowers they lived with as their potential bona fide partners. They surely expected economic security and social protection from their partners. But they assessed his provision of these important resources within a broader moral economy.[13] If their old men took care of them in good faith, they provided them, in equally good faith, with love and selfless devotion.

Age was simply considered one factor among many that shaped their relationships and made some men more desirable than others. The women did not find anything predatory in dating old widowers, nor did they talk about it in instrumental terms. Receiving help and support was simply the natural consequence of being "true women" willing to take care of their men.

During my fieldwork, I very often witnessed women providing care for their men well beyond what any interpretation of their actions in terms of instrumental interest would allow. Nor was such devotion a matter only of individual choice. I was impressed by the fact that the whole group of women regarded such partnerships as *substantially* valid. They were, for example, unwilling to condone any sexual infidelity on the part of the woman, even in the many cases in which the sexual life of the couple was tenuous at best. I also found that the older men often had the very same definition of the situation: they saw their economic and legal support not as a "price" they paid, but as a natural component of the reciprocity between two lovers. Actually, very old men sometimes proposed marriage as a way to protect the rights of the woman (who "truly" loved) from the predatory designs of uncaring offspring.

Among the migrant women, the story of Aneta had attained the status of a normative paradigm, a description of the world as it should be. During our afternoons in the park, whenever a newly arrived woman was present, Aneta was asked to recount her story. Aneta had emigrated when she was in her early fifties, in order to secure a reliable income for her daughter and two granddaughters. A delicate and shy woman, she had spent most of her working life as a clerk in a concrete factory. She entered Italy with a tourist visa, knowing she would be unable to return to Ukraine for years.

When she arrived in Naples, she was immediately asked to take care of a seventy-eight-year-old widower, a former night porter, who promised to treat her as "part of his family." She quickly accepted; with debts to repay and relatives in need, she wanted to start working right away. What she had not understood was that Carmelo, the widower she was to care for, was expecting to get a real wife, someone who could take the place of his deceased wife of fifty years. The woman who had arranged the job for her—in exchange for the usual fee of a month's salary—was a care worker herself, among the most trusted brokers in Naples. When Aneta accompanied her to his flat, she was surprised to find Carmelo's three adult children waiting for them to go all together to a nearby pizzeria to celebrate her arrival. They had their dinner together and left.

Aneta found herself in an unknown flat, with a tired old man waiting to be helped into bed. When she then moved to the small sofa in the living room, Carmelo was surprised. He explained by gestures that he expected her to sleep in his bed, where there was all the space she needed. "I won't harm you," Carmelo apparently said very pompously, making Aneta always laugh in retrospect.

During the night, however, the jaunty old man started caressing her. She was paralyzed, tired, and afraid to react. He was so frail that she feared that any reaction on her part might harm him. But he was sweet and passionate. Aneta always stressed that she did not really know why and how it happened, but they made love before dawn. And they kept doing it all the subsequent nights to come. They were married within a year.

From the very beginning, Carmelo expected everybody to treat Aneta respectfully, as his wife. She was given money to send home and money to manage the house. Carmelo's children, who had initially been worried he would become the prey of a gold-digger Slav, ended up appreciating her devotion to their father. One of them even said that his father "was living longer thanks to her love and care."

After some years, Carmelo's health failed. She assisted him until the very end. On his last night, they had to call for a doctor. He entered the room, thought Aneta was his care worker, and commanded her briskly to do something. Despite his agony, Carmelo used his last energies to correct the doctor, telling him, "she is not a care worker, she is my wife." These were the last words the man uttered. No matter how often she repeated the story, Aneta could not help shedding some tears at this point.

Aneta found that Carmelo had taken good care of her in his will; she inherited his tiny flat, some small savings, and a modest survivor's pension. The inheritance enabled her to move to Alpinetown and accept hourly paid jobs only in respectable families. She planned to return to Ukraine as soon as her flat there was ready, to live, thanks to his pension, a comfortable life taking care of her granddaughters. She fully felt like the widow of Carmelo, and she did not want to have other men.

Aneta's experience was clearly extraordinary, especially with regard to the very rare open-mindedness of Carmelo's children. Other women in similar situations usually had strong conflicts with the children of their husbands, who did not want to share any inheritance with the "Slav." Aneta's marriage had occurred in Naples, far away from Alpinetown. There was, moreover, no independent verification of the truthfulness of her account. Still, Aneta highlighted a model that many women considered both possible and fair. They felt Aneta was lucky because her devotion and feminine care had been properly recognized and respected. Equally intense relationships existed in Alpinetown.

Lavra, like Aneta, was also a fiftyish-looking woman from rural Ukraine. She tended to an older woman, Luigina, for some years until she had to be hospitalized. Luca, Luigina's brother, appreciated her patience with and devotion to his sister, so he let her stay in Luigina's flat while looking for another job. After a few months, Luca asked her whether she wanted to work for him; although he was still in good health, he was very frail. His sons did not like the idea of him staying completely alone. She started cleaning his apartment, taking care of the garden, and cooking for him, while working part-time as a housekeeper for other families in the neighborhood. They had dinner together, she checked that he was in bed with the TV set on, and then she returned to Luigina's flat.

On Valentine's Day in 2007, Lavra called me screaming that she had something deadly important to tell me. I had to come over immediately.

When I rang the bell, I was frightened that something terrible had happened. But when she opened the door, she held a bouquet of red roses that Luca had presented to her.

Lavra paced the room repeating that she did not know what to do. She had noticed that Luca was looking at her in a different way and often complimented her appearance. But she had thought it was flattery; "I'm a babushka, Martushka!" she exclaimed. We hugged and talked, and then she left to prepare dinner for Luca. They were married the same year, and she shifted from care worker to wife. They were a very close couple, and their home was always open to friends.

During my fieldwork, I came to know several of these couples, and although I never succeeded in shaking the feeling that something was strange, I often felt they enjoyed a warm and solid companionship with a high degree of mutual respect. These men were ready to sponsor their wives' children and had a more generous understanding of their family obligations back home. Nor were they absorbed by the demanding task of managing an immigrant family.

These couples, moreover, quickly became central to the whole group of migrant women. Unlike other women engaged in sustained relationships, their husbands did not have anything against them spending time with their compatriots. Their husbands were knowledgeable about local ways and were often willing to stand as guarantors for their wives' friends with prospective employers or landlords. They supported and assisted their wives when they wanted to organize something for the community.

These women quickly became the pillars of the fledging community infrastructure. The parish committee, for example, included a disproportionate number of women married to older Italian men who had been previously widowers. In the end, I was not particularly surprised that many women were able to see those whom they had been previously calling "the old pricks" as the best possible companions.

# FIVE

# Proper, Respectable Places: The Arduous Construction of Community Institutions

For many years, the women had no place in the city they could call their own. They gathered at particular places—specific corners of some public parks, the waiting rooms of the bus and train stations, a row of benches along one side of Alpinetown's main square—that only their presence marked as belonging to them. Besides the Sunday market in the parking lot, they organized their social life according to a very simple heuristic: when a woman was free, she would go around the various sites and stop when and where she found other women. If she met no one, she would return to her workplace with the feeling that she had wasted her rare, precious hours of freedom.[1]

Over time, a whole cluster of formalized places has slowly developed, along lines that would have been simply unthinkable in the beginning. A variety of associations and places of worship have created a supply of outlets and occasions where the women may congregate, according to structured schedules, for various purposes. The birth of these more formalized places has been experienced by most women as an important step toward a respectable, decent life. To have their own churches, to be able to relax in a private space, has always been considered by the women as progress.

The birth of these communitarian institutions, however, has not been the intensification or continuation of the previous forms and understandings of the women's sociability. It has implied, instead, the birth of additional forms, increasingly differentiated from, and often in competition with, the previous ones. The birth of associations has paved the way to a cleavage between "decent" and "indecent" sociabilities, which has quickly translated into a cleavage between "decent" and "indecent" women.

Owing to the fact that any association had to be identifiable as legitimate in the local environment, a second set of cleavages has appeared. In the political culture of Alpinetown, migrant associations are conceived along strictly "cultural" or "national" lines. Those women interested in becoming involved in associational life have progressively adopted the established way of classifying the world, thus fragmenting a large and fuzzy group of post-Soviet women into several clear-cut clusters defined along ethnonational and religious lines. They have become, somewhat in spite of themselves, a cluster of differentiated immigrant "communities."[2]

## If You Want to Stay Warm, You Need an Association

The women quickly discovered various organizations and agencies that might help to meet their needs. Alpinetown has a comparatively strong and well-organized network of social services, some of which were available to immigrants. The area has also a strong network of philanthropic organizations, most of them sponsored by the Catholic Church (and a few by leftist associations and trade unions), which were often willing to accept even irregular migrants among their clientele.

When a woman arrived in the city, previous migrants quickly informed her about what assistance was available and what would be most helpful. Some centers were good sources for secondhand clothes; others had excellent Italian-language teachers; some volunteers were better than others were at finding jobs when women needed them. A trade union office provided some assistance if employers refused to pay; an outpatient clinic provided healthcare; a hostel, founded many decades ago to protect rural Italian women migrating to the city, could still provide, when available, a clean bed for a few nights.

The staffs of these agencies were nearly always highly sympathetic to immigrants' plight. All of them claimed, I believe in good faith, that they were providing services meant to facilitate the active, egalitarian, empowering inclusion of their clients into the local society. The women had a distinctly different attitude: they appreciated the services provided and esteemed many of the volunteers. Some of them, like Piero, quickly become real embodiments of trust. At the same time, the women were also adamant that these organizations were distant from their own lives. Even the best persons who worked for them were so different from themselves that they could never feel at home in these groups or treat staff members or volunteers—even Piero—as their friends. They regarded these agencies as offering useful services, but they approached them strategically, in order to get the most out of them. They were places where they received things they needed according to rules and aims about which they had no say.[3]

Very soon, the women started feeling the need for a "respectable" place where they could meet during their free time: a place where they could find emotional support from someone who was fluent in their native language and could really "understand" them. That requirement, by definition, excluded all Italians. "Yes, I can go to Piero," Svetlana once said. "He is good. But I will never be able to express my anger to him in his language."

Iryna once told us that she "could not speak of [her difficulties with her newly arrived daughter] with some stupid social worker or teacher who has no idea of what it means for an army officer to become a *lavac-uli*. I cannot express how I feel in Italian . . . it simply does not come out the way it should." They granted that the established social services could solve some of their practical problems, but they could not substitute for a place where these women could find emotional comfort and public recognition.

They had informal gathering sites, but all were precarious. The few shared flats, when they started appearing as described in chapter 1, were reserved for friends already known, and in small numbers. When winter approached, it was simply too cold to meet outdoors. They often fantasized about having access to a stable place where they would be able to spend time among themselves, relaxing and talking over their problems—a place where they could "cook something together." At first, I thought that the problem could be easily solved. I knew there were places in Alpinetown designed to provide immigrants with social activities and psychological support, and that the Catholic diocese had been very active and open-minded in creating some spaces that could be accessed by immigrants. I expected we could migrate there during winter.

The women knew better. They claimed that those places were not really for them: those "social centers," although formally open to all immigrants, actually catered only to some immigrant groups. As they had been established over the years for dealing with previous waves of

immigration, they were, according to the women, ethnically and lin-
guistically marked: North Africans comprised a wide majority of users
of one of these spaces, Albanians frequented another, and a small social
center often hosted Latinos. The *oratorio* of one church was formally
opened to all immigrants but actually attended mostly by Filipinos.[4]
One association claimed to provide a space for all immigrant women,
but the women were highly suspicious, considered it a front for Italian
feminists, and did not want to go there.

The lack of a place where they felt welcome became a standard complaint the women voiced among themselves. Yeva was a former social
worker still proud of having been a chair of the local women's committee of the Communist Party in her youth. She felt that having a public
space they could collectively enjoy was indispensable for considering
themselves respected and respectable.

Very often, while in the waiting room, she repeated that she could not
believe, referring to the other spaces available to immigrants, that "[the
Italians] treat the *chórnenky* better than us." She took for granted that she
could not expect to be treated like the Italians, but she found it intoler-
able that other immigrant groups could enjoy something they lacked.
"Even the Albanians know where to go, so why does nobody think about
our situation?" was another way she framed her dissatisfaction.

Other women did not advance invidious comparisons but still
thought the lack of a collective space placed a serious strain on their
dignity. Some were more interested in defining the problem in practical
terms. "I cannot go on crying here on the bench where anybody can see
me and think that I am crazy! I am fed up with it!" Olga exclaimed after
a moment of despair in the park.

Eventually, some women began to complain that they did not have
any place to pray. Alla, a Moldovan who had formerly been among the
managers of a tile factory, was especially aware of the issue. She complained that she had to pray alone or go with her "grandpa"—the elderly
man she took care of—to the Roman Catholic Mass. She felt unable to
pray adequately there and alienated from a ritual she could not understand. She thought that other people stared at her when they saw her
making the sign of the cross in the Orthodox fashion.[5]

These complaints were voiced repeatedly, among many others, without anybody having any confidence that they could find a solution.
Around 2003, however, there was an important turning point. A Romanian group started to organize an Orthodox service in a little-used
church lent by the local bishop. This alleviated Alla's feeling of solitude but highlighted the lack of religious services for Ukrainians and for

those Moldovans who did not belong to the autocephalous Romanian Church. The success of Romanians in securing a recognized public space was felt both as proof that it was possible and as a symbol of the group's failure in gaining what it deserved. Some of the women started discussing in detail how they could acquire a space they could use freely for their social gatherings.

Originally, their plans were minimal. They just wanted a room where they could meet a couple of half-days a week, possibly with a kitchen. Some women asked around to see if they could find a place that satisfied these requirements. They started going around to the agencies they knew asking for their help. They soon discovered that any agency, public or private, took it for granted that such requests should be filed only by properly identifiable "immigrant associations." Although some spaces were available, they were inaccessible to single individuals.[6]

The women started to consider forming an association that would fulfill the expectations of the agencies and gain access to the benefits they could distribute. The idea, purely instrumental at first, quickly became an autonomous dream, a request for public recognition. They would have their own association, organize events, be able to defend their rights, and show Italians their culture and values. We spent hours deciding on the best name for the association. We even talked about sewing a flag for it.

This dream immediately encountered two major obstacles. Most of the women were irregular migrants, and they feared that public associational life could draw the attention of the police. Moreover, establishing a formal association would require financial, legal, and organizational resources beyond what was available to them. I thought their dream of an association would remain unfulfilled, but I underestimated the women's ingenuity.

Around a year after the inauguration of the Romanian Church, Alla and Yeva called my office number and hurriedly asked me to meet them in the main square. As these requests were usually made only for serious emergencies, I was worried that Yeva had encountered problems with the application her employer was filing for her legalization. They sounded happy, however, rather than anxious. When I arrived in the main square, Alla rushed to greet me and introduced me to Diana. "She will be our president! Martushka, we have found her!" I did not understand what was going on.

Diana was a well-groomed woman in her midfifties, wearing a dark blue dress and a pink pastel shirt. Makeup subtly accentuated her rosy cheeks, wide blue eyes, and ruby lips. Her hands, unlike those of most care workers, were smooth and well manicured. The freezing temperature justified her long fur coat. If she had not said she was Russian, I would have taken Diana for an Italian *signora* strolling through the city center shopping.

Her Italian was flawless, and she clearly knew Alpinetown well. I had never met her, and I was not sure why Alla and Svetlana were so eager to introduce us. She invited us to have coffee in a nearby café. While we walked, Yeva spoke excitedly of the shining future Diana would guarantee for all of us. I felt increasingly puzzled. When we sat at the table, Diana smiled and told her that perhaps she should explain to me why we were there.

As usual, we started trading our personal stories, a ritual necessary to establish common ground. Diana had grown up in an industrial city in a remote region of Russia where she started working as an interpreter. She married a Russian man, with whom she had two children. After the couple divorced, in the early 1980s, she fell in love with one of her customers, an Italian manager who worked for an Italian company that had an industrial plant in her city.

When the children grew up and left for good jobs elsewhere, she agreed to marry the Italian, quit her translation job, and accompany him on his assignments. Six years before our meeting, he retired early and they moved to a small village close to Alpinetown. Recently, she said, their relationship had soured.

Francesco, her husband, had become detached, irritable, hostile, and even aggressive. He had started criticizing her for everything. He did not want her children to contact her. He complained that the neighbors were surely thinking he was one of those "suckers cheated by a clever Slav harlot." When Eastern European women started arriving in the area, he forbade her to have any contact with them.

One day, Diana heard somebody speaking Russian in the market and stopped for some small talk. Shouting angrily in front of all passersby, her husband ordered her to stop immediately, screaming he had had enough of "you savage people" during the years he had been working in the Soviet Union. A couple of months ago, she continued, she had left their house in tears, while he threatened her with losing everything and living "barefoot" if she dumped him.

Having been a dedicated middle-class homemaker for so many years, she found herself lost in Alpinetown. She was sitting on a bench in the park in front of the station and crying when, in a weird reversal of roles, a *sidelka* stopped to speak with her. Mistaking Diana for an Italian *signora*, she asked in broken Italian what was wrong. Unable to speak, Diana kept sobbing. Uncertain about the matter, the woman called Piero, the only "help" she could think of. Piero helped Diana to find a place to sleep for the night and then found her an elderly woman to assist during the coming weeks. He also explained that, as a married woman, she had rights and sent her to a lawyer to claim them. Diana worked for the elderly woman for a few months. After the matter was settled in court, she found herself the owner of a small flat, with some savings in the bank, and a reasonable amount of alimony.

When Alla met Diana and mentioned to her their dream of forming an association, Diana saw all the pieces of her recent adventures coming together: her desire to see her culture recognized by the Italians, the plight of care workers, and the need for someone who could help with personal and family troubles. Diana decided she would found an association for Eastern European migrant women, a place where they could go and find others "of the same blood" and with the same experience. She quoted approvingly what Alla had said: only other Slavic women could really understand what they live through. No Italians, "not even Piero," could help; they inevitably judged and blamed them.

Diana also reframed the purpose of the new association: through the association, they would teach Alpinetown to appreciate their culture, the great artistic achievements of their peoples, and the sophisticated experiences the migrants could offer. She would provide the time, skills, and resources necessary to establish an association, while Alla would provide access to the women, whom Diana had just started meeting personally.

A few months later, a small photocopied leaflet announced that the Agape association had been founded to unite, support, "provide guidance" to, and represent Eastern European care workers.[7] Diana was the president. Iana, a Moldovan in her forties who had been a university teacher and was now a care worker, was the vice president. Alla, whose papers had just arrived, was the secretary. Yeva was the treasurer. The budget was less than 150 euros, and the legal address was Diana's small flat.

For some time, the association operated in ways that resembled the shared flats. It differed from gatherings in the park or the waiting room only because it took place in a heated room. On Sundays, women would visit Diana's flat after congregating in the parking lot. Anyone who wanted could spend two or three hours chatting, cooking some food to share, and praying in front of the Russian icons Diana had placed in a corridor. Women would come and go, tell their stories, ask for help, or pass around photos of their children. Frequently, someone would take a nap in Diana's bedroom.

After many months, through determined lobbying, Diana was able to persuade the authorities to provide a small space, to which the association moved. Diana, who spent nearly all her time working on behalf of the association, developed an ambitious agenda. She wanted Agape to be a space where women could gather but also, perhaps for her more importantly, to serve as a bridge to the local community, a way, as she repeated endlessly, of teaching Italians that these women were not merely *sidelki* but also carriers of a "great culture, sisters of Tolstoy and Tchaikovsky." Diana thought that only by claiming membership in such high culture could the women hope to gain respect from Italians.

The main problem was that such a grandiose cultural project did not hold much appeal for many of the group's members. The association drew disproportionately from two segments of the ever-expanding number of Eastern European migrants in Alpinetown. There were the isolated and the newly arrived, who looked at the association mostly as a source of low-cost emotional and practical support. A second group consisted of the older and more conservative women who had decided to remain in live-in care work to maintain their full commitment to their home areas. Both groups appreciated the association mostly as a place where they could spend their free time without incurring any expense. Women of both sorts were regulars, but they were not interested in high cultural consumption.

On the other hand, those women who had partners in Alpinetown, those who had invested in renting a shared flat, and the few who were living with their children tended to look at the association as one possibility among many, which conducted events that they would attend—or not—according to their interests and the alternatives available. High culture was rarely a priority for them, and even the idea of providing Russian courses for immigrant children never garnered the necessary support.

## Performing Respectability

One evening Diana called me to discuss a new idea she had for the association: offering cooking classes. Drawing upon her personal experience as an Eastern European woman who had been married for decades to an Italian, she contended that the women would run into troubles with the elderly people they took care of if they were not able to cook Italian food properly. "They cannot feed their grandpa borscht, *bliny*, pirogy, or *olivye*," she said. "They will run into trouble." If they wanted to find—and retain—a good job, they had to master Italian cooking.

Thinking about Gianni's disgust with Elena's practice of cooking pasta along with peeled tomatoes, I had to agree with her. The next Sunday,

Diana announced to the women that the association would offer a ten-week course in Italian cuisine, starting the next week. The women's enthusiasm dimmed only slightly when Diana announced that the participants had to pay for the ingredients. In order to ensure that the cost did not become excessive, we decided that nobody would have to bring extra food for the lunch. We would cook on Sunday morning and serve whatever we cooked for lunch.

As with most of the association activities, when she made the announcement Diana had no idea where the cooking class could be held or who would do the teaching. After a frantic search, Iana persuaded a priest in her neighborhood to allow the group to use the kitchen of his oratorio. Diana insisted that instructors had to be Italian, so I was charged with finding several Italians who were willing to spend the best part of a Sunday teaching Ukrainian ladies how to make relatively simple dishes. Invoking the natural solidarity that exists among graduate students, I recruited all my colleagues who could vaguely claim to know how to cook.

The women liked the idea and were quite friendly with the cooks. For them, the cooking classes became a way to interact with Italians on relatively equal footing. My colleagues were definitely younger, so the women did not feel judged by them. They alternated motherly reproaches with cheeky jokes. One morning, when the cook returned to the kitchen after taking a brief phone call, he found all the women smoking and drinking, both strictly prohibited inside the oratorio, instead of cutting the vegetables. Laughing, they pretended their cigarettes were knives. They were clearly enjoying the demotic sociability of the waiting room in a more comfortable setting, and the presence of young Italians did not make them more reserved.

In one case, however, the situation was starkly different. Toward the end of the course, I was running out of conscriptable colleagues. I had the idea to ask Rinaldo, a respected professor who had also a reputation as a very good cook. Although he was an unassuming and friendly person, he was distinctly older than the other cooks were. Diana, thrilled by his status as a university professor, quickly spread the news.

When Rinaldo and I entered the kitchen, all the women were already there but, instead of sitting and drinking coffee before starting to cook, they lined up with their aprons already on. Each of them introduced herself to Rinaldo, stating her name, where she had come from, and her former profession. In that moment, none of them was a *sidelka*: Iryna presented herself as a military officer, Iana as a professor, Yeva as a pharmacist, Inna as a music teacher, Diana as a translator, and so on. With my fellow graduate students, a name had been more than enough.

With Rinaldo, they clearly wanted to stress that they were educated professionals who appreciated his cultural status. We sat down and Rinaldo slowly started to explain how to make a good *soffritto*[8] for his dish. The women remained silent, and I noticed that they were taking notes in Italian. Finding such seriousness funny, I teased Iryna that this was the first time I had seen her so disciplined.

Usually she made fun of everything in a good-spirited way that others found amusing. Olga told me coldly to stop being childish; Iryna said loudly that she was very interested in what Rinaldo was saying and I should not be so impolite with one of my professors. They were following a completely different script from the one they had used with the younger graduate students. Fortunately, Rinaldo made them laugh by saying that my behavior did not bother him, as I was also very impertinent in the classroom.

When the soup was finished, the women prepared the table for our communal meal.

Rinaldo sat at the head of the table, and Diana and Iana sat next to him on each side. Many of the women had brought special Russian or Ukrainian delights they placed in front of him. Amazed, I reminded the women in Russian that we had agreed not to bring anything but the ingredients. Iana cunningly asked me to help her in the kitchen and, as soon as we were in the other room, bluntly told me to stop embarrassing them. It was an important occasion for all the women.

They were hosting an important person, a professor, she exclaimed, which was most unusual. They were grateful that he accepted their invitation and wanted to treat him respectfully, as he deserved. I replied that Rinaldo was a very friendly person and there was no need to be so formal with him; he was happy to spend some time with them and enjoy lunch together. Iana retorted coldly that she was not stupid; she knew very well that nobody would ever like to spend time with a group of desperate *sidelki*. Rinaldo was there only because I had asked him, and they wanted to host him like decent people and not like a bunch of weirdos.

When we returned to the table, Diana was conducting a formal series of toasts and talks about literature and music. I had just assisted at the first occasion on which the women had used the association to stage a claim to decency and moral worth in front of a high-status Italian. They felt that this performance could be successful only by sharply separating the self they presented to the natives from the reality of their everyday lives.[9]

## Surrendering to Nationalities

At the time Agape was founded, membership in the group of women was largely defined in terms of gender, fluency in some minimally understandable Slavic language, and some biographical link with the former Soviet Union. We referred to ourselves collectively as "the women," we freely shifted from Russian to Italian and vice versa, and we took for granted a stock of experiences such as having been youth pioneers or having sung certain songs. What really mattered, at least for most of the members, was their motherhood, their womanhood, and their difficulties as foreign care workers in Alpinetown. Agape's foundational leaflet, not by chance, claimed it was an association for foreign care workers, although some geographical reference was implicit in the fact it was printed only in Italian and Russian.

Diana, one of the few Russians in Alpinetown, was strongly committed to the vision of Agape as an association of Eastern European women, regardless of their ethnocultural origins. She took it for granted that, as in the collective life of the former USSR, national differences among us should be considered as mere variations of a common theme. For a long initial phase, when the association was mainly focused on providing a space in which women could congregate and support one another, this assumption appeared to work reasonably well. The language was the glue that held people together, and nobody really cared about the passports we were holding.

The context changed after the association had its own space and gained a minimal level of recognition from the local authorities. As part of the deal, Agape had to organize some initiatives reaching out to the local community. After the success of the cooking classes, Diana suggested that the association should promote an intercultural day when the women could invite the families they worked for to share a meal in the same church location. They would show their employers that they had something to give to local life in Alpinetown and impress them with their aesthetic taste. She added that a part of the day could be used for a public lecture and discussion of passages from Dostoevsky, demonstrating that, despite their current occupation, the *sidelki* were highly educated women who hailed from a great cultural tradition.

As often happened, the discussion that followed did not endorse Diana's highbrow aspirations. It quickly shifted to what initially seemed to me a much more mundane topic. What food should be chosen as the "typical dish" for the event? Diana assumed that she herself would choose a representative dish and that it would be something Russian. Alla suggested they should prepare a Ukrainian dish, as most of the *side-lki* were Ukrainian. Iana proposed a Moldovan dish, because this cuisine was distinctive and very few Italian families had had a chance to try it. Diana, taken by surprise, did not like the discussion at all. She vehemently opposed the idea of cooking several dishes, arguing that it would create a feeling of fragmentation that had to be avoided. She claimed that preparing a Russian dish was more than enough. They all knew how to prepare *pel'meni*, and surely they sometimes cooked it for themselves. The other women insisted that was wrong: what mattered was that Russians were a tiny minority among association members, while Ukrainians and Moldovans were the vast majority. Svetlana stressed that, although all of them spoke Russian, they were definitely not Russians. I tried to calm the situation by saying that our guests would not be able to tell the difference between *varenyky, coltunasi, pel'meni*, or *pirohy*.[10] Jokingly, I said that we could cook them whatever we wanted to and they would complain anyway because it was not spaghetti.

Nobody laughed. It slowly dawned on me that Diana took it for granted that Russian cuisine was the "high cuisine" for all of Eastern Europe, while she regarded Ukrainian and Moldovan foods as merely local, rural, and inferior variations. She saw these women's insistence on "their" dishes as irrational and backward, a sign of a persistent provincialism that could compromise the whole project of proving to Italians that they were educated people. The discussion ended in a stalemate, and the initiative was postponed.

A few months later, the same cleavage reappeared with more radical consequences. Again, Diana had discovered a precious opportunity. The priest of a church located near the place we had used for cooking classes had mentioned to her the existence of another small church nearby. Given the dwindling number of parishioners, it was largely unused. They had wondered if they could ask the diocese to lend it to the association to hold religious functions, along the template of what the diocese had done earlier for the Romanians.

Diana talked with some people in the diocese, who had said they understood the needs of "their Orthodox brothers." Seizing the opportunity, she announced that she had already found an Orthodox priest living in another Italian town who was willing to come once a month to celebrate Mass for them. The other women, however, reacted with a visible lack of enthusiasm. Iana, who had previously complained about the lack of religious functions for Moldovans, argued that many Moldovan women were already attending the Romanian Orthodox Masses and that she did not know whether they would want to shift to a ceremony with a "Russian priest."

Many women argued that they were Catholics, although of the Eastern rite, and had no interest in the whole project. In over two hours of heated discussion, only the handful of Russian women in the room supported the proposal. The others were either adamantly opposed to it or conceded merely that having a Russian Orthodox Mass was better than not having a Mass at all. Diana, visibly hurt, decided she would organize the religious functions anyway. She accepted, however, the mandate not to advertise the Russian Orthodox Masses as part of Agape activities.

Once these seeds of division had been planted, I started hearing complaints that Agape was not really a place for all *sidelki* but rather a place only for Russians. The advent of Russian Orthodox Masses had created a clear division: the women who attended these services had lunch together afterward, gathering as a distinct group. In this respect, the religious observance generated a line of ethnocultural cleavage.

The tension deepened over the ensuing months, as Diana acquired a more visible role in Alpinetown as the representative of Eastern European women. With her Italian citizenship, her fluency in Italian, and her ample free time, Diana was often invited to participate in initiatives on behalf of migrant care workers by local politicians and social service agencies, although her spell as a care worker had been brief and merely incidental. When her application to the local government for a small grant to enable Agape to sponsor cultural events was granted, Diana perceived it as recognition by the local society.

In order to fulfill the conditions of the grant, the association had to organize more activities that promoted cultural exchange with the natives. Any idea Diana proposed encountered opposition from the other women. Meetings were fraught with tension. "Russian language courses, Russian poetry, Russian religion . . . I am fed up of being Russified!" exclaimed Alla, who announced that she was no longer interested in participating in Agape. Diana maintained her control over the association, but women who did not share her belief in the superiority of Russian culture or nostalgia for the Soviet multiethnic tradition withdrew.

A few weeks after Alla left Agape, a leaflet appeared announcing the formation of Vykup, a "Ukrainian Christian association" headed by her. She had learned how to run an organization during her years in Agape, and she had recently married a retired Italian who provided her with both economic security and a secure footing in local society. He was delighted to support his wife in this new project by helping her to deal with Italians. Moreover, many of the Ukrainian migrant women had received their amnesty papers in the meantime, so they enjoyed a more secure position in Italy.

According to the leaflet printed to announce the birth of Vykup, the association aimed to preserve Ukrainian self-consciousness and contribute to the integration of care workers into Italian society. Although some of its activities were very similar to those Agape had tried to undertake, Vykup had a much more explicitly religious focus. While Diana claimed to promote an open, pluralistic association of women unified by their participation in a particular high culture, Alla claimed to protect a national identity rooted in a religious affiliation.

Vykup's first priority was to enable Greek Catholic Ukrainians in Alpinetown to attend Greek Catholic Mass regularly. They found a Polish priest who could celebrate Mass in the Greek Catholic rite and was willing to visit every fortnight. As most Ukrainian *sidelki* in Alpinetown had come from the Greek Catholic areas of Western Ukraine, the launch of these Masses sent a strong message of recognition. They found hospitality in a little-used Roman Catholic church and started planning the Masses. The priest agreed to host their service, which, like any other activity held in the building, was meant to be open to all *sidelki*, regardless of nationality or associational affiliation. Owing to the large number of Greek Catholic women, the Masses became immediately identified with Western Ukrainians and with Vykup. The priest also allowed Vykup to hold its activities in the nearby oratorio. Alla was not surprised by her success. She explained: "We [Western Ukrainians] are Catholic. It is natural for us to be in a Catholic church and to meet in a Catholic oratory." Agape had acquired its main space thanks to Diana's connections with the local government; Vykup obtained a space thanks to its religious ties with local Catholics.

These developments transformed the relationships among Eastern European care workers. After visiting the Sunday market, Ukrainian women had to decide between hanging around with their friends, going to the Greek Catholic Mass (which was followed by a well-organized lunch), or attending the religious and cultural events organized by Agape (also followed by lunch). Initially, and for most women, the increased number of options was positive, and they could choose every Sunday according to the specific offer and their personal contingencies.

Diana and Alla, on the contrary, expected the women attending their initiatives to be loyal followers, while often addressing the women who participated only in the other association as little less than traitors. Denunciations were bitter: Diana presented it as a battle between religion and culture, between petty nationalism and cultural openness. Alla thought it was just a continuation of the millennial struggles of Ukrainians to emancipate themselves from Russian imperialism. I had participated in the group for years without knowing the religious affiliation of any of the women, very often having only indirect clues about their "national" (in Soviet terms) membership. Suddenly such information had become crucial to avoid embarrassing gaffes.

I found myself in a difficult situation: Where was I supposed to go? How might the split affect my fieldwork? Fortunately, when I asked Alla and Diana if I could belong to both associations, they replied that of course I could; I was a useful resource and, after all, I was neither Russian nor Ukrainian, neither Greek Catholic nor Orthodox. I was not alone in trying to keep up my ties with both groups, but I was the only one who enjoyed a recognized status as legitimately in between.

The first Greek Catholic Easter Mass held in Alpinetown was a deeply emotional event, particularly for those women whose children would receive their first Easter communion since they had emigrated. Iryna decided to include me in her family along with her husband and her daughter. She prepared a basket containing salt, pepper, butter, eggs, cheese, salami, and bread, covered with a hand-embroidered tablecloth. A representative of the family had to bring the basket to the priest for his blessing, and Iryna decided I should do it even though I was not Greek Catholic. I was concerned, as I had basically no knowledge of the Eastern rites.

When I asked them for more information, I was puzzled that Iryna could provide only very fuzzy answers. Lena, her daughter, told me that nobody was interested in the ritual: it was something you do for your family and friends. Iryna said she hardly ever went to church in Ukraine but was thrilled because "our folk's" Mass was taking place in Alpinetown.[11] While we were on our way, Iryna judged my black clothes inappropriate and gave me a *vyshyvanka*, a traditional Ukrainian shirt, to wear.[12] When we arrived, the church was packed, and many women were wearing similar blouses. I estimated that there were at least 700 people in the church, the largest gathering to date. I asked Iryna if they were all Ukrainians. "Of course! This is our church," she replied. I said there were actually many Ukrainians who were Orthodox. She replied by shrugging, implying this was a minor detail.

The priest invited the representatives of the families to lay the baskets near the altar. I stood in line, reached the altar, deposited the basket, and waited there for his blessing. The puzzled priest had to ask me to move, as a long queue had formed behind me. Iryna was laughing. The Mass was fascinating, and the women were singing with evident joy. When I asked Iryna what the song, sung in Church Slavonic, was about, she responded merely "the usual Church stuff." At a certain point, she sent me back to the altar with even less instruction than before: "when the priest calls the row, you go, kiss the cross, and cross yourself." It seemed easy. I can do it! I thought to myself. While standing in the queue, I noticed several women I knew. Oksana waved at me and signaled her invitation to have a beer with her afterward; I replied with a nod, unsure that this conversation was appropriate in the church. Going down the aisle, I kept repeating the instructions, hoping to avoid any further major embarrassment. I failed miserably, as I crossed myself according to the Roman Catholic sequence. This time, however, both Iryna and the priest smiled warmly and I rushed to my seat as quickly as I could.

After more than two hours, the Mass ended. In the square, as we greeted one another and chatted, I met and hugged Alla, who was elated at the success of her initiative. She said that the Italian priest who lent them the church was impressed by how many people were attending the Mass and by their evident enthusiasm. She had told him Ukrainians were "true Christians," fortified by decades of communist persecution, while Italians were nominal Christians, spoiled by consumerism and materialism. "Now all women know we have a decent place to meet," said Alla, "we do not need to be embarrassed any more." I asked her what she meant, fearing she would launch into another tirade against the Russians. This time, Alla meant something completely different. The boundary she traced, which became increasingly salient in subsequent years, was between those who attended church regularly and participated in related social events and those who continued to spend their free time chatting and drinking in the public places where we had always gathered.

Like Diana, Alla was now ready to draw a distinction within the group between those women who would shift, now that they had the possibility, to "respectable" activities and sites and those who would refuse such opportunity to become respectable, preferring the previous, makeshift sociability. Since "decent places" were finally available, the women more active in their management started considering those who maintained the same routines increasingly as "indecent," "ignorant," or, sometimes, even "*blyat*."[13] To them, the Sunday open-air market and the benches in the park, which all had previously visited on a regular basis, quickly became a symbol of degradation. While at first the religious functions were planned in a way that made them compatible with visiting the parking lot, the schedule was subsequently modified so that going to church now constituted an alternative to spending a long time there. Participation in the church activities became a formalized choice.

## The Challenge of Intercultural Formats

Alla had identified the Ukrainian religious tradition as the functional equivalent of the "high culture" advocated by Diana. In facilitating the (selective) continuation of these traditions in Alpinetown, both Diana and Alla were responding to the low status of the group as a whole. They perceived their associations as instrumental in asserting the migrant women's right to be recognized as worthy, bona fide members of the local Italian community.

Within this collective claim to decency was also embedded a more internal claim: the better-educated, more established, and often older women tried to assert their authority over the other women and claimed the duty to discipline them. Participating in these associations was both a marker of social status and a self-proclaimed indicator of moral worth, and their activities functioned as an alternative to the open-air market and other sites of informal sociability, which they increasingly identified as disreputable.

If the community slowly became differentiated along moralized lines, the emergence of the cleavage between the leadership and the women helped, for a while, to hold its national differentiation in check. Women active in Agape and in Vykup quickly realized that they could not compete successfully with the makeshift sociability of the parking lot and the waiting room without organizing events that the women would find more enjoyable. As they lacked the necessary resources and labor, both associations, once established, ended up collaborating in organizing special events. The two associations shared the same ambition: they sought to reach the natives of Alpinetown, gaining recognition not only from the local authorities or from the diocese but also from the general population.

Fortified by the success of the Easter Mass, Alla decided it was time to launch a new initiative centered on Ukrainian Mother's Day, celebrated the second Sunday of May each year. At the following meeting, Alla assured members that many Italians would attend and journalists would publicize its success. The celebration of Mother's Day would be a "real intercultural event!" Vykup would show the citizens of Alpinetown that Ukrainians were not simply "*sidelki* getting drunk along the riverbanks and having sex with anyone."[14]

Around the same time, and with similar motivations, Diana launched the idea of participating in a multicultural festival organized by the Catholic Diocese. The culminating event of the festival was a parade in which each immigrant group in Alpinetown would demonstrate its own music and dancing. Agape would also serve food and sell small items. For the first time, Diana argued, the *sidelki* could assert their presence alongside the other immigrant groups in Alpinetown. To participate, however, Agape had to accept the way in which the Italian organizers categorized the world: places in the parade were allocated according to nationalities, and each national group was supposed to present its own culture and customs. As a result, Agape had to distribute participants along three segments of the parade, for Ukrainians, Moldovans, and Russians, respectively.[15]

For Mother's Day, Alla decided to have a traditional dance show performed by the Ukrainian youth of Alpinetown in a Catholic pastoral center that boasted a real, albeit a bit old-fashioned, theater. There would be Cossack dances followed by carefully staged dances portraying a traditional Ukrainian wedding. The problem was that there were not enough Ukrainian boys and girls in Alpinetown, as only a few women had been able to complete their family-reunification applications. Demography is destiny, and Alla had to give up the dream of ethnic homogeneity. Thanks to Lena, Iryna's daughter, a group was hastily arranged. It consisted of two Ukrainian boys, three Ukrainian girls, one Albanian girl, and three Italian girls Lena had recruited from among her classmates.

The participants practiced for several hours a day. Sofia and the other Vykup women advertised the event by putting up posters in the public places frequented by migrant women, in schools, and even in some cafés in the city center. The women received invitations to distribute to the members of the families they worked for. Several association members were assigned to prepare specific dishes for the reception. The day before the ceremony, Alla announced excitedly that she had received confirmations from all around the city, and some officials would attend.

On Mother's Day, I visited Iryna's flat to participate in dressing Lena in traditional Ukrainian clothing. Iryna was also preparing a large *olivye* salad, a cold dish she had selected as typical.[16] She said anxiously that she expected at least two of the families she was working for to participate. She wanted them to be impressed by the beauty and artistry of Lena's dancing. She claimed that someone was going to film the performance, so Lena's dancing would also be seen in Ukraine. "Can you imagine what a surprise for my parents! Their granddaughter, dressed so nice and dancing so skillfully. . . ."

The ceremony was a great success. Several hundred women participated, and the crowd was filled with a tangible undercurrent of emotion at being together to celebrate. Yet it was obvious that few, if any, Italians were in the audience, although the women had made a great effort to reach out to them. Almost none of the women's employers showed up. Besides a couple of priests representing the local church, the few Italians I was able to identify were partners of migrant women, and they did their best to keep their participation as short as possible. Some even refused to sample the food, claiming that it was "too heavy."

Meanwhile, as the festival approached, Diana had to face the fact that Agape's resources were insufficient to put on the expected show. After considerable thought, Diana decided that, rather than relinquish the opportunity to participate, she should agree to an armistice with Vykup. The performances that Ukrainians had prepared would be reused. To avoid acknowledging a full-fledged defeat, they added to the Ukrainian performance a gig by Maria and Sofia, Ukrainian by passport but self-identifying as Russians. They would sing "Kalinka," a Russian folk song that all women approved of and that was also well known to the Italian audience. Indeed, when they performed it, people started dancing all around the square.

Agape also organized a stand selling Russian delicatessen items, Moldovan cognac, *matryoshka* dolls, embroidered tablecloths and shirts, and, of course, vodka. Alla, Iana, and Diana took care of the stand for the entire two days, while dozens of women came along to help, bring food, take pictures, or simply thank them for what they were doing. Participation in the festival yielded a sizable amount of money, which was divided between the two associations.

Both experiences taught the associations a lesson that remained true in subsequent years. Activities organized directly by the associations could play an important role in offering the women internal recognition, but they utterly failed to foster intercultural contact and external recognition on their own terms. Their only chance of attracting an Italian audience was through participation in programs or initiatives organized by Italian associations or local government bodies.

Here, the women could hope to be acknowledged and accepted, but not on their own terms. They had to be willing to be treated as one group of immigrants among many others and to be pigeonholed as an undifferentiated national "community" defined by folk customs and traditional ideas but not, for example, by religion, education, or occupation. Within this political space, the women's ethnic associations could secure support only by articulating a vision of Eastern Europeans as "good immigrants," humble, traditional, hardworking, morally respectable, and religiously inspired. Both the collective reading of Dostoevsky that Diana dreamed of and the claim to social and professional modernity that many of the women wished to assert had no space to be heard.

## The Crucible of Leadership

The secession of Vykup paved the way to further subdivisions along ethnic and religious lines. Another, equally important, development revealed a change in the women's understanding of the rights and duties of leadership. At first, the women had treated Agape mainly as a place to congregate. They took for granted that Diana was the "boss," as she was paying for everything, and treated her with respect, but they conceived of her role mostly as a service provider. They expected Diana to invest her time, energies, and resources in assisting them. They were ready to blame her if she did not deliver what they wanted. Many women were willing to put up with her high culture project—indeed, even with her "Russification"—as long as she catered to them. None could afford to pay a membership fee, and most conceived of Agape as a place to receive something.

The leaders of the associations, however, had a very different idea of the associations' functions: both Diana and Alla thought that their associations were, above all, a way for them to collectively gain respect and recognition from the local community. They felt that the associations should focus on emotional, religious, and cultural matters, so the women could give up their disorderly social life. They felt that the women should be active participants, devoting their energies to implementing the associations' projects, without having much of a voice in defining them.

A few months after the festival, Iana, who was still Agape's vice president, suddenly announced that Moldovan women needed their own space. In order to cater to the religious needs of Moldovan women, she planned to organize a new association, Vira. This move did not come as a complete surprise. Many women were aware of Iana's growing criticism of the activities organized by Agape, and especially of Diana's leadership. A former university professor, Iana was outspokenly articulating the Soviet-era argument that the only legitimate criterion for social stratification was having higher education credentials. She acknowledged that Diana was putting a lot of energy into the association, drawing on her many personal connections and even some of her personal economic resources. She did not consider these elements important.

**163**

In her eyes, leadership positions were to be given to whoever could rightfully claim to be the most highly educated. She expected all the women in the association, including Diana, to behave deferentially toward her. When Agape was founded, Diana had given her the title of vice president mostly as a way of acknowledging the growing number of Moldovan women in Alpinetown. Iana had taken it as a recognition of her high cultural capital, and she openly stated that she considered it a step toward the presidency. After Alla had founded Vykup, however, Iana had grown more dissatisfied with her prospects within Agape.

I once asked Iana why she was leaving Agape just when the climate between Diana and Alla, and between Agape and Vykup, had markedly improved. I knew that she was not particularly keen on organizational activities and wondered how she could manage a new association. I told her that there was certainly enough space to accommodate whatever activities she wanted to conduct without going through the ordeal of creating a separate association.

Iana presented her association as complementary to Agape, not as a competitor. Reverting to her previous complaints, she argued that although most Moldovan women spoke Russian fluently, they were much closer to the Romanian Orthodox Church, which held regular functions in Alpinetown. Her new association would be a way for the Moldovans to participate and support the life of the Romanian Orthodox Church. There was more to the story. She told me she had fully understood that Italians—that is, the local government and philanthropic agencies—thought of immigrants exclusively in terms of "national" categories. "Have you any idea of how many times they have asked me why the Moldovans do not have their own associations?" she said. She also told me that she had acquired her papers years before and would soon marry an Italian and leave care work. She regarded taking responsibility for her people as a new way of becoming a *signora*, a way that required not severing links with the women but instead assuming responsibility for them.

Several weeks later, Iana invited me to attend the Romanian Orthodox Mass, which, she claimed, "had been opened" to all Moldovan women thanks to her efforts. As with the Russian and Ukrainian functions, the Romanian Mass was held in an underutilized Catholic Church that the diocese had lent to the organizing committee.

After the Catholic Mass was finished, the committee rushed in to transform the church interior to suit the Orthodox Christian ceremony. At the end of the ceremony, they had to dismantle everything and swiftly store the screen and icons to return the church to the priest in its original form. When I arrived, some minutes before the Mass started, the transformation was nearly complete. Iana handed me an embroidered scarf as we entered the building. Later, I asked Iana why she had done this when many women were entering the church without covering their heads. She replied that it was not mandatory, but rather customary, for married women to wear a scarf. When I remarked I was not married, Iana replied bluntly that I was old enough that I should have been. "You cannot behave like those girls with miniskirts and low-cut shirts," she said.

As we entered the building, I noticed that nearly everyone was buying candles, icons, and calendars from a table just outside the door. Iana and I lit candles for the dead and kissed the icons. Explaining that many participants had brought food and wine to give as alms in memory of the dead, she suggested that I should think about my own loved ones who had died. I was surprised to notice several women bringing the elderly men and women they were taking care of to the Mass. Iana explained that many of them liked the Orthodox rituals, and sometimes the Moldovan women accompanied them to the Catholic Mass first and then took them to "their" Mass. I recognized Rania, a Moldovan care worker, sitting close to her "Italian grandma." When she mimicked a sense of surprise at my being there, I smiled and pointed to Iana, implying that it was her fault. After Rania whispered into the old woman's ear, she smiled and waved to us.

The church was very crowded. When two boys circulated through the aisles carrying baskets, all the women dropped some money into them, looking at each other to see how much they had donated. When I asked Iana why they were so obviously inspecting what the others were giving, she replied that this was "our Church" and "you just cannot be stingy here." She then graciously suggested that I could contribute some money myself.

Toward the end of the Mass, I was startled when Iana whispered to me that the church was so crowded only because the women needed a place to gather peacefully among themselves. She quietly explained that she had hardly ever entered a church in Moldova; that "was something only old women do. If I am in Moldova, I would rather go to a concert or somewhere to dance." In Alpinetown, however, religious functions were respectable ways of being "among their own."

Indeed, after the Mass ended, we spent at least as much time congregating in the square in front of the church as we had spent inside it. Iana introduced me to several women whom I had previously seen around the city but had not spoken with before. Iana described them as among the strongest supporters of the new association and entrusted me to them as she went off to greet the many women in the square. Expecting that lunch would soon be served in the attached recreational center, I suggested that we go there before all the best food was eaten.

Dina explained that the oratory was reserved for the lunch of the Romanians; we were expected to go to the riverside park instead. Puzzled by this explanation, I asked why they would not feel at ease with the Romanians: after all, nearly all the Moldovan women in Alpinetown were also fluent in Romanian, and they had just finished praying together. They did not really reply, but I could tell they were uneasy. Dina quickly said she hoped that Iana would indeed succeed in establishing their own association. After all, she had been a university professor and Agape's vice president, and now she was marrying an Italian. "She has what is needed; she can make it," another woman commented.

Until a few months before, the women had almost never made distinctions among themselves according to their places of origin. As long as a migrant woman was a care worker and was able to speak a language they could understand, she was a woman, a *sidelka*. Moldovans, who were usually equally fluent in both Russian and Romanian, had always been considered fortunate because they could participate in two networks and rely on a wider set of contacts and opportunities. When Romania entered the EU, many of them had been able to claim Romanian citizenship, thus automatically becoming EU citizens entrusted with full civil, and some political, rights in Italy.

This had never been presented to me as a substantive ethnocultural difference, but rather as a fortunate coincidence, a stroke of luck. Now, the women had become accustomed to living in a world of separate ethnic entities. From their point of view, Moldovans' overlapping memberships had become a burden. When I asked what they were planning to do with their new association, they replied excitedly that Vira would be able to apply for funding and provide the women with sports and social activities. Ana, who was a good friend of Dina, said that she wanted Vira to organize some dancing parties so that "the women could come over and move a bit, have fun, listen to good music. They will feel more at home while being here." Geta suggested that Vira could organize classes in Italian. Evidently, these women did not share the strictly religious focus that Iana had announced was Vira's purpose. Very quickly, Vira grew similar to the other associations, trying to organize a variety of events and to be recognized as the representative of the "Moldovan community."

Iana presented Vira in this way to many individuals and agencies working with immigrants in Alpinetown, who she hoped would be willing to validate this claim. As she understood clearly, Italians thought of immigrant groups as having distinct ethnic identities and wanted to deal with them through separate associations.

Indeed, the greatest obstacle Iana encountered was the women themselves. She thought that, as president of the new association, she should identify opportunities and conduct public relations with local Italian institutions, while the women followed in her footsteps, taking responsibility for the implementation of those projects. At the initial meetings, she listed what had to be done on a chalkboard and tried to assign each task to someone. Standing by the chalkboard, she stared at the women sitting in their chairs and scolded them for their inadequacy. Women had to signal when they wanted to talk; the meeting style reminded me of an old-fashioned classroom. The women, on the contrary, perceived themselves mostly as the association's customers. They expected Iana to behave like Diana and Alla: that is, to invest significant personal and economic resources in order to deliver concrete services to them. Several initiatives floundered right away, and Iana and the women involved soon blamed one another for these failures.

Iana had claimed that, thanks to her educational credentials, she could strike a good deal with the much more numerous and better organized Romanians. Indeed, she was proud of her success, as the women participated regularly in the Romanian Mass, but she had no interest in negotiating shared use of the recreational center afterward. Instead, she said, she wanted a space for the Moldovans alone. Many women were dissatisfied with the situation. They said that they had been going to the Romanian Mass before Iana intervened and deeply resented the fact that they had to go eat along the riverside while Ukrainians and Romanians had lunch in their respective indoor sites.

A few months later, I encountered Anastacia, a youthful-looking Moldovan care worker, who proudly announced the advent of a new association, called simply Moldova. Her husband Maxim, one of the rare cases at the time of couples migrating together, had just started his own construction business. They had recently bought a small flat, and their children had been among the first Moldovan children to gain a family-reunification visa. Maxim often said he wanted to do something for the small but growing number of Moldovan children. He insisted that, after growing up in Alpinetown, they would "refuse to wash old asses like their moms." At the same time, he thought they needed closer contact with Moldovan culture. Anastacia proudly announced that Maxim had found a gym where they could hold a weekly dance class. "You know, where the Moldovans dance the earth trembles," she said proudly, quoting a Moldovan saying.[17] She was optimistic that many people would be interested in forming a traditional dance troupe.

When I asked why they had not organized this initiative with Vira, Anastacia replied that Iana was "unbearable, still living in Soviet times." She constantly "flouts around her being a professor." Laughing, she said that although she had been a "music teacher, and a very good one," she realized long ago that world had ended and now she was just someone who washed old asses for a living. Her husband had the resources and the contacts necessary to deliver what the women needed, and their attempt to cooperate with Iana had been unpleasant and unsuccessful.

Iana, who already knew about the new association, was furious. She expressed astonishment that this couple, both of them "ignorant people, little more than peasants," expected to represent Moldovans and contended that, because they had money to waste, they wanted to be paid respect they did not deserve. Yet while Vira became little more than a one-woman show, Moldova quickly became an active and effective association that organized a variety of events, often centered on traditional dances. A few years later, another group of Moldovans secured a space for their own religious functions and regular visits from a priest belonging to the Orthodox Church. A church committee, independent from Vira, was established to organize the Masses and the social events that followed them.

The growth in the number of women, and their increasing economic stability, eventually triggered a change in the social landscape of Alpinetown. Starting in 2010, I started to observe a growing number of events organized individually by private entrepreneurs. The Ukrainian son of one of the women started organizing special evenings in a working-class disco, during which Ukrainian pop music was played. These events became immediately popular among the children of the women and the youngest newcomers. A Moldovan woman soon started doing the same in another peeled-off disco in the outskirts of the town, this time playing "Romanian" turbofolk music.

A couple of years later, some leaflets announced the concert of a Ukrainian singer, who was doing a tour of the main emigration settlements in Italy and Greece. The price of the ticket, albeit low for Italian standards, was remarkably high in comparison to what had been acceptable only a few years before. The concert, however, was a success and other for-profit concerts followed once or twice a year.

A few months later, a shop specializing in Eastern European products opened, undercutting the need for many women to use the open-air market in the parking lot. The owner started to organize low-cost entertainment events, which he could easily advertise among his customers. His mix of old Italian evergreen, Eastern European pop music, and Romanian *manele* turned out to be especially popular among the women married to older Italians, who found these events somewhat familiar, close to the *balera* dancing of their youth. A one-man agency launched a program, initially targeted to the small number of Eastern European wedding parties celebrated in Alpinetown, which quickly expanded to cover other important ritual occasions.

The supply of professionally organized events contributed to further segmentation of the initial group. As it was particularly attractive to the more established families, it also cut the ground from under the feet of the associations, which had to rely nearly exclusively on the more isolated and less economically successful women for an audience.

## A Frail Associational World

Nearly two decades after the first Eastern European care workers arrived in Alpinetown, the initial group of women had separated into several distinctive, albeit interlocked, networks defined along ethnonational lines. For a while, Diana kept alive the idea of an umbrella organization that transcended specific identities and protected *sidelki* from degradation through their participation in a venerable high culture, but many women regarded that as a mere pretense. The development of other associations meant that Agape was increasingly identified as an organization for Russians.

All the women I knew expected Diana to act only in the interests of Russians. As very few *sidelki* were Russian, by passport or by self-identification, and many women increasingly used the services provided by Vykup, Vira, and Moldova, Agape found itself marginalized. Diana began to define its mission differently, slowly detaching it from the world of *sidelki*. It gradually became something closer to an Italian-Russian cultural association, with activities scheduled at times that did not fit with the schedules of care workers or cleaners. In 2016, it ceased activities altogether.

Vykup has survived and maintained some popularity among Ukrainian women. Its main focus is its religious mission, which is quite popular, although the post-Mass lunches are less attended than before. With Euromaidan, it has found a new dimension, supporting the fight against the Russian-backed insurgency. Since the start of the conflict, there have been some events promoting information on Russian aggression

**169**

(sometimes, but rarely, in collaboration with Italian groups), and the association has taken care of two wounded militants transported to Alpinetown for therapy. News about how to collect funds for the Ukrainian volunteer units has also circulated at Vykup events.[18]

The association has not overcome, however, its dependence on leaders with long immigration seniority, economic resources, enough free time, and good connections with local government and philanthropic bodies. Consequently, it remains very fragile, and its members are not consistently involved in associational life. The main problem is that the only stable constituency the association can rely upon are those women who have chosen to remain live-in care workers and focus their free time on religious observances and occasions for reproducing festivities and traditions from their countries of origin. As a consequence, Vykup must engage in a constant struggle to secure enough funding. The association, moreover, has not succeeded in gaining respect for the women by making natives interested in their culture, instead focusing more and more inwardly on events designed for its particular constituency.

Moldova, although its dance program has been quite popular for several years, is now in a state of suspended animation. The proximate cause has been that Anastacia and Maxim have moved to another Mediterranean country, leaving the association without its founding leaders. The reasons for which it has been unable to find an adequate replacement became clear to me when I attended its last major event, a few months before leaving Alpinetown.

The members had secured a small grant from the local authorities, to organize a one-day festival. They had contacted all groups in Alpinetown with even the slightest connection to folk dancing and invited them to share the stage with Eastern European immigrant troupes. They placed posters all around the city, including many Catholic parishes. They expressed real hope that the natives would participate, thus acknowledging the cultural value of their presence. The festival was certainly a success. The park was crowded, and the audience often started dancing along with the performers. Ukrainians, Moldovans, and Romanians were intermingling in the dance. Impressed by the merry mood, I noticed that, in addition to the women, several men and many children were participating.

The demographic composition of the group was significantly different from what it had been even only a decade before. It was equally evident that nearly all the participants were Eastern Europeans and that the few Italians I was able to meet were either professionally involved with intercultural initiatives or were partners of *sidelki* who were required to attend as part of their conjugal duties. Almost none of them were dancing.

Returning to my car, I came across Lena, Iryna's daughter, who had just left the stage after the performance of her Ukrainian group. She asked if she could use my car to change her clothes. While I covered the car window with a towel, she quickly changed from the traditional peasant garb she had worn for the dance into the miniskirt and leather jacket that represent the current uniform of Alpinetown teenagers. While using the rearview mirror to put on dark red lipstick and heavy black mascara, she told me how happy she was that the show had been a success. She loved to dance to the old stuff, especially the Cossack-inspired hopak. When she finished her makeup, Lena jumped out of the car and hurriedly kissed me goodbye. She was obviously excited and looking forward to the evening. She was late for her appointment with Vika and Olena, two other Ukrainian girls she had danced with at the festival. They were going to Alpinetown's main square, where some Italian classmates were waiting to take them dancing to techno music in the best-known disco of Alpinetown.

# Conclusion: From the Detritus of the Soviet Union into a New Social World

What happens when a number of middle-aged, educated women—most of them mothers or grandmothers—see the last remnants of their previous middle-class professional and family lives destroyed by the umpteenth sudden geopolitical crisis? When they migrate alone—outside of any official recruitment program, without relying on any established network of already settled relatives—to an area with no previous history of immigration from their lands? When any further physical contact with their families will have to wait for an adjustment of legal status in a far, unforeseeable future? When the only jobs open to them—live-in care work for elderly people—make them feel deeply polluted? When it requires spending their days and nights in flats that are home to other people, whose language and habits are largely unknown, and still be able to provide affectionate care for them? When their irregular status forces them to live in a twilight zone, void of any certified identity for claiming their rights?

There is a quick and—apparently—reasonable answer. These women will be overly concerned, indeed obsessed, with the practical pressures of everyday survival, with the pressing needs of making ends meet, of finding or keeping a job, of being able to save something to repay debts and support their families back home. They will submit, for force majeure, to the conditions, avoiding any aspiration that could become a liability. Driven by traditional understandings of maternal duties—and socialized to self-sacrifice by a long previous history of deprivation—they will live ascetic lives *here*. They will follow an overly instrumental orientation, framing the new environment only in terms of the resources they may acquire in it. The fruits of their work will gain them social recognition and respect only *there*, in their previous circles of recognition, among those that really matter for them, their relatives and friends "back home."

Many of the newly arrived women encountered in this book—such as Elena, in the first chapter—indeed describe their own lives through this simple binary. They think they are here only "to work," while what they call their "real life"—the emotional, meaningful, fulfilling one—takes place there, in absentia. They are mothers, victims of an unjust fate, working hard here in order to return there as soon as possible. They devoted a great deal of interactional energy to supporting each other, both in their instrumental orientation to *here* and in their devotion to *there*, not to mention their willingness to sanction each other for minimal transgressions to this narrative.

Many natives of Alpinetown, particularly those sympathetic to the plight of the women, make sense of the women using the very same binary. It is an explanatory device, a creditable account able to make sense of their being *here* but not fully *here*, of their being a social figure familiar enough to entrust them with the care of personal spaces and dear relatives, and yet alien enough to accept working conditions and salaries that would otherwise be inconceivable.[1] The distinction between a cold, instrumental *here* and an emotionally charged *there* also provides the ground for normative claims on their behalf.

In my encounters with social workers and volunteers, I have witnessed them employing such a distinction countless times, to win the confidence of potential employers. They associate the women with the positive polarities of a strong work ethic, attachment to maternal duties, fortitude in adversity, and self-sacrifice. They expect them to be modest, low-key, well-behaved, and deferential to the rule and the customs of the land that is hosting them.

I do not mean to underplay the severity of the condition in which the immigrant women live in Alpinetown or the reality of the instrumental attitudes that they may take on. For many years, scarcity restricted everyday choice. The description of themselves as *rab* (slaves) appeared to them, and sometimes even to me, at least plausible.

Nor do I want to deny the importance of motherhood in motivating their efforts. I have observed endless instances of self-sacrifice in favor of their children. Like many ethnographers before me, I very often wondered if—in their condition—I would ever have been able to do even half of the same for the sake of my children.

It is also true that the strict geographical disjunction between work and "real life," instrumental and consummatory orientations, and talk contrasting qualities of life *here* and *there* was a narrative very important to the women. It helped them to make sense of their trajectory and to articulate a claim to respect. But it is a fundamental error to take the distinction as accurately describing their preimmigration and Alpinetown lives, instead of appreciating it as a category of practice, a powerful, resonant rhetoric used in many situations in Alpinetown's social life.[2]

The women did not live their frantic search for ways to satisfy pressing material needs from their strong attachments to left-behind relatives. A contrast between life *here* and *there* became a valuable resource for them as they gave form to the experiences triggered by geographical mobility. And their instrumental practices in Alpinetown were not divorced from their needs for approval and admiration from others in actual, flesh-and-blood interactions. Those needs were not satisfied by sustaining relations with folks back in the homeland. No immigrant self can live exclusively on a diet of memories and Skype calls.[3] Geographical dislocation always *also* requires some kind of embodied settlement in the new reality, participation in some chain of physically co-present—smellable and touchable—interactions among peers.

Migrants treat their emigration sociability as simply a matter of convenience. The women I have chronicled here were not meeting with each other to bring about a change in their selves. They were just looking for an inexpensive way to spend the few hours they had free in an unknown city, to gain some crumbs of emotional support, and to experience the interactional warmth that comes from freely speaking one's mother tongue. Yet this everyday sociability—provided by other women in similar situations in specific, embodied sites and occasions—became a powerful mechanism of personal as well as social change, an important part of the "train of experience" that was bound to change them.[4]

Migrants may think of themselves as living in a suspended animation that will release them unscathed upon return, especially if they think their migration is temporary. In fact, however, the very same practicalities of everyday living in a new environment, in facing new encounters, in dealing with different types of promises and dangers, will inevitably require the elaboration of a new point of view on the social world. Living in a remarkably different place in a remarkably different social condition inevitably leads to observing oneself through the eyes of other—new and different—audiences.

After many years of fieldwork, I came to understand that their migration experience was shaped around pressures to work with a new set of identities, each including an embodied sense of what must be liked and what must be loathed, what is appropriate and what is offensive, what is decent and what is undignified. Over many years, the women have been able to transform a makeshift, tentative, and relatively undifferentiated perception of themselves as powerless and wrecked into a pluralistic set of competing social careers, each sustained by its own folk knowledge, morality, and, indeed, aesthetics. Even those women who most vividly remembered their original experiences in Alpinetown—working in live-in care, investing most of their resources *there*, practicing *here* only a low-cost, undifferentiated sociability—are not stuck in their initial orientation to life in the Italian town. They have not "remained" the same people they were in the beginning, if only because they have seen other women starting to do things differently and have not imitated them. Their looking back is part of the process of sensing how they have changed.

## A Social Psychology of the Immigration Experience

In contrast to forced migration, international labor migration is a process of social mobility through motility.[5] In the view of the Eastern European women who came to Alpinetown, the reason for their migration was straightforward: in Alpinetown they were able to earn more than three times (and often more than four times) what they could expect in the areas where they had been previously living.

As live-in care work brings with it free lodging and nutrition, their initial living costs in emigration were minimal. The women were equally adamant that the money they earned was slated to restore their middle-class status and lifestyle in their areas of origin. They would provide their relatives with adequate purchasing power, they would pay for the education of their children and grandchildren, and they would buy or renovate their houses and change their cars. In due course, the money they earned would make possible the acquisition of assets that could further strengthen the status of the family and insure it against future crises.

Initially they thought that, in the end, they would return unscathed, the very same persons in different and more valuable status locations. The women's aspirations to restore (and improve) the socioeconomic status of their families explain their strong motivation to face the risks (and the psychological stress) they had to face in crossing several legal, linguistic, social, and cultural boundaries in a short span of time.[6]

It would be wrong, however, to assume that the strength of their motivation could encase and insulate them from their new psychological and interactional circumstances. On the contrary, the aspirational project that sustained their lives had to be kept alive precisely through engaging within these circumstances, carving out a social space in which they could identify with others and find socially shared ways of confirming each other. The dynamics of mutual support became personally and socially transformative.

Social mobility, especially when pursued through geographical mobility, is never only a movement between structural locations: it always implies a delicate process of personal and interactional adjustment.[7] Any migration is a powerful impetus for personal change. Trying to succeed in social mobility implies anticipating—through observation, imitation, and sheer fantasizing—what it is like to be somebody else, how people should behave in different conditions. When they seek mobility, migrants are challenged in two ways: they must negotiate a new set of similarities in reference to new groups while struggling to maintain the expectations embedded in membership in the previous ones.[8] For the economic migrants in Alpinetown, as for many migrants elsewhere, the process entails a self-inflicted trauma of leaving the status of a competent, resourceful, bona fide member of a previous lifeworld to become a novice in an intertwined set of new ones.[9]

The economic migrant's process of change can be detailed by focusing on changes in the presentation of the self—the ways the migrant tries to control or guide the impressions that others take and to signal to others a version of self-understanding. During mobility, some previous elements, stage props, and scripts disappear, while others become available, to be appropriated and used in often unexpected ways.[10] Mobility implies also a radical change in significant audiences, whose criteria of interpretation are at least partly unknown. The migrant is thus exposed to ambiguities, uncertainty, and ambivalences in the ways performances may be appreciated and understood. There are new eyes, which objectify what they see according to different, and less known, schematizations and mythoi, to use Frantz Fanon's formulation. Migrants must change their presentation of the self, and by doing so, they will trigger changes in their ways of feeling, thinking, and acting.

A specific feature of the processes of international migration, however, makes the processes of personal transformation even more experientially significant. Migration usually exposes migrants to two distinct, and inconsistent, experiences of change in their own personal status.

The basic mechanism of labor migration is the exchange between participating in upward mobility (in the sending context) and downward mobility (in the receiving one).[11] Given the sizable costs of international mobility, migrant pioneers are seldom drawn from the lowest strata of the sending society. This is precisely the case for nearly all the women pioneers in Alpinetown, who previously had been members of the educated middle class in their formerly Soviet spaces.

Yet the incorporation of newly arrived immigrants in advanced economies usually takes place at the lowest rung of the receiving social hierarchy, through the filling of positions defined as 3D: dirty, dangerous, or demeaning.[12] The women of Alpinetown were employed at the very bottom of the immigration pecking order. Their previous accomplishments became invisible or unappreciated. In Italy they experienced an intense degradation of status.

During their settlement in Alpinetown, they had to learn how to cope with the challenges arising from the improvement of their social status in their places of origin and the experience of being exclusively identified (by natives and other immigrants alike) with their despised new status. In Alpinetown Eastern European women confronted pressures arising from the double movement of upward and downward mobility across ethnocultural and geopolitical boundaries, which triggered a strong pressure toward experimenting with new practices of the self.

The idea that geographical mobility triggers significant changes in the identity of those who experience it is far from new. Most available attempts to elaborate a psychology of immigration, however, are overly individualistic, relying on previous psychological traits to explain the subsequent paths to adjustment and acculturation.[13] Cross-cultural psychologists adopt a markedly holistic approach to cultural difference, making each migrant the bearer of an "original" culture, facing the problem of adjusting to live in an equally stable receiving culture.[14]

Different as they are, both approaches bear the important commonality of relying on a container view of the distinction between *here* and *there*, which underplays the importance of what happens *during* the migration process, in the interstitial encounters taking place in early settlement. They postulate that, when migrants arrive, they face a certain number of already defined paths of adjustment among which migrants will have to choose. The settlement of migrants appears driven, nearly exclusively, by what they were before migration and by what is open to them in the receiving society.

In contrast, I focus on the ways in which the interactional experiences during the early phases of settlement produce specific, local irritations that are to be faced through practical, embodied processes of self-transformation. Previous psychological traits and cultural resources are surely important. But they become relevant only through encounters among co-present individuals. I have consequently treated the experiences of the women as both a structural movement across social positions *and* as a rite of passage that transform migrants into "different people."[15]

Migration experiences follow—with varying intensities—the classical sequence of any rite of passage: there is a phase of separation, a transitional liminal period, and, hopefully, a subsequent reincorporation of the individual into a new personal status. The outcome is not necessarily "assimilation," a concept that often denies the novelty of the new social figures that emerge in the process, but it is surely deep change.[16] In coming to Alpinetown, women leaving Eastern European societies that decomposed after the historic end of the Soviet Union were already experiencing a painful process of separation from what they had considered previously secure and permanent features of their social being. The physical experience of moving across borders was simply the final experience of being cut away from their former social identities.[17]

The early years of their presence in Alpinetown continued what Van Gennep—the grandfather of the anthropological study of the rites of passage—has called "liminality."[18] The women were already living in a condition marked by high levels of uncertainty, ambivalence, and ambiguity. The experience of liminality, according to Victor Turner, must be a temporary experience, charged with high degrees of emotional intensity, characterized by the feeling of the contingency of one's self and being open to the possibility of new perceptions.[19]

Equally instructive are the differences between the transformation of the self during migration and the rituals studied by Van Gennep and Turner. In Van Gennep's analysis, the experience of liminality is—and has to be—strictly controlled both in temporal terms (as a passage toward a well-known outcome) and processually (it must be regulated by a "master of ceremonies" following a script with a strictly regulated sequence). In the transformational experience of the women, on the contrary, all these key elements of any rite of passage were utterly lacking. They had to fashion their new identities more serendipitously, without relying on the existence of a script and anticipation of their future states. The lack of an institutionalized master of ceremonies explains why, in going through their liminal experience, they had to rely on their own informal group as a kind of master of ceremonies of last resort.

## Fashioning a New Self in Emigration: The Importance of Studying Pioneers

Stressing the importance of the transformation of the self as an intrinsic dimension of the migration experience does not mean claiming that all migrants experience it in the same way. The pressure to build a new socially viable understanding of themselves takes different forms according to the organization of the migrant flows. The lives of the women pioneers I chronicle in this book are important precisely because several features of their experience have made them a group through which I could observe with special clarity a general phenomenon that usually appears in a more diluted form.[20]

Three features of their situation were particularly important: (1) they were unsponsored, "neoliberal" migrants, moving outside any administratively controlled program; (2) they were pioneers, moving to a new location where they could not rely on relatives or friends; and (3) they were, as soon as their tourist visas expired, irregular migrants with limited access to a legally certified identity. Their condition was lacking in many of the features that may moderate the migration shock and guide their identification with a preestablished set of social scripts. It also differentiated them from the better-known cases of women's migration: the migration of Asian women to the Gulf States through contract work schemes and the migration of Latinas toward the United States, both largely supported by preexisting networks of relatives.

As the women were part of an unsponsored migration flow, there was no agency officially and practically responsible for their recruitment, employment, and monitoring. Their case was sharply different from all instances of tightly planned migration flows, such as the European *Gastarbaiter* schemes of the last century and (in an even more systematic form) current female contract work in the Gulf States. In the latter case, the spells of sojourn are short and known in advance, social segregation is strictly enforced, and there is a well-functioning administrative and legal infrastructure targeted at keeping immigrants separate from the receiving society.

Many of these programs appear in fact to be quite successful in insulating migrants from the receiving society, dramatically curtailing their outgroup interactions. As these systems usually imply that all nonwork activities take place in formalized settings with other migrants of the same origin, contract work migration is designed to support the maintenance of previous identities, practices, and lifestyles. Still, even in these tightly controlled and temporary flows, there is evidence that the experience of immigration implies for many migrants an existential challenge that requires the shaping of a different personal narrative and self-perception. In Asian contract migration, for example, such changes often become visible and performable only upon return.[21]

Another important situational element in Alpinetown is that the women were all migrant pioneers, with no relatives, friends, or even acquaintances. This was likely one of the main structural differences between their experience and what has been recorded in many large-scale flows such as migration from Latin America to the United States.[22] Their settlement was different from the experience of immigrant followers who were moving to a location already shaped by the settled presence of a sizable number of established peers, with their tried paths, received wisdom, and established practices.

As I have shown with my comparison of Nastya and Olysa in the introduction, the ways in which pioneers must establish their new selves is different from the same process undergone by followers. Nastya, like nearly all the pioneers, had experienced a much more perilous liminal journey, having to build a new set of personal practices from scratch, often by trial and error, with the limited help that she could find from other women in similar situations.

For Olysa, on the contrary, as for most of the women who arrived later, the pressure to define a new identity often translated into pressure to align oneself with one of the available preformatted definitions, to negotiate in reference to a somewhat recognizable menu.[23] Olysa had, even before arrival, preliminary sensitizing knowledge of the diverging trajectories (the *signore*, those living in immigrant households, the singles orientated nearly exclusively to *there*) open to the women. She treated these trajectories naturalistically, as self-evident options to choose from, oblivious to the fact that they had been shaped (often by trial and error and at large personal cost) only a few years before through the experiences of pioneers like Nastya.[24]

To be sure, the existence of an established repertoire provided by an already developed local immigration subculture does not obliterate the biographical discontinuity implied by migration. Followers must also face the practical contingencies of psychological adjustment and the pressing need to fashion a different, displayable narrative of oneself suitable to the new environment.[25] The existence of an established reper-toire constitutes, however, a factor that, absorbing a large part of the shock, shapes differently the followers' process of fashioning their new sense of themselves upon emigration.

Last but not least, all the pioneer women experienced protracted spells of irregular migration status. This had two important consequences on the way they could negotiate, with themselves and with others, the meaning of their presence. First, they found themselves locked, some-times for a long period, in a state of legal nonexistence.[26] Although the chances of actual deportation were minimal, the sense of precariousness was not. As in the case of the Salvadorian and Guatemalan immigrants in the United States studied by Cecilia Menjivar, the sense of legal pre-cariousness ramified in nearly all spheres of their social lives, making them especially sensitive to any behavior they could interpret as a sense of disrespect.[27]

The other equally important implication was that the women could not, for the whole spell of their irregular status, visit their families back home, nor could they be visited by them. The early years of their settle-ment, in other words, were marked by a complete physical separation from their original circle of recognition, with whom they could stay in contact only through telephone and Skype conversations and through the money and goods shipped via the network of minivans. This pro-tracted physical separation made even more powerful the feeling of sep-aration from their previous selves, and it made even more pressing their search for a legitimate foothold in Alpinetown.

## Easier Said than Done: The Challenges of Fashioning a New Self in a Novel Environment

The claim that pressures to produce new presentations of the self are an endemic feature of the migration experience is only a part of a satisfac-tory explanation. It opens the question of how such production is actu-ally achieved in specific, interaction-bound contexts. The ways in which migrants actually shape these identities—acting among different spaces and along different times—are characterized by contradictory styles and distinctive practices.[28]

The specific contents and style of the presentation the women adopted—deeply cherished and constantly enforced among them—was an outcome far from obvious. Knowledge of their previous social and cultural background would not have allowed the prediction of its forms.

The specifics of the new conditions did not shape it directly. It was a contingent accomplishment, something that acquired its meaning precisely from the fact that it could have happened differently.[29]

The women's construction of new ways of perceiving and presenting themselves was a long and emotionally charged process of trial and error. They could select only those features of their previous selves they both cherished and found workable under the new conditions. They could appropriate, often with the help of some dose of imagination, some new elements and opportunities they had encountered and which they sensed could be useful as a ground for claiming respect. The result was a form of presentation of the self that strongly characterized them as different from both their previous selves and the socially typified categories, often perceived in strongly essentialist terms, they did not want to be associated with.

The evolving form in which ex–Soviet Union women presented themselves in Alpinetown seemed to many natives, and to many other immigrants, shocking. It centered, as detailed in chapters 2 and 3, on the adoption of a highly hyperfeminine style and on the endemic adoption of displayable consumption as an index of moral worth. It was a blatantly materialistic, strongly sexualized, and intentionally conspicuous presentation of self. It also prescribed a (strongly policed) form of sexual stratification, which openly employed race and wealth as selective factors for allocating prospective partners to sharply differentiated types of interaction.

During my fieldwork, I found this way of self-presentation puzzling. It contrasted both with my own normative conceptions of the good life and with my mundane expectations of what would have been appropriate for women of their age and condition. I found it difficult to reconcile with what I knew of them, of their actual strength in self-sacrificing, of their devotion to conservative notions of family and coupledom. I could not help, moreover, finding it counterproductive. It seemed designed nearly perfectly to strengthen the stereotype of the luscious Slavic gold digger, a widespread stereotype making their position in the labor market more vulnerable as well as contributing to the public stigma that they felt was so demeaning. It ran, eventually, against the first precept for an irregular migrant: do your best to go unnoticed.

Observing them through the process, I slowly realized that the hyperfeminine, materialistic, and in many ways intentionally gross presentation of themselves was, above all, a way of drawing boundaries against both *here* and *there*. Through its elaboration, the women were carving out for themselves a social space—neither *here* nor *there*—that buffered them from the rigid expectations placed on them by people in both sending and the receiving locations. They created a space for themselves, in which they could turn their existential situation of liminality into an arena where new expectations and claims to decency could be put forward and tried out, first among themselves and subsequently with others.

Their new presentation of self drew a silent boundary against *there*, the place where they were considered *only* as mothers and breadwinners. Such a boundary created space for a sense of their lives in Alpinetown, a place where they could legitimately aspire to care for themselves, a place where they were not viewed as old babushkas but (potentially, at least) as full-fledged women, worthy of male desire and commitment. The importance of this boundary grew with time, as the women—after repaying their most pressing debts—slowly had to learn how to keep under control the ever-rising expectations of their relatives *there*.

At the same time, this presentation of the self established a boundary against *here*, protecting them from the definitions offered, sometimes with the best of intentions, by their employers, by the people they occasionally met in the streets, and by the personnel of the various philanthropic agencies they relied on. The women felt perpetually under their gaze, and they did not like what they thought that these gazes were seeing in them. They felt defined as destitute migrants arriving from backward places, badly needing either strict controls or paternalistic protection. In their role of providing low-cost care, they felt like second-class substitutes for Italian women.

Their adopted presentation of self responded by stressing that they were, above all, full-fledged, sophisticated women. They worked as care workers but they were not care workers. They were sophisticated and educated women, they were "white," and they could freely compete with the mannish Italian women.

As long as they could maintain such boundaries, they could advocate within the carved space both a notion of self-worth and a claim to a decent place in the sexual, moral, and social orders of Alpinetown. These boundaries were important for two reasons. They protected them—during their experimentation—from the risk of feeling ashamed, a ubiquitous and paralyzing possibility that cast its shadow over all their individual interactions with the new environment. It also allowed for a self-conscious alternative to the local standards, such that they could avoid the risk of humiliation endemic in trying to adopt the (largely unknown) Alpinetown styles, which Italian women seemed to master with ease.

Why did this double boundary have to be drawn in a highly sexualized and materialistic way? A starting point for solving the puzzle is to acknowledge, paraphrasing Marx, that the women crafted their own presentation of self but that they did so under conditions not of their own choosing. They had to fashion their presentation of self within the constraints and resources available in the environment they were slowly adapting to. As with any presentation of the self, these constraints consisted of three types. There were the internal constraints, the banks of experience solidified in their own previous biography, to which they could reconnect in some new way. There were the expectations of the new audiences, the anticipation of how they would be seen by others.[30]

Finally, there were the often-neglected practical requirements of visibility and performativity. The women needed something that could actually be displayed and performed on the given stage, with the props and scripts available at the concrete sites where they were located. Among what could be displayed and felt, the most important were the props that could allow them some form of everyday pleasure, a materialized form of experience as sensually different as possible from the physical reality of decaying bodies and incipient death they were constantly in contact with during their work time.

When I started meeting the very first women in the streets of Alpinetown, I soon realized they were reasonably aware of the difficulties entailed in the kind of jobs they could find and the consequences of the undocumented legal status they would fall into when their tourist visas expired. What they ignored, however, was that some features of their personal identities that they held dear would quickly prove useless in the new conditions, and that any attempt to activate them could turn into a liability. Such discovery was the original "presentational shock" they had to go through. As detailed in chapter 1, the first women arriving in Alpinetown made no mystery of being socioeconomically destitute, nor did they keep hidden what they thought about their current occupation.

The acknowledgment of these elements was part of a complex, heroic narrative that gave meaning to their tribulation and sustained their self-image. They expected to be considered European, civilized, mature, and highly educated mothers, self-sacrificing for their children. They expected that the wide gulf between what they were and what, in their words, they were forced to do for the sake of their children would command a certain degree of sympathy, if not admiration.

In their very first weeks in Alpinetown, they discovered painfully that this narrative was viable only within the small group of other women like themselves. Natives—and especially their employers—did not feel any need to distinguish them from any other migrants working in Alpinetown, nor to treat their current condition as an unfortunate, temporary one. On the contrary, they treated their being care workers naturalistically, as something literally descriptive of their being.

Nearly all the pioneer women were highly educated, with at least a college degree, who were bound to work in a very underappreciated sector. Their educational credentials were often higher than those of their employers, as they nearly always provided services for elders of the lower-middle class or even the working class. The educational system they had gone through was somewhat similar to the Italian one, thus making them expect that others could easily recognize the status attached to their qualifications.

The women quickly discovered, however, that their educational advantages did not trigger any overall respect. Some employers did not even believe they had been professionals in their previous lives, or that they were college educated.[31] Few of them cared. Some considered it an exotic curiosity, something they could mention sarcastically to visitors, even in the presence of the women. If the women mentioned their education too often, most employers would grow irritated, as if the women were being snobbish. The very few that took the women's educational and professional experience seriously feared that such a status would make it easier for them to walk away and thus started looking for replacements. The source of the women's pride was actually, in the new conditions, a liability they had to keep under control.

The women were hurt by the lack of significance of their education during the settlement process. Even if few of the women admitted it explicitly, many of them had hoped in the beginning that their employment in care work would be, although long, temporary. They had the hidden expectation, revealed only upon disappointment, that as soon as they learned the language, adjusted their legal statuses, and repaid their debts, they would be able to find jobs more congruent with their professional skills and previous lives. As soon as their knowledge of the new environment increased, they realized that the actual chances of occupational mobility were quite slim.

With very few exceptions, their educational titles were not valid in Italy. Even when it was possible, to have them recognized required an uncertain, lengthy, and expensive process. As the few women who enrolled in educational programs in Alpinetown quickly discovered, even if they acquired some Italian credentials, they would turn out to be useless, as the demand for skilled workers in Italy is limited and de facto reserved for natives.[32] Their chances of occupational mobility were nearly nonexistent.[33] The women had to accept that their educational accomplishments simply did not matter in their lives in Alpinetown, serving only as a reminder of what they had lost.

A similarly painful, and even more unexpected, discovery concerned the importance of motherhood. As their work required living in close and personal contact with some natives, often playing the role of an ersatz relative, they felt they had the right to behave toward them in personal terms. The elders they cared for and their relatives, however, were plainly not interested in knowing more than strictly necessary about them. As Nica quickly learned, her employers perceived the women's motherhood as an organizational nuisance for their daily routines, rather than as a ground for recognition. In certain cases—as particularly evident in the case of Vika—their being long-distance mothers could even be used against them, triggering little degradation ceremonies.[34] Finally, to show "excessive" attachment to their left-behind children, or to display sorrow over the distance, would make some employers fear they would not last long in their employment, thus motivating preemptive searches for substitutes.

The experience of this indifference did not become weaker when the women started widening their social circles. Actually, one of the first things learned in the group from the very first women who had found lovers in Alpinetown was that they were typically cold about whatever concerned their life before emigration and recalcitrant to any involvement with their children.

The first phase of settlement was consequently marked by the discovery that education and motherhood, two features of their selves the women held dearly, did not play well with the new audiences. They had, moreover, an unavoidable Achilles' heel: both education and motherhood in emigration are experiences of absence, and absences are never easy to display onstage. The women initially tried to present themselves as educated women and self-sacrificing mothers. They failed, and they had to acknowledge that the reactions to their dignity claims on these grounds ranged from indifference to irritation.

At the same time, as I have already described in chapter 3, the women also made another—and luckily more exciting—discovery. They discovered that in Alpinetown, they were still considered "women," potential objects of male desire. The discovery of "having returned to be women again" was very important experientially. Most women had been through many years of romantic neglect, and nearly all of them had resigned themselves to babushka status.

After a while, during our walks through the city, I could nearly physically sense the excitement and turmoil they felt, the sensual attraction of observing and being observed, the readiness to interpret even the slightest sign of attention as an indicium of sexual attraction. The elaboration of this discovery greatly enriched our internal communicative repertoire. The jocular pleasures of "being women again" in fact provided an alternative to the tragic frame employed to interpret their humiliation as care workers.

During our strolls, we could point out to each other some of the men we encountered, we could discuss how we thought they would be in bed, and we would joke about which of us had caught a man's (alleged) attention. The few times I dared to say that we were behaving like a bunch of aroused teenagers in the streets, the reactions of the women were ecstatic. Rather than feeling offended by my remarks, they thought it was an unexpected boon to be appreciated and enjoyed in full. The signs of interest they received were generalized to the entire male audience. I quickly learned that I did not dare to correct their impressions, pointing out how many (although not all) instances they interpreted as forms of sexual interest seemed to me trivial signs of mere curiosity or courtesy. The group had started building its own perceptive premises, and I could not simultaneously participate in it and challenge them.

Long before any instance of actual romance, the women started to prepare for our strolls by taking care of their appearances. Our practice of strolling for hours had been originally motivated by the lack of any other inexpensive alternative. It quickly became *also* a conscious and well-staged form of display. It started minimally, with some lipstick and well-groomed hair. It grew in frequency and sophistication, involving a whole ritualistic apparatus—posture, clothes, makeup, hairstyle—characterized by the refusal of whatever might appear mannish or ambiguous.

The performances, besides being fun and emotionally rewarding, provided the women with a new and unexpected arena for securing a ground for recognition in the new environment. It became a way to reassure themselves, even more than their largely unknown audiences, that real life, the life where an adequate amount of recognition and respect is granted, was only suspended. What the women had been unable to achieve with their claim of being educated middle-class mothers they could—perhaps—obtain by practicing their resurrected womanhood.

The elaboration of a hyperfeminine self, moreover, allowed them to draw two additional boundaries that were very important to them. First, the traits—traditionalism, rurality, modesty, and humility—usually attached by natives to the image of the foreign care worker were radically at odds with the conspicuous and hyperfeminine presentation the women were progressively shaping for themselves. It helped them to stress both that they could not be reduced to their work *and* that they were different from the previous (and better established in the local labor market) waves of immigrant care workers.

Their presentation of self acquired a sense of vindication on their claim to respect on what they conceived as racial grounds, as it opposed them to the many domestic workers from the Philippines and Sri Lanka. It also established a difference between the women—civilized urban dwellers—and the many domestic workers from Romania and Albania, whom the women considered impossibly rural, "people just out of the stable."

All these immigrant groups enjoyed, in fact, a better status than the women could aspire to at the time. Besides the fact that Romanians would soon become EU citizens, the large majority of these groups had been in Alpinetown for many more years, spoke Italian fluently, had been able to adjust their legal status, and had usually left live-in care work to shift to the more prestigious hourly paid work for a pool of employers. Besides their better occupational and legal standing, they were groups who had acquired a secure footing in the urban environment, with many reunited families and their own associations and churches.

Through their performances, challenging the modest and humble presentation of themselves that had marked the previous settlement of other groups of domestic workers, the women were clearly compensating for their comparative disadvantage (as well as advancing a claim based on what they understood as their more fair-skinned, Caucasian superiority).

The performances, at the same time, allowed them to draw an equally important boundary against Italian women they saw as mannish. In fact, if a main focus of the Eastern European immigrant women's performances was the male gaze, an equally important process was making disparaging comparisons between their increasingly flamboyant attire and that of the Italian "half-women" who crossed their path. They increasingly categorized Italian women as selfish, stressed, and unable to love and take care of their relatives, and they assumed that their sloppy and androgynous style revealed precisely this character.

The women elaborated a very simple and effective framework: The Italian women's (perceived) unfeminine style was the epiphany of their lack of respect for and devotion to their husbands and, more generally, their households. The boundary with Italian women became, with time, increasingly moralized. They defined more and more explicitly the difference between Eastern European and Italian women as deeper than a matter of style or taste. They interpreted it as a contrast between real, deserving women—who, all their difficulties notwithstanding, were still women who took care of their appearances, making efforts to uphold their womanhood—and masculine, selfish women who, although wealthy, failed to perform their most basic gender duties.

The importance given by the women to the male gaze and the boundary drawn against the Italian women sustained each other. The women started to claim in a ritual fashion that Italian men were attracted to them precisely because they recognized in their superior femininity the marks of passionate love and wifely devotion that Italian women sorely lacked. Hyperfemininity had become an oppositional stance that supported both a claim to respect and a legitimation of mating as a form of social mobility.

Consumption became a dominant element of their self-image along a similar, and intertwined, dynamic. The adoption of a strongly consumerist stance was another way in which the women drew a boundary against Italians, most frequently symbolized by the stereotype of the stingy employer who, albeit wealthy, was not interested in acquiring "nice things." They did not deserve the world of plenty they inhabited, and to which they were oblivious, taking it for granted.

The immigrant women, on the contrary, had the right to be scrupulously and materially proud of whatever they acquired, as proof of their current achievements as well as indicia of their right to claim a better future. The various ways in which the goods the women acquired could be displayed was an important area for their attempt to shape their presentation of self, detaching them from the role of care workers and supporting their claims and aspirations to deserve better.

In the beginning, the women were largely undifferentiated. They treated each other as mothers and regarded such a role as egalitarian. As shown in chapter 2, initially, their expenditure was nearly exclusively concentrated on their sending areas, and the choices made were remarkably similar. Going on Sundays to the minivans to send money and goods to the homeland was the most important act of the week. It was important to them that they could do it together, at approximately the same time, as the physical act of sending their parcels could be—and was—observed by the other women, busy in doing the same. They could show that they were good mothers and reassure each other that their emigration was not a failure.

From the beginning, however, there were also goods that could not be displayed. These were the goods that, although accepted, should not be displayed, such as the (usually secondhand) goods that many, likely most, women received from their employers. The women usually accepted the offers, as they were goods the women desired but could not afford. Such gifts, however, challenged the group norm that employers—as distinct from the elderly persons they were caring for—always had to be described among them as spoiled brats, cold and mean people. As Snizhana learned at great cost, these goods had to be kept strictly private.

Conspicuous consumption became an important dimension of their presentation of self in a subsequent phase, sandwiched in between the initial phase of settlement (in which they had literally nothing to spend on themselves) and the times during which they faced more long-term choices, such as renting a flat. The women suddenly realized that they had some room for consumption for their own use. They used this opportunity mostly for sustaining their new practices of self-presentation.

Their consumption, in fact, was highly selective. For example, they modified only marginally the quality of the food and drinks we consumed together. Besides very cheap cell phones, they did not invest in electronics, even when having some items would have helped maintain contact with their relatives or alleviate their solitude during the long days in the house of the elderly they assisted. The increased consumption was in the beginning nearly all focused on cosmetics and clothes—in touchable and actionable stage props useful for sustaining their feminine identity.

In the consumption process, the role of the group as master of ceremonies was particularly evident. As shown in chapter 2, the women maintained for the new goods the same rituals they had established previously for the goods they were buying for their children and relatives. Shopping was not complete without physically presenting newly acquired goods to the other women.

The women would meet, each carrying their shopping bags. One of them would begin taking out one item at the time to circulate among the other women. Clothes would be touched and tried out, perfumes smelled, creams and lipsticks opened and admired for their texture and color. In the meantime, the proud owner would tell the story of how it had been bought, with whom, and what she had found intriguing about it. The other women would nod appreciatively before the owner returned the item to the bag, taking out a new item to show off.

When the first woman had completed the show, another one could start with her bags. Even with a small number of women, this ritual could easily take hours, during which the women could celebrate together—

with all their senses—their strength and capacity to improve themselves and their condition. The presentation of the goods bought to be shipped home was mostly meaningful to the women as a way to reassure each other that their emigration was working and their relatives were living better.

The celebration of the goods bought for personal consumption, although similar in the ritual procedure, had a different, aspirational meaning. The women perceived the goods they acquired as strengthening their capacity to perform adequately in front of a male audience, and they performed at the same time in front of the other women, entrusting them with certifying the quality and appropriateness of their consumption, of making it tangible proof of their resistance to the condition of *lavaculi*. Through the weekly display of their newly acquired goods, they supported each other in their willingness to work toward further social mobility.[35]

In sum, the hyperfeminine and materialistic style adopted by the women in their presentation of self was an interactional process grounded in the carving of an interstitial social space able to shield them from the competing pressures of *here* and *there*. The experience of such a safe space was important to the women because it sustained them as members of an aspirational subculture, laying a claim to an amount of recognition and appreciation regardless of their positioning at the very bottom of the migration pecking order. And because it allowed them to distinguish themselves both from their occupation and from other groups—Italian women, other immigrants, babushkas—they feared being assimilated. As the space they had generated for themselves had different moral and aesthetic criteria, the women felt that experimenting within it was possible without incurring constant humiliation.

Hyperfemininity and conspicuous consumption were not necessarily the only elements of potential identity the women cherished: the roles of educated women, of mothers and of wives, would have been at least as meaningful and desirable. These latter roles, however, were experiences of absence. Womanhood and consumption, on the contrary, could be successfully, corporeally exhibited in Alpinetown. They had the advantage of being eminently displayable and performable.

Hyperfemininity was something they could work on, something inscribable on their bodies that they could feed through specific sensual practices. As a never-ending transformational project, it provided a daily confirmation of not giving in to what they feared most, of not giving up on the claim that they deserved better. Publicly, visible consumption provided an equally important arena for protecting themselves from the uncertainty of the migration process, as well as providing physical, sensually experienced feedback about their progress.

## Interaction, Rational Adaptation, and Culture

Struggling to make sense of my observations about the evolving hyperfeminine, materialistic style increasingly adopted by the women, I often discussed with my supervisors and colleagues my interpretations of what was going on among the women. I tried to explain to them what I thought was the development of a localized aspirational subculture, geared to insulate the women from their current occupational status as well as to stimulate them to keep alive a sense of entitlement to a better future. As often happens in academic discussions, many of them suggested on many occasions that I could be utterly wrong. Some of them advanced two alternative schemes, which roughly correspond to the current prevailing divide in social and psychological accounts of the migration experience.

Some colleagues claimed that what the women were doing should be understood as a form of rational adaptation. The hyperfeminine presentation of the self involved instrumental activities targeted at signaling to potential partners their presence and availability. The romantic market in Alpinetown was clearly shaped by asymmetric information, and the women, in such a view, were simply sending a message that some of their still unknown individual characteristics could be valuable to potential Italian male "buyers."[36]

Some others suggested instead that the women's presentation of self was a legacy of their pre-emigration experiences, a transplant of their inherited "culture." What I was observing was actually only the reproduction and selective adaptation of the notions of womanhood and consumption they had been socialized to appreciate. The women were simply transplanting them in a new context, following their embodied tastes, oblivious to the fact that they could interpret *here* in a different, and maybe counterproductive, way.[37]

Both challenges to my view, located in powerful theoretical traditions, are suggestive and elegant. I want consequently to spell out explicitly why I think the mechanisms they invoke are necessary—but far from sufficient—elements in explaining what I actually observed and accounted for in this book. They cannot substitute for a historical and localized interactional analysis.

The suggestion that the new presentation of the self had an instrumental meaning—an advertisement geared to promote contacts with potential partners—was certainly plausible. The women were not living in a delusion. They rightly understood, much better than I had myself, that they had some chance to participate in a romantic market; in Alpinetown they were not considered too old to be women, maybe even wives. They also rightly perceived that there were indeed a number of potential male partners—usually older, usually less educated, but still living a somewhat middle-class lifestyle—who were attracted to them. Even if they tended to overestimate the size of this niche, it nevertheless existed and provided a real possibility of advancement.

When some of the women started having personal contact with Italian men, they correctly reported that their potential partners were either long-term singles, divorced, or unhappily married. These men were attracted to them precisely because they expected them to be different from "Italian women." They also realized that their fair-skinned complexion and Caucasian identity could offer a comparative advantage against the women of other groups in what they perceived as a competition for scarce resources.

To acknowledge that the women wanted to signal something, however, does not imply accepting an instrumentalist interpretation of their performances. During my fieldwork, I easily observed many elements that, while compatible with the desire of being identified as valuable women, were definitely not instrumental. The first is that the hyperfeminine frenzy the women stimulated in each other ramified in several private practices, which were known only by the woman who enacted them.

The best example is the use of the thong, briefly discussed in chapter 2, which many women used as a talisman to protect them from the desexualizing environment of care work. Its value was precisely in the fact that it was unobservable to outsiders, while still being there to remind the women that their being was different from their occupation.

The same consideration applies to the attraction for the extremely high-heeled shoes Olga bought in her first visit to Pittarello, setting an example many other women subsequently imitated, as soon as they could afford some voluptuary expenses. These were shoes that the women could not expect to use in their current lives and that actually—to my knowledge—have never been used in public. They were shoes, to quote Olga, the women could use "only in bed." Their importance was not in their possible use as props for their current performances but rather in the fact that acquiring them was felt as preparation for a life in which, indeed, such high-heeled shoes could be worn as a matter of course.

A second element standing against any interpretation of their presentations as rational strategy is that the hyperfeminine presentation was of equal importance on occasions in which a male audience could be expected *and* on the strictly in-group occasions, in which no man would ever participate. As the women were living in an economy of scarcity, props were never wasted lightly. Still, I never noticed a significant difference in the investment carried out for preparing themselves for external or internal performances. The hyperfeminine, defiant outlook was as important in interaction among the women—where it expressively reassured themselves of their self-worth and aspirations—as it was in public interactions, where it could *also* work as a signaling mechanism.

An instrumental interpretation, moreover, fails to account for the fact that the women were aware of the fact that native men perceived many of these performances as utterly inappropriate, as "pushy" or overbearing, as a somewhat aggressive use of the public space. If hyperfemininity signaled anything to Italian men, it was the idea they were "cheap" women, hardly material for building the kind of long-term relationship the women aspired to.

If the signaling hypothesis were correct, there should be some kind of fit developing over time between the specifics of the women's presentations and the criteria employed by potential partners to interpret the signal. In fact, even when a certain number of relationships came into being, there was still no fit between what was practiced in-group and what the Italian partners expected from a potentially viable companion. The women were well aware of their potential partners' expectations, thus ruling out ignorance.

In my days as a chaperone, when I accompanied the women on their first dates with men they hoped could become serious about them, I observed that the women regularly dressed down in comparison to what they used to practice during our strolls. An integral part of becoming a *signora*, moreover, was to drop out of any kind of hyperfemininity altogether, switching to more low-key and less cocky appearances. The meaning of hyperfeminine performances and blatant consumption must consequently be understood internally—for what these activities contributed to the individual women and to the group—rather than as rational dating and mating strategies.

The other alternative explanation often presented to me was that what I was observing could be explained in terms of previous socialization, as transplanted habitus, which also initially seemed quite plausible. As I explained in the latter part of the introduction, the scarcity of consumer goods and the genderless sexism of Soviet times were two endemic topoi in the women's recollection of their youth. Many of them, moreover, had participated actively in the sociocultural changes of the transition, working as shuttle traders of consumer goods and adhering to the new Eastern European ideals of femininity that rejected both rurality and communism as gray and unsexy.[38]

The idea of a subcultural transplant sounded even more plausible as the women themselves used it as legitimation for what we were doing. In answering my thousand queries, they usually replied matter-of-factly that it was just how a "real woman should dress" or "that's the way we do it in Ukraine (or Moldova, or Belarus, or Georgia, or . . .)." During my trips to Ukraine and Moldova, I could readily observe many external similarities between the notions of feminine beauty endorsed in the two contexts. I have no doubt many of the props used in Alpinetown were clearly rooted in homeland subcultures.

But the frequent use of a largely homeland repertoire, in terms of props and aesthetic criteria, did not determine the meaning that their performances had in Alpinetown. As I discovered during my trips to their hometowns, the ways in which the same repertoire could be enacted in the two contexts gave a different meaning even to relatively similar presentation of the self.

Throughout my fieldwork, I often wanted to have a chance to observe the women in their sending contexts. This wish was unfulfilled for a long time. Most women were unauthorized migrants and thus unable to travel back to their countries of origin. I was able to travel back with some of the women once they acquired legal status, when they received final papers through one of the amnesties launched by the Italian government. Participating in these trips, from the buying of gifts for those back home to some of the actual visits, was one of the most interesting and moving experiences in my fieldwork.

The trips represented the first times the women could reconnect with their children or grandchildren—some of them fairly grown up by then. It was also the first time they could see the outcome of their emigration, in terms of flats being bought or restored, household appliances being used, family statuses enhanced. Going along with them, I quickly realized the loss of significance of hyperfeminine rituals during the times we spent there.[39] Most of the things that they had always presented to me as essential in Alpinetown, in terms of dress code, makeup, and defiant attitude, became less important.

The display of womanhood, of course, did not disappear. But it was enacted in a remarkably, although subtly, different way. Shopping remained an important practice. It was, however, a different kind of experience. A main activity during these trips home for all the women who had daughters was going shopping with them, a process through which they tried to restore a channel of mother-daughter transmission of proper womanhood. Dresses, cosmetics, and underwear were among the most common gifts for female relatives. Moreover, nearly all the return trips implied some kind of event—usually a night out—in which all the tricks and tools I had learned in Alpinetown were strictly enforced and expected, with an even more frantic energy. On these occasions, the overall style of the performance was not controversial. It was celebratory, a performance targeted only and especially to family and friends. It was part of showing themselves as members of dignified households.

I also noticed the women were much less concerned with their everyday appearances—they, including Iryna, often went to throw out the garbage *without* wearing makeup. They policed the other women (and me) very rarely. They accepted a more complex and pluralistic vision of the womanhood ideal, for example, wearing discreet colors or proudly endorsing items of Italian fashion they had previously despised. In their hometowns, womanhood could be performed without so much hyper-feminine effort.

My first reaction to the observation of these differences was to attribute them to the effects of local systems of social control. I had heard many complaints about the gossip in their towns and villages concerning the low morality of the women while they were abroad. I was also aware—from my reading of local newspapers and debates on the internet—that emigrant women in Ukraine and Moldova were often portrayed as more interested in consumption than in family integrity and, not infrequently, as loose women. I thus assumed their change could be explained as an attempt to ward off criticism by adopting a low-key, modest way of presenting themselves.

My observations did not really support my speculations. The women I was travelling with were neither modest nor low-key. They took active pride in bolstering the level of consumption during their stays at home, often indulging in acts that were openly instances of conspicuous consumption. Their shopping performances, however, were different and more relaxed than in Alpinetown. They knew they were considered big spenders, enjoying a kind of superior economic citizenship. They felt at ease in navigating the local shopping scene, which they knew well, and took for granted that shopkeepers and sales assistants would treat them with respect. The difficulties and humiliations of their working life were far away and hidden, while the level of consumption they could guarantee their families was highly visible and provided a strong source of recognition.

The result was a significant change in the style of their consumption, less based in constant comparisons and more oriented to a savvy, judicious choice. While shopping, they were not concerned with being identified as destitute *lavaculi*. They wanted to be understood as sophisticated, expert consumers.

The decrease in hyperfeminine performances, moreover, had nothing to do with privacy concerns about their romantic lives in Italy. The women did not hesitate to show off the existence of an Italian mate, if they had one (and sometimes even if they did not), and to stress publicly his socioeconomic status. They would call him from the tables of the local café, thus ensuring widespread publicity about their Italian man. They often jokingly invited other women of their circle to emigrate, luring them with the chance of finding new and better partners. Some of them openly criticized the Slavic partners of their stay-behind childhood friends, often causing minor—or major—irritations and even a few quarrels.

I slowly concluded that my mistake had been looking in the wrong direction. Possibly because of my own prejudices about the economic "backwardness" of the sending areas, I had tried to explain the differences I noticed by the presence, in their hometowns, of mechanisms that repressed certain ways of acting, thinking, and feeling. The differences could be explained much better by focusing on the mechanisms that granted the women *there* both a larger and more complex panel of identities and a deeper distance from the polluting features of their lives in Alpinetown.

While in Italy, they constantly had to reaffirm their womanhood as a way to detach themselves from the roles of care workers, absent mothers, lovers of married men. During their trips home, on the contrary, the hyperfeminine emphasis could become weaker—and the differences from the style of Italian women less relevant—because it was just one item on a much larger actionable menu. In their hometowns, the women returned as mothers, in a physical, displayable way. They returned as respected members of (now) middle-class households. As the distance helped to keep latent the fact that many of their relationships involved married men, they could present themselves as satisfied women. They had many more elements to draw upon, and they enjoyed the greater narrative choices they could use.

The strongest element against the hypothesis of hyperfemininity and materialism as transplanted habitus can be found in the fact that both phenomena changed considerably over time. The women have demonstrated a remarkable degree of plasticity. When the original group slowly differentiated along several paths, most women changed their presentation of the self accordingly.

Small but sizable groups of women became *signore*, a process that has required leaving behind—as Dasha had done—much of the distinctive, defiant attitude toward assimilation into the middle-class Italian pattern of subtly understated femininity and rationalized consumption. Some, like Natasha and Nastenka, who entered relationships with men the group regarded as unsuitable dropped from the group altogether and adopted different—much more individualized—ways of presenting themselves. The women, like Iryna or Maria, who have become the backbone of the Eastern European "immigrant communities"—the networks of families with Eastern European men and reunited children—maintained many of the props and scripts I was introduced to, but they shaped them into performances now reserved for collective occasions. Within the community, the same props came to signify the proud standing of a woman as a member of a dignified household.

Many other women, particularly those who remained in live-in care work, slowly adjusted to local expectations about proper care workers' presentation of the self (and to their own aging), often renouncing any flamboyant attire to return to a somewhat babushka-like iconicity. A few, like Olga and Sofia, maintained the hyperfeminine, defiant outlook. Nearly all the daughters of the women I know appear identical, at least to the adult eye, to other working-class teenagers in Alpinetown.

The specific presentation of the self I have chronicled has thus played an important function in the process of settlement, helping them to become "different people." Far from being a habitus transplanted, determining the entire immigrant career of the women, the hyperfeminine performances have played a transitional role for managing their liminal conditions, sustaining the women—and the group—while allowing experiments with many other ways of presenting themselves. Unsurprisingly, their rise and demise have had strong implication also for the dynamic and structural importance of the group itself.

## The Natural History of the Immigrant Group

As the ex–Soviet Union immigrant women changed their ways of presenting themselves in Alpinetown, the structure and functioning of the group in which they participated also evolved. The two evolutions were closely intertwined.

For a long period, the group absorbed the near totality of the women's free time. Their congregations created sites where they could feel at ease, protected from embarrassment. Peers provided the crews necessary for most of the individuals' performances of new selves. The group was the backstage where they could design, discuss, and innovate their selves without revealing themselves to unwanted third parties. It was the only audience available for their enactment of some highly cherished roles. Collaboratively the women provided information, support, and guidance—and, when possible, material aid—both to newly arrived women and, during crises, to those more established. The group provided the women with many inexpensive opportunities for luxuriant, demotic entertainment, a precious balance to the many hours they spent alone, entrusted with the care of old, frail, often dying bodies.[40]

Collectively they offered each other sympathetic reactions during times of feeling lonely, destitute, or overburdened. The group provided recognition and admiration for whatever achievements the women could show off. Before participating in the women's gatherings, I had never felt such familiar warmth among a relatively large group of people who had, in fact, come to know each other quite recently. Aside from work, the group was the main anchor of their lives.

At the same time, their gatherings were not free festivals. The group expected a high degree of loyalty from its members and policed them quite intrusively, at least in certain matters. As Snizhana learned with her dishwasher, as I have told in chapter 1, and as I myself experienced in my naïve encounter with Amir, recounted in chapter 2, the risk of ostracism, of expulsion from the group, was an ever-present possibility, which could sometimes be exercised preemptively.

In their rituals of displaying acquired goods, the women granted each other recognition and respect, but they also expected a moral monopoly on the validation of each single shopping—and dressing, and working, and mating . . . —decision. None was above the judgement of the group. Iryna was surely among the women who enjoyed, since the very beginning, more prestige and status in the group. Still, when she decided to date—and subsequently marry—Avel, she had to go through a wideranging ordeal of unsympathetic comments, prophecies of doom, and nasty jokes that seriously compromised her standing. Any woman felt entitled to treat her paternalistically, degrading her to the role of a novice.

Even on lesser matters, women quite constantly observed and criticized each other, pressuring errant members back into line. The group assumed and constantly reproduced an expectation of total and full-fledged similarity among the women, with very little room for variations in understanding. I was often shocked to realize that no individual leader triggered or was enforcing the tight discipline. Some women, of course, were keener on policing than others. But overall it was a decentralized process, where any single member could be—and, surely, many of them have been at one time or another—the enforcer.

The combination of precious moral support with possibilities for experimenting with new senses of self and strict enforcement of group identities explains the strength of the group and its capacity to provide in difficult conditions an infrastructure able to support the development of a subculture that was at the same time oppositional and aspirational. Precisely through providing such a breeding ground it also paved the way to its own demise, its segmentation into a variety of migration trajectories, each shaped by a different morality and aesthetic.

When the group was first constituted through encounters in the streets, it provided the women with a strong sense of empowerment. It provided them with a touchable sense that they were not alone, a feared feeling that was particularly strong precisely in the few hours of free time in which they could not help realizing that they had nothing to do. Above all, it provided them with protection from the discomfort of not knowing the rules of appropriate behavior.

Before the group, the fear of shame had been a main obstacle in any interaction in their new environment. The women feared whomever they encountered would recognize them as *lavaculi* and judge them accordingly. These fears did not abate spontaneously with repeated interactions because women could suspect—sometimes correctly—that apparent kindness masked a sense of condescending superiority.

The fear of shame, moreover, was bound to reappear constantly, as I documented in chapters 2 and 5, whenever the women entered a new site in Alpinetown. The group protected the women from such risk in at least two ways. It supplied companions, crews with which the women could venture into new sites or enact performances in the public space that, just because shared among peers, had to be judged through internally generated criteria of respectability and worth. It provided, moreover, an oppositional subculture that allocated the blame for any unsuccessful interaction to the Italians involved, thus sanitizing the shame and turning it into an expression of oppression and not of interactional incompetence.[41]

Equally importantly, the group provided the women with a comparative space that could help them against the shame inflicted *there* by the ever-rising expectations of their stay-behind relatives. When acting in isolation, they were always exposed to the guilt of not sending enough remittances, of not being sacrificing enough mothers. Many relatives— often their mothers, to whom they usually entrusted their children— felt it was their right to complain openly of not receiving enough. Often, their relatives would autonomously raise the level of expenses they incurred, asking the women to foot the bill. Before the group existed, most women felt powerless. Any refusal would make them feel heartless. Within the group, they could observe what the other women were doing and develop an understanding of what should be a proper amount of support.

The group heavily policed the women, pushing them to sacrifice for their children. At the same time, it policed, equally strongly, the instances of "excessive" sacrifice, stressing often that their relatives, otherwise unrestrained, "would treat you as a cash machine." It enforced a sense of proper motherhood that prescribed strong, but more emotionally detached, support for their relatives, willing to provide generously for their children but also to prevent them from being "spoiled" by their remittances.[42] The group functioned as a buffer zone between *here* and *there* that was able to balance the shaming power of both localities.

The same double reference was crucial in the ability of the group to sustain the women in their aspirations concerning social mobility both *there* and *here*, in strengthening their upward social mobility in the sending area and in managing prospectively their experiences of downward mobility in Alpinetown. These ambitions, which are key motivating factors in any process of social mobility, were for the women particularly challenging, as they required the capacity for *not* learning from the environment, from the myriad of everyday disappointments, in order to preserve and reproduce an investment in a different future.[43]

As for their orientations to those left *there*, the group provided the women an appreciation for their efforts and recognition of their achievements. The praise and admiration they conferred on the other women for their remittances was a vicarious substitute of the boosting in social status the women expected to achieve in their place of origin, but which they could not experience directly. The messages the women exchanged with each other confirmed they were indeed experiencing upward mobility in their hometowns, thus strengthening their resolve.

As for *here*, the group allowed the women to confirm to each other that—their current marginality notwithstanding—they would eventually be able to acquire respect and recognition in the future, if they tried hard enough. The group provided a shell, an armor against the current polluting conditions. It also strengthened the willingness to advance claims to respect, the capacity of every single woman—no matter how destitute—to construct in time a new powerfully attractive self. It was a deeply democratic ideal: within each woman, they preached to each other, there was a *signora* waiting to be appreciated.

The group supported the women in their difficulties in thousands of small ways. During our meetings, women could cry, complain, display weaknesses, and even be mean with each other. What they could not do, however, was display any instance of behavior that could be read as a form of surrender, as acceptance of their current condition as an inescapable fate. They had to believe they had the power, if they kept trying, to change themselves and their lives.

The willingness to sustain the aspirational projects of the women, even at considerable cost, was particularly evident in the strictly policed norm against mating with inappropriate men. In the group, few rules were as systematically enforced as the ones, described in chapter 4, restricting relations with *chórnenky* to strictly sexual liaisons. The norm clearly was clearly inspired by a strategy of social closure on "racial" grounds.[44] Through such interdiction, the women advanced a claim to "white" status, and consequently a right to be chosen as long-term partners by Italians, not for their being exotic—as is often recorded in many instances of female migration—but for their being attractive according to Italians' own standards.

The women conferred much importance on their Caucasian appearance. They never passed up an occasion to stress how some of their phenotypical features—being often blonde, tall, with a fair complexion and blue or green eyes—could make them not only easily pass as Italian but also be recognized as attractive in the traditional local gender stratification. It reinforced the idea that Italian men could easily conceive of them as prospective partners.

The effect of treating Caucasian appearance as normative preserved the aspirations to become a *signora* in a second, more empirically evident, sense. In Alpinetown, the number of potential Italian partners they could hope to date was small, and reaching them was difficult. The number of potential immigrant partners was large and it was much easier to enter into contact with them, as they attended mostly the same urban sites. The norm consequently worked as a barrier against the easiest mating option. By sustaining the norm, the women pushed each other to keep trying, against all reasonable odds, to reach the status of *signora*, renouncing other, potentially more accessible, alternatives.

The internal cohesion of the group, and its ability to sustain and police the aspirational project of the women, seemed to me a taken-for-granted feature of their lives. The women were so deeply embedded in the activities of the group that for a long time I did not expect it to morph into something else in the medium term. It did.

In the arc of a few years, as I document in chapters 4 and 5, the group that had attained a well-defined existence, with clear boundaries, repetitive practices, shared symbols, and enforceable norms, has slowly dissolved—not with a bang, but with a whimper—into a galaxy of individuals and cliques connected by weak links or disjointed altogether. Each of them has established different forms of settlement in Alpinetown and differentiated elements of personal understanding and public presentation.

At the same time that it appeared quite powerful, as I documented in chapters 4 and 5, the group faced some major challenges. One of them can be identified, following Durkheim, in the increase of the moral density of the group. The group was born when the Eastern European women in the Alpinetown areas numbered a few dozen, and it gained strength through their involvement in the enactment of frequent face-to-face rituals. The rapid increase in the number of women—today in the thousands—led inevitably to a proliferation of different sites, which slowly developed their own differential membership: each would frequent some but not other sites. Further differentiation grew out of the fact that different women found themselves in different phases of their immigration biographies. Over time the set was composed of different immigration cohorts. From one to the other, individuals increasingly had vastly different migration seniorities and different levels of knowledge about the new environment. To integrate them into a single unified social life became increasingly difficult.

Equally important, if paradoxically, the demise of the group was made possible by its own previous strengths. Shielding the women from the paralyzing effects of shame and pressuring them to maintain and pursue their aspirations to more stable and respected forms of belonging, the group played an important role in easing their experiences in the new location. The differential effects of these experiences have in turn led to a growing diversity in the women's everyday life.

When the group was born, the women led very similar lives, thus legitimizing a strong mechanical form of solidarity with identical norms meant to regulate similar aspirations. Over time, however, the women travelled diverging paths, each embodying differentiated experiences, up to the point at which these experiences could no longer be regulated by the decentralized enforcement of an undifferentiated set of norms and models of behavior.

Besides the changes in occupation and housing, chronicled in chapter 1, equally important relational differentiation followed the experience of new shopping practices, narrated in chapter 2, and in their romantic lives, recounted in chapters 3 and 4. Some of these transformations required the women to leave the group as a matter of course, as in the case of the *signore*, or in a more suffered way, as it was for the women who mated with inappropriate males. In these cases, loss of membership in the group was an on/off affair. With other processes, such as the adoption of specific forms of shopping practices or the pressure to give priority to more family-friendly forms of sociability, the weakening of participation was a more uneven and impalpable process.

Their attempts to secure a foothold in the associational and religious life of Alpinetown, analyzed in chapter 5, led to a decline in the mechanic solidarity among the women. The local opportunity structure was predicated on a way to recognize immigrant identities that did not fit with the ways in which the women had self-organized previously. These principles of association overrode those created autonomously by the women themselves. Over time, newly arriving immigrant women could rely on specific personal networks and organizations, no longer needing to identify with the informal group.

The strength and power of the group had been impressive. Still, there was no formal mandate or external subsidy behind it. Its participatory life was wholly dependent on implicit, intimately felt spiritual and/or emotional needs. As an informal group evolving from makeshift sociability, it had functioned only thanks to the willingness of the individual women to remake it constantly, to submit to it, and to be eager to provide materials for its rituals. The increasing diversity in the paths travelled by different groups of women could not help weakening its very foundations.

The demise of the group may appear to be a dreary end for what had been such an important source of support for the women. This, however, would romanticize the women's experience, not only because the group was born under conditions of material scarcity and social isolation that are today—in their current, more prosaic lives—markedly improved. Rather, I see its natural history as typical of a transitional institution, which plays an important part in the process of settlement precisely because it facilitates the transition of the participants out of their liminal status toward more stable, albeit not necessarily happier, statuses.

The group allowed the women to develop a presence in Alpinetown that, just because it was purposefully defiant and distinctive, absorbed most risks of shame, thus making the women less averse to experiment with new possibilities in the new environment. It helped pioneers establish routes in the new location that later newcomers experienced as natural, taken-for-granted strategies. The contours of the group's natural history confirm, in a very micro, interactional way, the original discovery of the Chicago school that ethnic institutions—precisely through their distinctive, and sometimes defiant, modalities of operations—are not to be seen as an obstacle to integration in the host society but rather as a possible channel toward it. I hope my book has both vindicated the importance of this kind of transient institution and conveyed the knowledge that its life is by no means a trivial interactional accomplishment.

# Acknowledgments

When I open a new book, the acknowledgments are usually the first thing I read. I look for names I know. I fantasize about those I've never heard of. I always wonder if they really helped the author in writing the book. I always suspect authors overstretch their gratitude.

Yet my list is definitely long and, still, understretched. I simply would not have been able to write this book—and pester my subjects for so long—without the help of many colleagues, friends, and institutions. I want to thank Marzio Barbagli, my supervisor for the dissertation that started this project. I'm thankful to the graduate program and the people in it that have helped me all along: Ivano Bison, Raimondo Catanzaro, Mario Diani, Gianfranco Poggi, and Giuseppe Sciortino. The fellowship I subsequently enjoyed, by the Istituto Cattaneo in Bologna and by the Research Fund of the Provincia Autonoma di Trento, paid my bills for many years, keeping the project going.

Ethnography fieldwork requires entering the field, but also being able to leave it. I am grateful to the Fulbright Commission, the Urban Ethnography Workshop at Yale University, and the Institute for Migration, Diversity and Welfare of Malmo University for hosting me when I needed time for getting out, reading, thinking, and (painfully) writing.

This book would have not been the same without the long discussions with Jeffrey Alexander, Elijah Anderson, Jack Katz, and Philip Smith. I need also to thank Nancy Anderson, Asher Colombo, Ronald Eyerman, Nicholas Harney, Nadya Jaworski, David Kertzer, Peter Kivisto, Igor Kon, Claudio Giunta, Elisa Martini, Grey Osterud, Chiara Saraceno,

Eleonora Vlach, and Paul Willis for having read drafts of my chapters. Jack Katz has been the greatest commentator, adviser, and critic an author could hope (or fear) to encounter. He has patiently read draft after draft of my work. He has always identified all the weak spots and always pointed out whatever needed to be rewritten. If the world were ruled by justice, he would be listed as a coauthor.

The Department of Psychology and Cognitive Sciences at the University of Trento is the closest empirical approximation to the interdisciplinary ideal that many predicate (yet few try to practice). It gave me the possibility to meet colleagues from diverse disciplines, with different perspectives. With its academic organization strongly oriented toward research, it has supported me at every step. I am particularly thankful to Maria Paola Paladino, Remo Job, Paola Venuti, Silvia Fargion, and Jeroen Vaes for their support and friendship.

The libraries at Yale and Trento have been key to my work all these years. I love these places, and I am deeply grateful for all the help I received from their librarians in finding rare or unlikely texts.

Boris Cvajner, Gorka Ostojić, and Borut Cvajner have always been living examples of how migrant family ties can be emotionally and intellectually stimulating over and through distance.

Decades ago, when I was thinking about starting this project, I suddenly saw the moment of my greatness flicker. And, in short, I was afraid. I spent weeks uncertain and feeling helpless, wondering if I should really do it. Until I met somebody who just laughed and told me, "Why just not to try to do it and see if it works? It could be fun." As in the worst chick lit, many years later the guy became my partner and the clumsy father of our son Arjuna. Thanks for those laughs.

I am worried about how many people I have forgotten. If you do not find your name here, please do not be disappointed. I promise I will include you in the following editions.

And finally, this work would not exist without the countless hours that so many women have dedicated to me. My greatest thanks go to them. Дякую! Благодарю вас! მადლობა! Дзякуй!

# Appendix:
# How I Conducted
# My Study

Ethnographic research often has humble, unexpected starting points. Ethnographic projects may be already well on their way when they start being recognizable as purposeful, carefully designed, intentional activities. In my case, the roots of a long ethnographic experience lie in several fortuitous encounters in the streets of Alpinetown that started at the end of the 1990s, years before the formal beginning of my research.

My initial encounter with post-Soviet women migrants was an unexpected but felicitous occurrence. I had studied Russian in my youth but had not had many occasions to practice it since then. One day, while window-shopping in the center of Alpinetown, I heard two women—Zoryana and Olga—speaking between themselves something that reminded me of Russian. I stopped for some small talk, more concerned with how rusty my knowledge of the language was than with the information I was acquiring.

The two women, however, were as surprised as I was. They said they were Ukrainians, and they had arrived independently of one another a few weeks before, after a short spell in Naples, to work as live-in care workers for elderly couples in Alpinetown. They too were recent acquaintances. That day was actually the first stroll they were taking together. They asked who I was and why I was able to speak what they (rather charitably) said was good Russian. I told them I was Croatian, that I had studied Russian when I was young, and that I had arrived in Alpinetown in the early 1990s holding a refugee visa.[1]

We decided to have a stroll together along the main streets of the town. I was excited to have a chance to practice my Russian, and they were equally interested in meeting someone who was, from their point of view, a longtime resident. We talked, and we decided we would meet again.

In the subsequent weeks, I came across other women like them in the streets of Alpinetown. I discovered that, as with Zoryana and Olga, it was enough to say a few words in Russian to start a friendly conversation.

One of the things I most vividly remember about those first months was the fact that the women often didn't realize there were other people from the same place of origin in town. One day, while walking with Olga, we met another woman with whom I had had a brief conversation some days before, Lavra. When I introduced her to Olga, they quickly realized they were actually from the same town on the border between Ukraine and Moldova. They had no idea that their emigration had taken place roughly at the same time.

Month after month, their number was growing. When I met the first of the women in the streets, local administration and philanthropic agencies dealing with immigrants did not even have a category for them, as there was practically no (recent) previous history of migration from the states of the former USSR to Italy. When they had to fill out a form, clerks and volunteers would often count them as Polish or Romanian.[2]

When, years later, I officially started my research project, their *recorded* number was already more than three hundred, to which a sizable number of irregular migrants could be added. In 2018, official data certified that immigrants from the former Soviet space, even not counting those with irregular legal status and those who have acquired citizenship in the meantime, are among the largest groups of non-EU immigrants in the area, numbering more than 5,500. Three quarters of them are women, a majority with considerable migration seniority. Despite the economic downturn experienced by Italy, their number has kept growing even during the crisis, albeit at a reduced rate.[3]

The shift from participation in a network of friends and acquaintances to a professional project occurred when I decided to quit my job as a clerk and apply to graduate school. Rushing to prepare the application, I discovered quite late that I also had to include a "research project." Knowing I could change it later, I decided the shortest way to write up a project was to make my new friends its topic. What had started as a cluster of friendships was to become my professional interest. This was a fateful decision, as the topic would turn out to be quite sticky, reluctant to be changed.

Although it may sound paradoxical, as soon as I drafted my proposal, I started for the first time to be worried about my role in the group. I was friendly enough with the women I had met in the years before, who found it normal to consider me a natural part of the environment. But what would happen with the growing number of newcomers? Would I really be able to participate in the group as fully as a decent ethnography would require? Would the newly arrived women accept me as somebody observing and writing about them? Since the very beginning, I had occupied a liminal position, neither an insider nor an outsider.

My personal background was Yugoslav, not Soviet. I spoke Russian, but it was not my mother tongue. I was an immigrant, but I had arrived much earlier. I was a foreigner, but my naturalization as an Italian citizen was in process. I had been a care worker myself, but I had been employed for years in white-collar jobs. They were living in the homes of their employers, while I enjoyed the luxury of a flat all to myself. I had never worried about these differences before, but now I feared they might be interpreted as placing me in a higher social status, thus creating a barrier between them and me.

In reality, I quickly realized that, given I was younger than most of them, still single, and without children, my professional achievements did not really matter. One of the new women, when Iryna introduced me to her, pointed out that at my age she already had a ten-year-old child. Another, more cheekily, declared that at my age she "had already been divorced twice." Many others found my (in their opinion) sloppy and unfeminine way of dressing funny to criticize.

To my surprise, far from being a matter of invidious comparison, the women framed me as naïve, unfortunate, young, and in need of womanly help and advice. I gratefully embraced and maintained this status of novice for many years, as it gave me ample room to ask silly questions.

I was equally surprised that the reason for my presence was hardly an issue. When I received the news that my application had been accepted by the graduate school, I rushed to the waiting room and announced it. I said I was planning "to write a book about us" in order to complete my graduate studies. Nobody really cared about the news, and we quickly shifted to a more interesting topic. I was helped by the fact that the group was recent and participation in it highly variable: at certain times, we were some dozens, at others, just four or five. Many people entered the group for a few months, and then a change of job—a very frequent event given the occupation—could easily imply a change of residence and a weakening of participation. After a while, I was just someone who was there, and wave after wave of newcomers took me for granted.

During the years of my (unexpectedly long) fieldwork, I found myself participating in the life of the group in a rather pervasive way. As I have described in the previous chapters, I did it in a variety of roles: I strolled and window-shopped regularly with the crew of women. I worked with Iryna, selling the items of direct sales companies (mainly cosmetics and underwear). I helped organize initiatives in the associations and traveled back to homelands with the minivans. I acted as a chaperone on the women's first dates, participated in barbecues in mountain parks, attended church functions and disco nights, brokered medical appointments and provided ad hoc legal counsel, visited dime stores and discount supermarkets, participated in the informal Eastern European open-air market supplied by the regular minivan traders. I hosted women in my apartment and was hosted by the few who—in due course—had a place to receive guests. As is the case with most ethnographers, while involved in fieldwork I struggled to keep an accurate record of what was happening and to justify my research in the light of broader intellectual concerns.[4]

The original timeline placed the end of my project at the end of 2008, when I was going to defend my doctoral dissertation. As it happens, as soon as I was completing a hastily drafted dissertation, I applied for a postdoc position to continue my fieldwork. Many things were happening, and I felt I had not observed the women long enough to identify a solid pattern of change in their lives. I thought another two years would suffice. When they expired, I discovered I needed even more.

New cohorts of women had arrived, the group had started differentiating into multiple sites and cliques, many women had stabilized their romantic relationships, the first sons and daughters had joined their mothers in Alpinetown, and some of them were approaching adolescence. Moreover, many of the pioneers were now facing a new set of transitions in their life course. Some of them had become old in emigration and wondered about what would happen with retirement, some others had sons and daughters approaching adulthood, and many had married or started stable cohabitation. I wanted to understand how they were giving form and meaning to such transitions within their emigration experience.[5]

Luckily, I was awarded a four-year fellowship that allowed me to keep participating to the lives of the women. As Iryna was ready to joke, "You will keep adding chapters to your book until we are dead." Dasha wondered if I would go on "pestering us" all my life. People had just grown accustomed to my presence and had become oblivious to my project. In fact, year after year, the project had become a long-term ethnography, following the women pioneers for a sizable portion of their lives, while at the same time adding detailed observations on the followers who had joined them.[6]

Over the years, however, both the activities and the sites of my fieldwork have changed, as a consequence of the development of differentiated paths the women could follow. In the beginning, the fieldwork implied participating in a single group, whose members were living remarkably similar lives. We would meet in the designated places, and being there was all that was required. Even when a plurality of sites became marked by the presence of the women, it was accepted that the proper way of participating in the group would be to stroll among them, chat with whoever was there, and move, if one felt like it, to another site. For many years, there was simply no competition among them.

Over the years, as I have recounted in the book, the group slowly fragmented into a plurality of sites, many of them increasingly reserved for one or more cliques. The growing exclusivity of several subgroups of women—linked to increasingly differentiated migratory careers and each giving birth to distinct social and moral worlds—became not only a theoretical focus but also a practical problem. As always with ethnography, the two dimensions were inextricably intertwined. As I have documented, participation in the group slowly changed, with fewer communal gatherings and much more frequent individual exchanges, telephone calls, and selective gatherings.

The group slowly melted down into a variety of different worlds in which differences could be ignored (as I did at the party narrated in the prologue) only at peril. My ethnographic work became less tied to a specific set of ties and practices, and more defined by participation in a wider collection of activities linked to the diverging careers of the various subgroups of women.

Three periods abroad, thanks to the generosity of the Fulbright Program, of the Urban Ethnography Workshop of Yale University, and of the University of Malmo, helped me to slowly disengage from the field and gain sufficient distance to complete this book.

# Notes

PROLOGUE

1.  Euromaidan has been a revolt, centered in Independence (Maidan) square in Kiev, against the decision by president Viktor Yanukovych to refuse signing an association agreement with the European Union. Starting in November 2013, the confrontation become particularly bloody on February 18, 2014, when a significant number of casualties were recorded. Yanukovych was later overthrown in the morning of February 22. The day after the main clashes in Kiev, a vigil was held in Alpinetown. More than two hundred women attended. It was the first political initiative the women had ever attended, let alone organized. I was away and did not personally attend the event. I observed, however, that all the women I was in contact with immediately posted on their Facebook page pictures of them holding candles or waving the Ukrainian flag. As the outcome of the fight was at the time uncertain, there was some defiance in their attitude.

INTRODUCTION

1.  The name of the town, as all personal and organizational names used in the book, is a pseudonym. Details on my fieldwork are available in the appendix at the end of the text.
2.  "Putin deplores collapse of USSR," BBC News website, April 25, 2005, http://news.bbc.co.uk/2/hi/4480745.stm.
3.  For the notion of context of reception, see Portes and Rumbaut (1996).
4.  For a discussion on the social psychological understanding of migration as a lived experience, see Cabaniss and Cameron (2018) and Suarez Orozco (1997).

5. Strategic research materials (SRMs) are defined by Merton as those "strategic research sites, objects, or events that exhibit the phenomena to be explained or interpreted to such advantage and in such accessible form that they enable the fruitful investigation of previously stubborn problems and the discovery of new problems for further inquiry" (1987, 1–2).

6. In fact, a main reason for the neglect of this dimension lies precisely in the fact that most social science research is focused on already established "communities" or "ethnicities." In short, researchers usually study the living conditions, organization, and experiences of "followers," those who have been able to rely on the networks, knowledge, and infrastructures provided by earlier migrants. Very few studies try to reconstruct the natural history of the group and the differences between the experiences of the various waves of immigrants. For some important exceptions, which have been particularly important as inspirations for my work, see Adams (1987), Anghel (2013), Chamberlain (1997), Hagan (1998), and Smith (2006).

7. In migration studies, this phenomenon is referred to as "cumulative causation." It is a process identified as early as 1964 in studies of Italian emigration to the United States; see MacDonald and MacDonald (1964). It has been explored and systematized by Douglas Massey's pathbreaking analyses of the dynamics of Mexican migration to the United States; see Massey et al. (1990).

8. On the connections between migrating social networks and occupational concentration in specific niches, see Tilly (2000) and Tilly and Brown (1967).

9. See Petersen (1958).

10. The arrival of pioneers does not automatically imply significant new waves of arrivals. In fact, not all migrant pioneers trigger subsequent arrivals. Even when they do, pioneers often filter prospective migrants, thus shaping the composition of further migration. They may act as bridgeheads as well as gatekeepers. The role of previous contacts varies remarkably according to the kind of social networks involved (urban networks being on the whole less conducive to cumulative causation than rural ones), the gender composition of the networks themselves, and the kind of human capital embodied in pioneers and early adopters. See Fussell and Massey (2004), Hagan (1998), and Lindstrom and López Ramírez (2010).

11. For a review of studies on pioneers, see Bakewell et al. (2011).

12. "Pioneer" must be understood as a relative, not absolute, category. Over the years—as with Ruslana (chapter 1), Galina (chapter 2), and Diana (chapter 5)—I have met a very small number of individuals who actually arrived much earlier than the other women, still in Soviet times or in the immediate aftermath. They had not played any role, however, in triggering further arrivals nor had they contributed to the birth of the group. In fact, the women, and myself, had been oblivious to their existence in the Alpine-town area for years.

13. For a classic statement, see Tilly (2007).
14. The symbolic frames and interactional traditions employed by migrants are also path-dependent from the series of experiences undergone by pioneers and early followers. Remus Anghel's rich study of the changes in Romanian migration to Western Europe provides a fascinating account of the role played by early waves of pioneers in shaping the aspirations, perceptions, and strategies of subsequent migrants. See Anghel (2013). On the importance of social networks in migration processes, see also Bashi (2007).
15. I adapt such a distinction from Jeffrey Alexander's work on collective trauma; see Alexander (2012). For a review of studies, see Sciortino (2019).
16. For the notion of migration as a shock, and an analysis of the role played by social networks in managing it, see Choldin (1973).
17. All quoted sentences try to approximate actual utterances, but they are never fully reliable transcripts. While participating in the interactions, I tried to record the women's words, and parts of the verbal exchanges they involved, typing messages on my cell phone or scribbling them on pieces of paper while the conversation was unfolding or in its immediate aftermath. Most of the time, however, I have written my fieldnotes from memory later in the day, some hours after the events.
18. Many women nicknamed the elderly people they assisted "papa" or "mama," thus familiarizing their relationships with them and casting themselves in the morally positive role of the caring daughter.
19. On the importance of shame as a feeling of having lost any protective cultural clothing, see Katz (1999, 142ss).
20. I was constantly puzzled, in the beginning, by the frequent references to "slavery" in the talk of the women. During my first trip to Ukraine, I happened to witness a ceremony commemorating the experiences of forced laborers during the Second World War. In a subsequent trip, I attended a discussion about forced labor in the USSR. In both cases, the speakers and audiences positively moralized the suffering as part of national myth building, seeing it as an instance of personal sacrifice and spiritual strength in facing an unjust fate. The women in Alpinetown had creatively adapted a widely available and shared frame for giving meaning to their emigration experiences. For an analysis of the meaning of "slavery" in post-Soviet societies, see Grinchenko (2015).
21. Many women, for example, expected to be able to call for their children before they were fourteen years old, so that they could start Italian high school. Most of them, however, did not have the requirements by then. Quite a few of them, indeed, were unable to satisfy the requirements even when their children were getting close to eighteen, the final legal deadline for family reunification. Very often, when they, the mothers, were ready, their children, often thanks to years of remittances, had developed different plans. The mismatch between the sense of time for emigrants and that of their relatives is not peculiar to the post-Soviet women. For similar findings in the case of US-Mexico migration, see Dreby (2010).

22. See Donato and Gabaccia (2015), Donato et al. (2011), and Houstoun et al. (1984). A critique of the historical evidence about the novelty of the "feminization of migration" is provided by Schrover (2013).

23. Over the decades, in each specific phase and each specific locale, there have been shifts and changes in the gender composition of immigrant inflows. In Western Europe, for example, gender ratios have fluctuated remarkably in reaction to phases of the business cycle, variations in the specific type of labor demanded (very often along very gendered lines), and policy regulations. See Kofman et al. (2000) and Schrover (2013).

24. See Bretell (2016) and Lutz (2010).

25. See Diner (1983) and Jackson (1984). For other examples of female-dominated flows, see Harzig (1997), Wehner (1995), and Sarti (2004). For a systematic review, see Lutz (2010).

26. See Thomas and Znaniecki (1918), Thomas (1923), and Park and Miller (1921).

27. See Lee (1966).

28. Although it was (sometimes) acknowledged that migrant women would often participate in the labor force, their mobility was nonetheless considered less inspired by work opportunities; see Morokvasic (1984) and Anthias (2000).

29. The available literature is critically reviewed by Donato and Gabaccia (2015), Lutz (2010), and Mahler and Pessar (2006).

30. See Cerrutti and Massey (2001), Hondagneu-Sotelo (1994), and Herrera (2013).

31. There is evidence that the choice to delay the migration of the wife is usually a husband's preference and that income-producing motivations acquire primacy among migrating daughters, if not among wives; see Hondagneu-Sotelo (1992). For the finding that most women are active in the labor market upon arrival, see Chavez (1992).

32. Even in largely male-triggered flows, there are women migrating alone, often able to activate subsequently independent migratory chains; see Kanaiaupuni (2000). In some other corridors, particularly from countries where kinship structures are more matrifocal, flows may be more gender-balanced, through assorted individual movements or through couples migrating together from the very beginning; see, among others, Massey et al. (2006).

33. Women-dominated flows tend to originate in sending areas characterized by a more active presence of women in the salaried occupations, as well as by less pervasive patriarchal norms of family stability.

34. See, as classical examples, George (2005), Repak (1995), and Parreñas (2001). Migration from the Philippines provides a good example of the differential impact of having women as pioneers. As the earlier waves of emigrants had been women employed in domestic services, male followers have often been channeled into this sector also, becoming employed in a

set of occupations that would have not been considered suitable for men in the sending area; see Constable (1997a). For a comparative study, see Bartolomei (2010).

35. See Bloch (2018), Gamburd (2000), Faier (2009), and Keough (2016) for other studies of women-dominated flows.

36. See Park (1928).

37. See Bloch (2018) and Cvajner (2011). Similar dynamics, in which homeland traditions are creatively reinterpreted, have been documented among Filipina emigrants in Hong Kong and Singapore; see Constable (1997b) and Yeoh and Huang (1998).

38. See Hondagneu-Sotelo (1994) and Mahler and Pessar (2006). It can be argued that migration also triggers gender changes when one of the partners is geographically immobile (and independently from his or her own subsequent movement). For example, the absence of emigrated husbands implied a significant restructuring of gender expectations in Southern Italian sending communities during the period of mass emigration; see Reeder (2003) and Piselli (1981).

39. See Pessar (1999).

40. See Hirsch (2003).

41. See González-López (2005).

42. See Menjivar (1999), Schmalzbauer (2011), and George (2005).

43. See Donato (1992) and Donato (2010).

44. See Repak (1995). In still other cases, men acquire increasing power over subsequent arrivals because they are inserted into more dynamic and less atomized labor markers; see Hagan (1998).

45. Reunited husbands may tend to compensate for such changes by monopolizing status roles in the ethnic infrastructure, where they may enforce increasingly strict interpretations of traditional gender norms. In other instances, the women themselves may try to compensate for the external gender imbalance framing their (higher) incomes as temporary and complementary. For a classic study of these developments, see George (2005).

46. See Smith and his analysis of a "pioniera" migrant coming to the US alone and with no interest in family reunification. See Smith (2006).

47. For an early argument along these lines, see Curran and Rivero-Fuentes (2003).

48. See Donato et al. (2014) and Donato (1992).

49. See Donato (1992) and Hofmann and Buckley (2013). For the importance of family life in migration decisions, see also Parreñas (2015). Even where there are substantial numbers of reunited husbands, women pioneers may still regard being single as actually the most fortunate and prestigious occurrence.

50. For other cases where emigration follows, or works as an alternative to, the dissolution of the couple, see Repak (1995) and Tacoli (1999).

51. For a general overview of the historical evolution of a global market for household services, see Hoerder et al. (2015). For the connection between

demand for domestic services and women-led migration, see Momsen (1999).

52. Such reliance on nearly exclusively ethnic sociability contributes to reinforcing the vision of the newly arrived migrant as defined by specific, strongly instrumental attitudes. Michael Piore, in his classic 1979 study, claimed newly arrived migrants, especially if they think of their migration as temporary, are focused nearly exclusively on material incentives. Migration is only the search for economic resources to convert into social status back home. In his well-known formulation, the recent immigrant is "a true economic man, probably the closest thing in real life to the homo oeconomicus of economic theory" (Piore 1979, 54).

53. See Gordon (1964). Migration experiences, however, have always been more complex, with a staggering variety of forms of sociability and intergroup contacts. For a systematic review, see Hoerder (2002).

54. There is nothing particularly new in stressing the social differences in work conditions typical of domestic services and the impact they have on the immigrant experience. There is, indeed, a wide literature on how employment in domestic service has shaped the migration experience of European women migrating to the Americas. See, among others, Lintelman (1995), Wehner (1995), and Diner (1983). For a similar argument concerning Latina care workers in the US, see Ibarra (2002).

55. Care work requires, nearly by definition, a temporal and spatial proximity between carer and cared. For a detailed discussion of care work as a specific form of body work, see Twigg (2000) and Twigg et al. (2011). For ethnographic studies of the implication of care work for the shaping of migration experiences, see Świtek (2016) and Ibarra (2002).

56. See Ibarra (2002) and Hondagneu-Sotelo (2001).

57. See Cvajner (2009; 2012).

58. Besides *badanti*, many natives used the term *slave* (i.e., Slavs) to refer to the women. The women found it derogatory and heavily resented it. In Medieval Latin, starting at the end of the sixteenth century, the geographical term *Slavus* (present day Slav) and the condition of *slavum* (present day *slave*) become slowly synonymous, owing to the function of the Balkans and the Black Sea as major reservoirs of enslaved labor. Starting with the Enlightenment, moreover, Western European elites increasingly adopted a symbolic distinction between Western and Eastern Europe, associating the latter with backwardness, tribalism, authoritarianism, and exoticism. Eastern Europeans were "orientalized," in Edward Said's sense of the term; see Said (1979). For the subsequent development of this framing, see Wolff (1994) and Kuus (2004). In gendered terms, Eastern Europe has been frequently associated in Italian discourse with a varying combination of primitivism, traditionalism, subordination of women and sexual profligacy, a fraught combination of moral condemnation, and envy or desire. The

gold digger stereotype, however, is far from being restricted to the Slavs' women (Stephens and Phillips 2003).

59. The notion of "face" is at the center of Erving Goffman's well-known essay on face work; see Goffman (1967). His analysis highlights how inconsistencies in the available face create an endemic risk of embarrassment and misrecognition, forcing potential victims to stay guarded. This is precisely the structural condition of an emigrant in a new context, especially in the early phases of the settlement process.

60. The history of post-Soviet women migration is still to be written. For some important studies, see Baganha and Fonseca (2004), Bloch (2016), Keough (2016), Solari (2018), and Fedyuk and Kindler (2016).

61. Smaller numbers of women had passports from Belarus, Georgia, and Kazakhstan. While many of the women were individually quite proud of their "new" states, membership in our group paid little or no attention to actual political boundaries. They defined as "us" any woman who could draw on the same Soviet stock of common knowledge and experience. This is why I use, as many of them would do, the adjective "Soviet" as a common denominator for all of them. I use "Soviet" in the same way I happen to use "Yugoslav" to define myself and other people of my age who grew up in the territories of the former Yugoslav federation. Eastern Europe has no scarcity of ghosts.

62. See Snyder (2010).

63. See the detailed study of consumer culture in the former Soviet Union provided by Chernishova (2013), which effectively dispels the myth of the Soviet consumer as passive and fatalistic. On the significance of consumption in the late Soviet Union, see also Zaslavski (1981).

64. These informal entrepreneurial activities usually involved some form of geographical mobility, as women would travel long distances to major cities in other republics to acquire goods that could then be resold for a profit in their own towns. These practices were common to most communist countries, well beyond the Soviet bloc. When I was a child in a coastal town in Croatia, a major source of sought after goods, mostly clothing items and the occasional rock music record, were traders, often women, who would cross the border with Italy, visit the cheap emporiums in Trieste (known in the city as *i negozi per slavi*, i.e., shops for Slavs), buy clothes, put them on one over the other, and cross back over the border. In the case of the Soviet Union, such trade implied travelling to large cities, often better stocked, or to provinces specializing in the production of certain goods.

65. The combination is explicit in the 1977 Constitution of the Soviet Union, which described women as "hard-working mothers who raise their children and take care of the house."

66. The ways in which the vision of women as workers and as mothers could coexist was very different in the various socialist states. The Soviet Union was the first country to legalize abortion in 1920, although it was banned

again from 1936 to 1955. After this second legalization, the Soviet Union had the highest rate of abortion in the world. Contraceptives were available and divorce was possible, albeit not always easily. Ceausescu's Romania, on the contrary, outlawed abortion, seriously reduced the possibilities for divorce, and strongly supported the traditional family as part of its pronatalist goals. The tension between official discourse and toleration for gender inequality seems, however, to have been a constant across the communist bloc. For a detailed study of socialist Romania, see Gal and Kligman (2000).

67. One of the few Soviet scholars of sexuality, Igor Kon, defined the combination of formal equality between men and women combined with the severe proscription against women's physicality as "genderless sexism"; see Kon and Riordan (1993).

68. See Shtern and Stern (1981) and Rotkirch (2004).

69. See Cvajner (2011), Davidenko (2017), and Porteous (2017). Something very similar happened in other postcommunist countries, including the Balkans. See Ibroscheva (2013).

70. The "emancipatory" feeling of hyperfeminine displays is not a monopoly of post-Soviet women. In their research with Bosnian refugees women in the US, Huisman and Hondagneu-Sotelo observed a similar phenomenon, where the adoption of a hyperfeminine style was perceived as a symbol of modernity and independent femininity (Huisman and Hondagneu-Sotelo 2005).

71. See the International Monetary Fund estimates at "5. Report for Selected Countries and Subjects," October 2007, http://www.imf.org/external/pubs/ft/weo/2007/02/weodata/weorept.aspx?pr.x=49&pr.y=7&sy=1992&ey=1999&scsm=1&ssd=1&sort=country&ds=.&br=1&c=913%2C926%2C921&s=NGDP_R%2CPPPGDP&grp=0&a=#cs4.

72. See Leon et al. (1997).

73. See Gorny and Ruspini (2004) and Thranhardt (1996).

74. For Istanbul, see Bloch (2011), Aktar and Ögelman (1994), and Yükseker (2007). For Poland, see Iglicka (2001). The role of Naples has been studied by Schmoll (2004). For related developments in the post-Soviet, Central Asian republic of Kazakhstan, see Kuehnast and Nechemias (2004).

75. During the 1980s, the rate of divorce in the Soviet Union was second only to that of the United States (but possibly higher, as there were a large number of de facto divorces). See Lutz et al. (1993).

76. For similar considerations in the former USSR republic of Georgia, see Hofmann and Buckley (2013).

77. *Babushka*, literally "grandma," is colloquially used to refer to elderly, sexless women with traditional, "rural" attitudes. It may be sometimes used tenderly, as a sign of respect for older women. Most of the time, however, the women used babushka to refer to whatever they were not. Ironically, the term has been appropriated by an Italian entrepreneur for a job-listing website for domestic workers (http://www.babushka.it).

78. The policy was formally discontinued in 2003, following a political scandal that included a request for the resignation of the foreign minister Joschka fischer and the opening of an official review of German visa policy by the European Commission; see Finotelli (2007). When the Volmer directive was discontinued, it was simply too late, as hundreds of thousands of Eastern European immigrants were already settled in the various countries of Western Europe and able to sponsor further arrivals. On EU visa policy, see Finotelli and Sciortino (2013). On the consequences of the Volmer directive, see Cvajner and Sciortino (2010a) and Nikolova (2012).

79. See World Bank (2016).

80. See Duvell (2006).

81. https://ec.europa.eu/eurostat/web/asylum-and-managed-migration/data/main-tables.

82. See Fedyuk and Kindler (2016).

CHAPTER ONE

1. It is always difficult to confidently say to what degree the group of people studied by an ethnographer is "representative" of a wider social category. I can however stress that other independently carried out studies involving post-Soviet domestic workers have found a very similar profile for pioneers in other Italian cities. See Degiuli (2016), Mazzacurati (2005), Näre (2011), Solari (2018), and Vianello (2009). A similar profile for Ukrainian and Moldovan pioneers has also been painted by the first large-scale study of foreign domestic workers in Italy; see Catanzaro and Colombo (2009). In addition, a similar profile has also surfaced in studies of Eastern European women migrants in other Western European cities; see Bloch (2018), Nikolova (2012), Heyse (2011), Keough (2016), Hellerman (2006), and Baganha and Fonseca (2004).

2. The differentiation in the occupational lives of the women was minimal. Although some of the elderly enjoyed better health, and some employers could be particularly open-minded, the differences in their work conditions, in their salaries, and in their schedules were negligible.

3. On the connectedness of the sending and receiving migration contexts, see Waldinger (2015a).

4. For the notion of migration career, originally elaborated in the 1920s by the Chicago school of sociology, see Cvajner and Sciortino (2010b) and Martinello and Rea (2014).

5. The cost of migration in the early 2000s could vary from 350 to 2,200 Euros, contingent upon a multiplicity of factors, including the financial resources of the prospective migrant. The price usually included document preparation, the visa, and transportation. For some estimates of the costs of migration based on surveys carried out in Moldova, see Cuc et al. (2005) and CBS-AXA (2005).

6. If they had made the right agreement with a reliable agent, somebody would meet them at the bus. They would be brought to a flat for a short resting period and they would learn some basic Italian before being dispatched to work for an Italian family somewhere in Southern Italy. Assistance in obtaining a job would have to be paid for with an additional fee, usually equivalent to a month's salary. If, on the contrary, they had been able to secure only a visa and a bus ticket, they had to start frantically looking for a job on the spot. Within hours of their arrival, without knowing where they would sleep the very same night, they had to find a household interested in their services. To find such a family required the help of one of several "agencies" operating in Naples or one of the myriad of independent contractors—usually women who had been or still were care workers themselves—who were selling the same service directly at the bus stop or in one of the city squares. If they had entrusted their fate to a questionable agent, or if the agencies and contractors judged them to be unfit for domestic service, their first days in Naples could become an excruciating calvary. The women who failed to enter the care-work market had in fact only the alternative of scraping together a hard living as agricultural day laborers, living in shacks, paid little if any salary, at the mercy of a long chain of recruiters.

7. This nearly exclusive concentration of former USSR women in live-in care work is a consequence of their late arrival in the Italian labor market. Household services are a traditional magnet for foreign workers in Italy: the first recorded presence of foreign workers in the country, at the end of the 1960s, was precisely in domestic services. See Andall (2000) and Parreñas (2001). When, in 2000–2001, emigration from Ukraine and Moldova to Italy became substantial, the "best" segments of the market for domestic service market were already filled by foreign workers from other shores (in particular from the Philippines, Sri Lanka, Poland, and the Balkans). Workers from these groups were well entrenched in the local labor markets and enjoyed an established reputation that they could use to hoard opportunities for their own newcomers. Ukrainian and Moldovan women had to enter the least appealing sector of the market: full time, around-the-clock, residential care work for lower middle-class and working-class elderly people.

8. In fact, Elena still lives in Alpinetown, where her children, now young adults, have joined her. When she succeeded in getting her papers and organized her first trip home after more than three years of absence, her husband notified her that he had found another woman and was moving in with her.

9. On the importance of philanthropic agencies in managing the largely informal supply of care work for Italian families, see Ambrosini (2000).

10. See Douglas (1991).

11. For an ethnographic account of this dimension of domestic work, see Näre (2009).

12. The women lacked what Erving Goffman would call a territory of the self, a "field of things" or a "preserve" to which they could claim "entitlement to possess, control, use, or dispose of" (1966, 27–30). Working mostly for working-class households, their lack of privacy was often compounded by the small size of the flats. Still, as Goffman rightly stresses, the boundaries of such territories are not a matter of size but of social recognition. Even those who could enjoy some architectonically secluded space often could not really call it their own, not even temporarily.

13. Olena Fedyuk has examined the role of photographs, including what she calls "Ukrainian corners," in the everyday life of Ukrainians in Italy. She mentions the presence in them of national or political symbols (such as the Ukrainian flag or a picture of Yulia Tymoshenko), which I never encountered in Alpinetown; see Fedyuk (2012).

14. Unsurprisingly, many citizens of Alpinetown found the behavior of the "Slavs" aggressive and rude. Many perceived their use of the public space as proof of incivility. Some letters published in the local newspapers framed the issue in terms of *degrado* (a combination of social divesture and urban decay). For the debate on the uses of public space by informal immigrant groups in various cities, see Dines (2002), Yücesoy (2008), and Yeoh and Huang (1998).

15. It is important to note that, in the previous lives of the women, there was simply no experience of domestic service. In the USSR, to have a house cleaner or a nanny hired privately was extremely rare. Care work was a state-regulated activity, especially in terms of child-care facilities. Outside of the domain of the state, it was the preserve of grandparents, who usually retired between fifty-five and sixty years of age and were expected to take care of household chores and grandchildren. Indeed, the market for household services in the territories of the former USSR is still quite young, confined to urban areas, and often still regarded suspiciously. See Zdravomyslova (2010).

16. The constant reference to sacrificial motherhood as a key element of their identities allowed them to root their experiences in deeply felt values, making them martyrs and saviors at the same time. On the importance of the symbol of the sacrificing mother, see Denisova and Mukhina (2010). For a similar discussion, yet targeting Ukrainian migration, see Fedyuk (2012). Some authors have stressed how, with the breakdown of the USSR, there has been in Ukraine a strong, state-sponsored effort to construct a vision of the nation strictly intertwined with the enforcement of a very traditionalist view of motherhood. A new celebrity, the pagan goddess Berehynia, is sometime mentioned as part of such effort; see Solari (2011) and Rubchak (2009). Although the efforts by various agencies to construct a Berehynia tradition is easy to document, I confine myself to the observation that the women I studied seemed to have quietly and happily done without her. A similar imagination is often found also in migrants accounts of Latina motherhood (Hondagneu-Sotelo and Avila 1997).

17. The polluting nature of care work has been noted by many researchers. Domestic workers deal with this pollution in different ways. Salzinger, for example, found that Latinas who joined domestic work actively tried to cast off the stigma of being a care worker by professionalizing their image (Salzinger 1991). Solari (2006) has similarly analyzed the use of both religious and professional arguments to legitimize care work among Ukrainian migrants. While the women would have easily accepted a vision of themselves as caring professionals, their employment in the household—rather than in an organization such as a hospital or a nursing home—denied them such legitimacy.

18. On the physicality of care work, see Twigg (2000). In her detailed ethnography of Indonesian care workers in Japan, Beata witek has detailed the challenges of body work when it takes place across ethnic boundaries.

19. Twigg, in her vivid descriptions of the hairless body parts, saggy breasts, and falling skin encountered by careworkers as a mundane, everyday occurrence highlights how care work is based on managing dirt and disgust (Twigg 2000, 395).

20. In the case of the women, being irregular migrants did not necessarily mean fearing deportation. The women were obviously scared of being deported. However, they also quickly realized that middle-aged Eastern European women working as care workers were definitely not a priority for law enforcement officials. The common sense among the women was that the police would go after them only if they did something obviously wrong, or if they seriously annoyed somebody powerful. After a while, the women learned how to be streetwise. Some discovered that they could make quite an impression on police officers on street duty—usually young, southern males—if they acted as stiff grandmothers. When they were too young for such a role, the women reckoned that flirtatiously emphasizing their powerlessness could also go a long way. Irregular status was a heavy burden because it implied the impossibility of establishing a sure foothold in the new environment and, above all, of traveling back to their homelands to visit their relatives and children. From the expiration of their visas and until the moment at which they would eventually be able to get their papers, their chances of any personal contact with their families were minimal. They were constantly telling stories about women who had been unable to return to their hometowns to see their dying parents. While this had actually happened to only a few women, the possibility frightened everyone. They evoked the possibility of such an event to signify the indignity of their conditions. For descriptions of the interactions between Eastern European women and police officials, see Harney (2012).

21. Amnesties are a frequent feature of immigration policy in many countries, although Italian politicians seem to have been particularly fond of this instrument. See Barbagli et al. (2004). For a comparative survey of European regularization programs, see Blaschke (2008) and Levinson (2005).

22. Shrinking family budgets may easily translate into less demand for cleaning services, while the demand for care work is remarkably rigid. Unsurprisingly, the recent downturn in the Italian economy has implied for many women who had moved to hourly-paid work for a pool of employers a return to residential care work.

23. The average monthly salary for a live-in care worker was equivalent, in purchasing power, to less than 800–900 US dollars per month, plus room and board. The luckiest ones could expect to receive the equivalent of around 1,100 US dollars, plus room and board. The newly arrived and those badly in need would settle for anything above the equivalent of 550–700 US dollars. I have used here the 2014 purchasing power parities for actual individual consumption as estimated by the OECD.

24. An Italian *dama di compagnia* is something similar to the ladies in waiting in Elizabethan times, a personal assistant of aristocratic rank. It can be used also to mean a chaperone, in charge of social and cultural activities. Ilda is the first living person I ever heard use such a term, previously known to me only from classic works of Italian literature.

25. A specific feature of the lives of the women is the closeness to death. The women feared the death of their relatives and being unable to return to help them. They also feared the death of the elderly they were caring for. See Fedyuk (2009).

26. In the literature on women-led migration, great emphasis is placed on so-called "global care chains" or the "international division of reproductive labor." The argument is that women migrating to wealthy countries to perform care work create a shortage of care work in their own households. This shortage is managed by hiring, in turn, poorer women to provide care for the left-behind relatives of the migrant woman. Women-led migration would thus create a global commodification of care; see Parreñas (2000) and Ehrenreich and Hochschild (2004). In my fieldwork, I have not found any evidence of such a process of commodification. The children of the women in this study stayed with relatives, usually the parents of the woman and, more rarely, aunts or cousins. The only case of "exchange" I found was a Moldovan woman who had invited a friend to live in her flat in Chişinău for free in exchange for looking after her seventeen-year-old daughter. It did not work well.

27. According to Italian migration laws, any regular immigrant has the right to apply for family reunification, provided she fulfills certain income and housing conditions. Family reunification is defined by the Italian Constitution and by the European Charter of Human Rights as an individual right. There is consequently no quota or contingent, and any resident immigrant that satisfies the conditions listed in the law may obtain a visa for her relatives. On the importance of family-reunification rights for European immigration policies, see Hollifield et al. (2014). For the specific problems encountered by domestic workers in this area, see Kontos (2012).

CHAPTER TWO

1. On shopping as a group activity, see Hine (2002).
2. Only a small minority of the women dissented from such a blunt, matter-of-fact link between the control of assets and attribution of personal worth. They were usually the older and more educated women, who remained loyal to the Soviet idea that education, not wealth, was the only legitimate criterion for allocating status and recognition. The few times they tried to use such an argument, the other women were ready to dismiss it as irremediably obsolete. I further elaborate the competing claims grounded in education vs. wealth in chapter 5, as the cleavage was bound to become one of the burning issues in the women's attempts to establish their own community institutions.
3. On the Holodomor, and its role in the history of Eastern Europe, see Snyder (2010).
4. I learned later, especially during my trips to Ukraine and Moldova, that such a feeling was far from being an oddity. In 2009, the Pew Global Attitudes Project surveyed, twenty years after the fall of the Berlin Wall, public opinion in many postsocialist and post-Soviet countries. The survey unfortunately did not include Moldova and Belarus. In Ukraine, however, a majority of the interviewees declared that the situation was worse than under communism. Less than half of the interviewees, moreover, declared that the socioeconomic change had been positive; see Pew Global Attitudes Project (2009).
5. Soviet consumer culture has been the object of several historical studies that have highlighted how social relationships adapted in various ways to the economy of shortage that defined the Soviet Union. The most complete and fascinating analysis I have found is Chernishova (2013). See also Field (2007) and Gurova (2018). A useful collection of essays covering the whole communist bloc can be found in Bren and Neuburger (2012).
6. When talking about shop attendants and cashiers, Marinela—along with many other women—used the term *sovok*, a word that implied both a certain style of behavior (rude, negligent, lazy, and occasionally cruel) and an explanation of it (being a nickname for *Soviet*). The same term was often used by the women to explain the many shortcomings of Eastern European men.
7. The habit of always carrying a string shopping bag in order to be prepared if confronted with the unexpected availability of scarce items was so widespread that this kind of bag acquired a specific name (*"avos'ka,"* from *"avos,"* i.e., perhaps). Their use had apparently started already under Khrushchev; see Reid (2007). Old habits, moreover, die hard. Recently, when travelling to the post-Soviet territory with a colleague, I could observe his puzzlement in the local market noticing that colorful *avos'ke* were sold again (and widely used) as trendy shopping bags.

8.  The best Soviet literary text on queuing, seen as a specific Soviet institution, is the short story by Vladimir Sorokov, written in 1983 but only published two years later in Paris; see Sorokov (1988 [1983]).
9.  For an ethnographic account of the swift transition, see Ghodsee (2006).
10. It is roughly the equivalent purchasing power of 14 to 25 US dollars.
11. Other researchers working on different kinds of women-led migration have also found that the development of a discretionary expenditure for "personal" needs takes place after the women have paid the most urgent debts and have transferred a substantial volume of remittances. In her study of filipina migrant women in Asia, Oishi has found that migrant women started experimenting with the shopping opportunities encountered in the new social arena only after their debts had been at least partly repaid. They justified their shopping, arguing that their husbands would have wasted any higher remittances on "monkey business" such as alcohol, gambling, and prostitution; see Oishi (2005).
12. Less than half a mile away, in another parking lot deserted on Sunday morning, a similar scene welcomed the Moldovan women. The Romanians used to have their own networks of minivans and a related meeting point. When the country become a prospective member of the European Union, and Romanian citizens started to enjoy the benefits of visa-free travel, the minivan service was quickly displaced by the launch of regular bus and cargo service.
13. Similar migrant institutions have appeared over more or less the same years in other European cities, catering to the growing presence of Eastern European women. For an ethnographic description of a similar open-air market in Rome, see Solari (2011) and Weber (2004). According to Solari, the market in Rome was also a place of homeland political mobilization, something I have never observed in Alpinetown.
14. His close friends also knew he had modified his van, adding a special tube underneath in which a person without papers could cross the EU border, at the time running between Hungary and Austria. Clandestine emigrants used this service to enter Italy; so did women without papers who needed to return to Ukraine because of some emergency. Ivan was very proud of his van's specially designed tube, which he claimed was impossible to detect.
15. Her specialization was far from being bizarre. On the contrary, I can attest Iryna had correctly anticipated that, when the women started to spend some money on "themselves," lingerie and cosmetics were among the first goods they looked for. Larissa Remennick, in her research on Soviet Jewish emigrants in several destinations, has documented a similar pattern. She writes that the consumption desires the women manifested upon arrival derived from having been "deprived of most normal means to care for the body, health and beauty." She highlights how "Soviet women invested great effort and cash on cosmetics and clothes" (Remennick 2007, 268).

On the importance of cosmetics and lingerie for the women in Alpine-town, see also Cvajner (2011).

16. It was not always profitable, however. Iryna always spoke of her sales in strictly economic terms, as a way of raising her income and achieving social mobility. Still, the more I spent time with her, the more it became clear that, although money was important, selling was more important for her self-esteem than for her wallet. As she was selling nearly exclusively to other *sidelki*, her market base was neither large nor prosperous. She had to spend considerable time collecting payments, often waiting several months. When I estimated the income generated by Iryna's business activity, I quickly realized that the money she made was comparable to, or even less than, what she would have earned working the same number of hours as a housekeeper, which has remained to this day her primary occupation.

17. To identify "emancipated" womanhood with the attainment of economic dependency, withdrawal from any public sphere, and identification with a male-centered sexuality may seem absurd to many "Western" readers. Still, it is a widespread stance across the gender discourse of Eastern and Central Europe, endorsed by a variety of ideological factions and thinkers, and surely quite popular among the women I spent time with (see chapters 3 and 4). Analysts of Eastern European gender regimes usually describe it as a backlash against the Soviet-enforced model of the woman as de-feminized worker and matriarch; see Ibroscheva (2013), Ashwin (2000), and Zhurzhenko et al. (2004). Another important source is the variety of popular positions in the gender debate of Eastern Europe that advocates a woman's role as concentrated on motherhood and in the reconstruction of the traditional "Slavic family" endangered by decades of Soviet rationaliz-ing oppression. Sometimes, such an argument is intertwined with a nation-alist argument that sees in motherhood the key to the survival of damaged national cultures. Given the standard and endemic opposition in Soviet ideological production between the Soviet family and the (alleged) "house-wife" model of capitalist countries, it is not surprising that the life of the *signora* could be perceived by the women as a symbol of modernization.

18. In all my travel to post-Soviet territories with the women, a visit to the open-air market has always been unavoidable. Women have always proudly introduced me to the local open markets not only as sites of quality shop-ping but also as places of women-centered sociability. Although the women have described the open-air market as a "tradition" of their countries, most of their experience with open-air markets was actually post-1991. There were informal open-air markets with dozens of stalls selling a wide range of goods from the Soviet Union, but they were mostly confined to items sold directly by the producers. Other forms of informal trade were managed individually and more discreetly. Only after 1989 did the liberalization of prices, the legalization of trade, and the opening of the market create the conditions for the emergence of a large number of informal open-air mar-

kets, where basically everything could be bought and sold. The emergence of open-air markets during the transition has been strictly intertwined with the emergence of heavily gendered survival strategies. Women managed (as they do still today) most of the stalls in these markets. See Darii (2008), Sik and Wallace (1999), and Aidis (2003). A collection of ethnographic studies of everyday market activities during the transition can be found in Mandel and Humphrey (2002).

19. Although customers never arrive before 8:00, sellers must come early to secure the space they want since the authorities distribute locations on a first-come, first-served basis. Many sellers hire an assistant to safeguard their spot from potential competitors.

20. In marketing research, there is a growing body of literature concerning the choice of commercial outlets by different groups and types of immigrants; see Ahmad (2003), Ger and Ostergard (1998), and Chattaraman and Lennon (2008). Much of it, however, tends to explain immigrant choices holistically, as the consequence of certain cultural traits or as elements in a broader identity strategy. Very little attention is paid to the local, sensory, and emotional experience of women with given categories of outlets.

21. Women who shopped at Lidl began to regard the fact that their employers did not shop at Lidl as further proof of their silliness. One day, Natasha arrived at the benches in the main square with a juicy anecdote: that morning she had suggested her "old grandma" go to Lidl to buy her groceries. Her employer had replied quite stiffly that she did not like the place because it was full of immigrants. "She forgets that I am also an immigrant," Natasha laughed. For them, Lidl was an Italian experience, but the Italians were stupid enough "to spend more money for the same products."

22. The chain, which currently has forty-four stores in Italy and nine in Croatia, is owned by the third generation of the same family and has a clear commercial identity: it offers a wide range of choices, reasonable prices, fashionable products, and locations accessible to those who do not have a car. Recently, Pittarello has opened some very large shops that resemble a scaled-down version of a superstore.

23. "Puttana" is an Italian word pointing both to paid prostitution and to a behavioral tendency toward low-quality promiscuity. Most women initially used the word "blyat" for the same purposes. Over the years, however, an increasing number of women adopted the Italian word even when talking in their language, an early sign of assimilation. They have kept the use of "blyat" as an intercalary word and an unspecified curse.

24. Benetton is an Italian clothing brand that has gained international visibility with a mix of provocative advertising, a wide range of colors, and affordable prices. They sell goods in the middle price range: with the sale discount, the sweaters would be quite affordable. For the Benetton market image, see Vignali et al. (1993).

25. I had just acquired Italian citizenship a few weeks before.

1. The truth of the maxim has been endlessly rediscovered in social science, under the heading of "homophily." See the classic work of Lazarsfeld and Merton (1954). For a review of contemporary research, see McPherson, et al. (2001).

2. According to international survey programs, acceptance of homosexuality in the former USSR countries is remarkably low; see Golovakha et al. (2007). A dominant frame in discussing the issue is the depiction of homosexuality as an issue of morality, sometimes with strongly anti-Western and nationalistic tones; see Martsenyuk (2013). Among the women, I never caught much interest in the morality frame. Perhaps owing to their biographical and educational background, the women were adamant homosexuality was a health issue, a condition deserving medical treatment. They subscribed in full to what had been the dominant frame in Soviet sexology, starting from the 1920s. See Bernstein (2007), Kon and Riordan (1993), and Stulhofer (2004). For a wider discussion of lesbian life in the USSR and its successor states, see Stella (2015).

3. In the conclusion I analyze the role of the hyperfeminine style in more detail. Studies concerning other types of migratory flows have identified other occurrences in which migrant women endorse what Robert Connell has called "emphasized femininity." See Huisman and Hondragneu-Sotelo (2005), Franz (2003), and Remennick (2007).

4. Although most of them had divorced, sometimes more than once, their experience of a failed marriage had actually strengthened their commitment to the norm of traditional coupledom. All the women claimed that ill-fated husbands, and the temper of the times, had failed them. They considered, however, that traditional marriage was the right and natural thing, while contemporary Eastern European reality was wrong. Any decent woman could only keep trying.

5. This attitude was particularly striking when we talked about domestic violence, something that a sizable minority of them had experienced. In some cases, they justified the "incidents" as an exaggerated retribution for women's failures to act as proper caregivers. In most cases, wife abuse was explained away, even by women who had been victims themselves, as an unfortunate consequence of alcoholism. Men were never held responsible. On domestic violence in Ukraine, see Barrett et al. (2012). For an attempt to estimate the diffusion of the phenomenon, see Ismayilova and El-Bassel (2013).

6. On the popularity of the Decembrists in Russia, and especially in Soviet popular culture, see Trigos (2009).

7. The women who had liaisons with Italians were usually quite positive about their romantic attitude and dating sophistication. When pushed by the others to reveal something more intimate, they usually complained

about the fact that "the Italians" were obsessed with foreplay, particularly with oral sex, and expected to devote a large proportion of their sexual time to it (Cvajner 2016). There is no way to assess how much this reflected a real difference in sexual cultures or whether it was mere bragging. In his ethnography of Romanian construction workers in the Italian city of Bologna, Domenico Perrotta found that the Italians' "obsession" with oral sex (and, in the other direction, the unsophisticated approach to penetrative sex of the Romanians) was a matter of frequent reciprocal jokes among Italian and Romanian workers on construction sites; see Perrotta (2011).

8. The women looked down on masturbation as an ineffective and unhealthy habit. Again, their approach was consistent with the predicates of Soviet sexual education, which has always defined masturbation as a loss of vital energies and as a potential cause of bodily and mental illnesses; see Bernstein (2007) and Shtern and Stern (1981).

9. To do so, I found helpful the analysis carried out by Huisman and Hondagneu-Sotelo (2005).

10. On the connection between the self and the mask, I have found the analysis of Alessandro Pizzorno particularly useful; see Pizzorno (2010).

11. Being a woman thus has an important collective dimension. Appearance is not the surface of an inner self but rather a publicly verifiable effort, certified and cosigned by female friends as well as by men. The male gaze, to be sure, must validate beauty, and the women openly sought this kind of recognition. They seized upon all indications of male desire in public—even the most explicit. But the male gaze is only one form of recognition, and not necessarily the most valued one. An equally important source of recognition derives from membership in a group of women sharing the same ideal. Other women's opinions are considered more reliable, being more impartial, while men, many women disconsolately declared, "are interested only in what you have between your legs." See also Porteous (2017).

12. On the importance of sexual hierarchies, see Levi-Martin and George (2006) and Green (2014). For an application in migration studies, see Cvajner (2016).

13. The original definition of public goods in economic theory as goods that enjoy the properties of nonrivalry and nonexcludability was provided by Paul Samuelson (1954).

14. The women had no problems with making such racial distinctions as a matter of obvious "natural" difference. The western regions of the former USSR have had little or no contact with North African and other African groups, who were present in very limited numbers in the Soviet Union and usually concentrated in the largest metropolises; see fikes and Lemon (2002) and Matusevich (2007). Many women, moreover, used explicitly "African" references as symbols of sufferance and backwardness, a use attested in other research, such as that of Solari (2011). The few women who actively resisted racial categorizations were the oldest and most educated,

who had remained somewhat loyal to the internationalist ideology of the USSR. Lesya, a former principal with a doctorate in philosophy, once tried loudly to remind the women that the great poet Pushkin was the offspring of a former slave from Cameroon who had risen to prominence in the Tsarist court. The women appreciated the conversation but remained unconvinced. On the diffusion of hierarchical notions of race in the territories of the former USSR, see Zakharov and Law (2017).

CHAPTER FOUR

1.  Of more than a hundred women I have been able to follow systematically during my fieldwork, five have returned to their homelands with the prospects of some kind of stable partnership.
2.  A hidden part of such definition was the exclusion of non-"European" former Soviet populations from this category: people with Central Asian ancestries were considered foreign, "*chórnenky*," no matter what their passport or the language they spoke. The latter group, however, was very rare in Alpinetown, and they hardly ever interacted with the women. Only later, with the establishment of the cultural and social associations described in the next chapter, did more restrictive, "national" categories become slowly more popular, although never uncontested.
3.  Iryna has always maintained a certain degree of ambiguity over the precise sequence of events. She has never said if Ahmed's jealousy was justified or if she became sexually involved with Avel only after he sprang valiantly to her defense.
4.  Transnistria is a breakaway territory located on a strip of land between the River Dniester and the eastern Moldovan border with Ukraine. The Pridnestrovian Moldavian Republic is internationally recognized by only a handful of states. Its security is currently "temporarily" guaranteed by a three-party (Russia, Moldova, Transnistria) Joint Control Commission. While lacking international recognition, Transnistria works internally as a presidential republic, with its own government, parliament, military, police, postal system, currency, flag, national anthem, and coat of arms. Its survival is contingent upon the Russian Federation's financial, military, and organizational aid. In recent years, an increasing number of its citizens have also received Russian passports. At the time of the events narrated, however, Avel—like most Transnistrians—was in a legal limbo.
5.  "Macedonian" is a social, not a geographical, category. Many of the men were indeed arriving from the FYROM, or Former Yugoslav Republic of Macedonia, as the Yugoslav successor state is internationally known. But the women excluded from such a category the many Macedonians of Albanian ancestry, while they included in it the former Yugoslavs from other successor states who worked in the quarries.

6. As far as I know, the men were never legally divorced, a distinct procedure that in Italy required at the time a three-year formal waiting period (called *separazione*).
7. Indeed, many of them had previously had affairs with Italian women that had been terminated precisely because their lovers wanted them to divorce.
8. The first time I had the chance to talk with him alone, we had both been invited to stay after Mass at a Greek Catholic church. As part of an initiative to welcome immigrants, a newly formed group of Ukrainian children performed traditional dances. A few minutes before the show, Dasha asked me to sit on the other side of Gianfranco, who did not know anybody in the room. Gianfranco was obviously irritated and bored. He told me several times he was there only because Dasha had pestered him, but he did not like to meet new people or deal with new customs. Mistaking me for an Italian, he insisted that immigrants who live in Italy should speak Italian and explained that he did not want Dasha to speak any other language. After the show, he stayed in the corner, looking conspicuously at the clock, until Dasha gave up and left with him.
9. The project never materialized.
10. A significant number of mixed marriages in Italy involve older and less educated Italian males marrying younger and more educated foreign spouses. See Guetto and Azzolini (2015).
11. There is a vast literature on what are usually called "fraudulent marriages" in Anglo-Saxon legislation. Marriages are considered "fraudulent" if contracted solely for the sake of obtaining legal residency and eventual eligibility for citizenship. In these cases, the native-born spouse is usually paid for entering into the marriage, and the couple never lives together, but divorces as soon as possible. In the case of the Eastern European (women) migrants in Italy, the whole structure of the problem seems to be different. The more frequent concerns—often involving very old Italian men marrying relatively younger women—are the loss of inheritance (a concern often voiced by relatives) and the cost of the women being able to enjoy a pension as survivors for decades (a concern often voiced by the government).
12. In 2009, Italian immigration laws were tightened to make the marriage of irregular migrants more difficult (Act 94/09), sharply reducing the number of mixed marriages in subsequent years. The provisions were, however, declared illegitimate by the Italian Constitutional Court three years later (act 245/2011). For a detailed analysis of mixed marriages in Italy, see Istat (2014). There are currently several legislative initiatives targeted to curtail access to survivor pensions, either requiring a certain number of years of marriage to qualify, or making them available only to older, postretirement age, survivors. None of them has yet been approved.
13. The notion of a "moral economy," originally elaborated by the English social historian E. P. Thompson, has been used to investigate the regulation

of both care work and irregular migration. See Näre (2011) and Chauvin and Garcés-Mascareñas (2012).

CHAPTER FIVE

1. One of the very first items the women would buy as soon as they could afford it was a cell phone. Still, only close friends would call one another to make an appointment.

2. In her study of Russian-Jewish emigrants in New York in the 1980s, Fran Markowitz finds a similar dynamic. Her emigrants arrived in New York as individuals, demonstrating little or no interest in building their own community institutions. Still, during their process of settlement—and facing the expectations of US citizens and institutions—they ended up building exactly what they had tried to avoid: a collective sense of themselves as a group and a set of institutionalized relationships defined by this collective sense. See Markowitz (1993).

3. Several analyses of welfare agencies, including many nonprofit or philanthropic ones, have stressed the existence of a silent conflict between the professional staff and their "clients." The staff has its own perception of the needs of the clients, and work within a usually implicit, but nonetheless binding, definition of which of these needs are legitimate and which ones are "excessive" or "unreasonable." As with any organization, moreover, these services are highly sensitive to the migrants respecting their routines and organizational rules. The staff of each organization I observed had their own local classification of their clients as "*bravi*" (i.e., rule followers) or "*casinisti*" (i.e., troublemakers). Although these dynamics are common to the entire welfare provision sector, they appear to be more fateful in the case of the Italian philanthropic services catering to migrants. Here, most services are delivered in kind rather than in cash and street bureaucrats enjoy wide discretionary power; see Ambrosini (2000).

4. An *oratorio* is a pastoral center, usually built close to a Catholic Church. As its purposes are the teaching of Catholic doctrines and the recreational activities of parishioners (especially children), an oratorio often includes a kitchen and some common rooms. Sometimes there is also some kind of soccer field. In rare cases, it may also have a theater or a bar.

5. Orthodox Christian (and Eastern-rite Roman Catholics, like many of the Ukrainian women) are taught to touch their right shoulder first, then their left. Roman Catholics first touch their left shoulder. Orthodox, moreover, use three fingers together, to symbolize the trinity, while Roman Catholics use the flat palm, to symbolize the five sores of Christ. The difference emerged sometime in the sixteenth century, and it has become a main marker of religious difference. I discovered the importance of this difference in my youth, when during the Balkan wars Serbian and Croatian

fighters styled their opposite signs of identification by adapting the two different religious gestures.

6.  In other places, individuals would be accepted as paying guests, as if they were organizing a private party, while associations could access the same spaces for free.

7.  As with all personal names, the association names are also pseudonyms.

8.  A mixture of chopped and sautéed onions, carrots, and celery. It is a key ingredient for many Italian dishes.

9.  A few weeks later, I asked Rinaldo about his experience. I told him I had found how the group had behaved with him, so different from usual, weird. Rinaldo, who was one of the most laid back and ironic academics I have ever met, said the ritual had reminded him of his youthful trip with a leftist delegation to the former communist bloc. He said the toasts and formalities were the same. Only at the time, he added, "we had been the deferential ones."

10. They are all variations of stuffed dumplings using unleavened dough. The first three appear in Ukraine, Moldova, and Russia, respectively. The last is closer to the Polish *pierogi* and is typical of Western Ukraine.

11. Sociologists of religion have often noted that migrants may assign much more importance to religious places of worship and rituals in emigration than they did in the homeland. For a review of studies in this regard, see Kivisto (2014).

12. The women would colloquially refer to the traditional Ukrainian embroidered shirt, part of the Ukrainian national costume, as a *"vyshyvanka."* These shirts are usually made of white cotton and can be distinguished by specific local embroidery features. The *vyshyvanka* reflects not only its Ukrainian origin but also the particular region in which it was made.

13. As in the other cases already described, this term did not refer to prostitution as such, but rather to the hyperfeminine performances, long chatting and drinking sessions, and tolerance for casual sex that had quickly become, in their view, incompatible with the claim to be educated mothers interested only in the welfare of their children.

14. I was surprised by Alla's harsh judgment, as most of us—indeed Alla herself—were still frequenting the riverbanks regularly. Not to mention that Alla had always been, and still was, one of the keenest critics of my alleged lack of sexual appetite. Most women, however, were not scandalized by what Alla was saying. They regarded her statements as merely rhetorical, as something that Alla, given her new role as leader of a Christian association, was supposed to say. They did not take Alla's injunctions seriously, nor did they expect to stop enjoying their customary activities.

15. This created a problem for the smaller numbers of women who had Belarusian and Georgian passports, or who were ethnic Russians from other former USSR successor states. They were not large enough in number to claim

a differentiated spot, and consequently, if they wanted to participate, they had to claim some degree of cultural closeness to one of the main groups.

16. Ironically, most recipe books classify it as "Russian." It was actually invented, or at least codified, by a French chef named Lucien Olivier, who was the chef of the restaurant Hermitage in Moscow in the 1860s.

17. On the importance of dance in the life of the Moldovan community, see Piovesan (2011).

18. This is worth stressing, as the associations I observed have always had the peculiar feature of not being involved in any systematic project oriented toward the homeland. There is a growing debate on the role of hometown associations in promoting development projects in their places of origin; see Waldinger et al. (2008) and Levitt and Lamba-Nieves (2013). In the case of the women, the activities of their associations have always been targeted at Alpinetown. While I heard the women sometimes talking about collecting funds for certain goals in their homeland—usually restoring a church or paying scholarships to orphans—these activities have never been frequent or systematic.

## CONCLUSION

1. The ambivalence of migration, in which the economic usefulness of migrants is made possible precisely by the perception of their sociocultural difference, has been analyzed in detail by Aristide Zolberg (1987).

2. For the importance of this distinction, see Brubaker (2004).

3. Regardless of the communication opportunities provided by new technologies, the idea of a migrant being for a long period both an embodied pursuer of material incentives *here* and a disembodied, exclusively mental, member of circles of recognition *there* remains unconvincing. For a study of the cross-border connections of emigrants, see Waldinger (2015b).

4. For the concept of train of experience, see William James (1988).

5. See Jasso (2011).

6. The amount of psychological stress and personal strain faced by international migrants can be considerable. See Nicklett and Burgard (2009) and Mirsky et al (2007). It is interesting that these findings seem to apply even to privileged migrants such as expatriate Western workers. See Truman et al. (2011).

7. The idea that social mobility leaves permanent scars on the psychology of the mobile individual—owing to her inability to be fully at ease with the norms and practices of her new social class—is one of the most common topoi of classical Western novels. In sociology, it is first advanced by Emile Durkheim (1951) in his classic study of suicide and made systematic by Pitirim Sorokin (1959). After a long period of neglect, this interpretation of the psychological consequences of social mobility has been made popular again by Pierre Bourdieu (2004), with his notion of a "*habitus clivé,*" a sense of the self torn by contradiction and divisions as a consequence of

the experience of radical change in social position. A main problem of this line of argument is, however, that researchers have been unable to find any empirical evidence of *permanent* psychological trauma caused by social mobility, especially when upwardly mobile persons may associate with others who are experiencing similar trajectories. See Goldthorpe (1980), Houle (2011), and Houle and Martin (2011). The lack of permanent scars, however, does not imply the absence of a remarkable amount of psychological strain and stress associated with any *process* of social mobility, both upward and downward. Rather, it is evidence of the importance of taking into account the significance of psychosocial transformations as an integral part of the interactional dimension of social mobility. For studies of how mobile individuals find ways of interpreting the expectations, fears, and anxieties of their new positions, see Newman (1988), Jones (2003), Ryan and Sackrey (1996), Bettie (2014), and Friedman (2015).

8. For an analysis of class mobility in these terms, see Friedman (2015).

9. On this point see Cabaniss and Cameron (2018).

10. In her study of new immigrants in the United States, Guillermina Jasso has found that they appropriated, in their interaction with interviewers, their legal role in the migration process as elements of their presentation of their selves. They presented themselves as principal applicants for visa requests, in highly gendered and nation-specific ways. Men, for example, are more likely to describe themselves as principals, even when they are not actually so. Women, on the contrary, underdeclare such status, even when it is the case. See Jasso (2011).

11. See Lamont (2000).

12. The popular acronym 3D is originally 3K, the English expression being the translation of the earlier Japanese definition of *kitanai* (dirty), *kiken* (dangerous), and *kitsui* (demanding). See Connell (1993).

13. See Boneva and Frieze (2001) and Jokela (2009).

14. For a critical review of psychological approaches to migration, see Berry (1997; 2001) and Suarez Orozco (1997).

15. The notion of a rite of passage, and the sequence I follow here, was been identified by Van Gennep (1981) more than a century ago and made popular again by Victor Turner (1965). The concept has already been used in migration studies, mostly by scholars interested in migration systems where international mobility has become part of a successful transition to manhood. For the Mexico-US case, see Kandel and Massey (2002) and Epstein and Gang (2010). Similar dynamics have been found by Monsutti (2007) for Afghanistan. See also Chavez (1992) and Menjivar (2006).

16. The classic vision of assimilation as the end state of migration processes is discussed by Gordon (1964). For the contemporary debate on assimilation, see Brubaker (2004) and Kivisto (2004).

17. While together, especially in the beginning, all the stories we exchanged were narratives of loss: of their jobs, of their husbands, of their savings

and assets, of their status as modernized and urban professionals. Maria, a fiftyish Ukrainian woman who had been formerly a high-school teacher, was one of the favorite storytellers in the initial group. In the early years, the women would nearly always ask her to tell her story to the newly arrived, and all of us would follow her performance attentively, no matter how many times we had already heard it. She would start the story in Soviet times, when her family enjoyed a stable, middle-class status; they had an independent flat, owned a car, and spent a week each year vacationing on the Black Sea. After the collapse, however, they had difficulty merely surviving and all their properties were eventually sold. At the end of the 1990s, earlier than most, Maria accepted an offer from a "middleman" to immigrate to Western Europe to work as a babysitter. When she arrived at the meeting point with him, she suddenly discovered that she could not bring with her even the smallest piece of luggage, as she had to cross the first border in a hidden compartment in the back of a van. The last thing she saw before the door closed on her were her two suitcases abandoned on the side of the street. She subsequently entered the EU wrapped in blankets and clinging to the bottom of a train. The middleman took away her passport—stripped her of her certified identity—until she was able, several months later, to repay her debts. When Maria told her story, even though years had passed—and even though she had told the story many times—she was still traumatized, not so much by the risks she had taken as by the demeaning conditions she had been exposed to. She insisted that she resented having been forced to travel "like a ghost" although she had tried in vain to explain to the middleman that she was "a mother and a teacher." She had been, however, forced to travel "like a criminal, a prostitute." What I always found interesting in the popularity of Maria's story was that she was an outlier. Nearly all the women, in fact, had entered the EU legally with a tourist visa and subsequently overstayed. Maria was not articulating a common, shared experience. Rather, her story offered a good opportunity for the other women to consider their own sense of separation and loss. Besides her remarkable qualities as a storyteller, Maria epitomized the sense of humiliation all had felt.

18. See Van Gennep (1961).
19. Turner (1967). Uncertainty has been identified for decades as an endemic feature of migrant behavior. See Williams and Baláž (2012) and O'Connell (1997). The interest in the ambiguities and ambivalences of the migration experience is more recent, even if precedents may be found in the writings of the Chicago school. See Uehling (2002), Tymczuk (2013), and Kivisto and La Vecchia-Mikkola (2013).
20. For the importance of cases that offer the possibility to observe a phenomenon otherwise diluted, see Katz (2012).
21. For the case of Filipino workers in the Gulf States, see Aguilar (1999).

22. Most studies of women migrating from Latin America rely on social networks directed to localities that already have a sizable presence of conationals. See González-López (2005), Hirsch (2003), Hondagneu-Sotelo (1994), and Cerrutti and Massey (2001). For the differences implied by migrating to "new immigration destinations," see Dreby and Schmalzbauer (2013) and Schmalzbauer (2009).

23. This is the case more frequently studied by rational-choice models of migration, which usually frame settlement as a choice between assimilation and ethnic retention, between remaining within the immigrant "community" and entering new aspirations and new networks of sociability. See Esser (2007).

24. Interestingly, the women pioneers themselves shared this naturalization process. When they instructed the newcomers, an activity they found both necessary and pleasant, they always presented the paths open to them as obvious, empirically self-evident choices, never as something they had discovered and made possible through creativity and effort.

25. Robert Park's notion of the "marginal man," torn between two identities, was actually coined to describe the experience of already settled groups, largely composed of followers. See Park (1928). The same applies to the notion of "double absence"—of being neither here nor there—proposed by Abdelmalek Sayad in his influential account of the experience of Algerians in France. See Sayad (1999).

26. The shortest spell of irregular status among the women was a little more than a year. On average, they had been irregular for three years, with many cases reaching five or six years of undocumented living.

27. See Menjívar (2006).

28. See Sciortino (2012). Ethnographic exemplars of immigrant groups drawing remarkably different boundaries from what I have identified with the women can be found—among many others—in Espiritu (2001) for Filipinos in the United States, in Schierup and Ålund (1986) for Yugoslav migrants in Scandinavia, in Sayad (1999) for Algerians in France, and in Hondagneu-Sotelo (1994) for Mexican women in the United States.

29. For a theory of meaning as contingent selection, see Luhmann (1976). For an application to migration processes, see Bommes (2013).

30. Harold Garfinkel, in his pathbreaking dissertation, defined the structure of the external constraints perfectly: "The big question is not whether actors understand each other or not. The fact is that they do understand each other, that they will understand each other, but the catch is that they will understand each other regardless of how they would like to be understood" (1952, 367).

31. I also initially had the same suspicions, although I did my best not to reveal them in any way. The women, however, were quickly aware of the fact that they were often not believed. In 2004, there were rumors in Alpinetown that

a temporary employment agency would soon start recruiting foreign women with a proper educational background. Many women asked me to help them with preparing and translating their dossier. Nearly all the women, while handing me their original diplomas, told me sometimes jokingly, sometimes harshly, that I could double-check their educational credentials myself. A few days later, it turned out that the agency was actually a scam.

32. On the lack of a demand for immigrant labor for middle and upper occupational positions in the Italian labor market, see Reyneri and Fullin (2011) and Saraceno et al. (2013).

33. Most women, even after nearly two decades, still work in household services, as care workers or cleaners. Some of them have moved on to work for companies specializing in cleaning offices and commercial spaces. Very few, usually daughters reunited with their mothers at a young age, are employed in bars and shops. The only significant cases of substantial social mobility are the *signore*.

34. For the meaning and structure of degradation ceremonies, see Garfinkel (1952).

35. At a later stage in the process of settlement, an even more desired—but potentially more divisive—category of goods entered the women's circuit. It was composed of the goods *some* women acquired as tokens of appreciation offered by others, particularly by males. In contrast to what they acquired themselves, these goods were not important in terms of economic value, although often they were indeed expensive. They were important, and highly prized by the women, for their aspirational meaning, because they meant a step toward future development. The ways in which the women could display these goods, and requests for confirmation from the others could be advanced, were sharply distinctive. The women who had received these gifts displayed them more indirectly, waiting for some other woman to notice and ask about them. The owners would always answer with a declaration that they were unsolicited gifts, "*sorprese*" as the women started to call them, adopting an Italian word. The women who could show them off had to walk a fine line: they wanted to have these goods assessed as a confirmation of their femininity, but in order to achieve that they had to present them in a more collective, altruistic way, as proof that the path they all aspired to walk was indeed real and that it contained rewards all women could—at least in principle—achieve.

36. The centrality of signaling under conditions of imperfect information was elaborated originally in the economics of labor markets. For its original formulation, see Spence (1973). It has been subsequently adapted to a host of management issues; see Connelly et al. (2011). In recent years, under the influence of rational-choice approaches, it has been often used to explain gender displays and personal performances. See Mialon (2012) and Bird and Smith (2005).

37. The idea of the habitus as a system of durable, transposable dispositions, able to shape individual attitudes, tastes, and behavior over long period of time and beyond changes in social conditions, is particularly crucial in the work of Pierre Bourdieu (1990). It is increasingly used along these lines in migration studies. See Kelly and Lusis (2006), Marshall and Foster (2002), and Oliver and O'Reilly (2010).

38. See Kis (2005), Ibroscheva (2013), and Zhurzhenko (2001).

39. On the importance of "going along" as a research strategy, see Kusenbach (2003).

40. See Exley and Allen (2007).

41. The importance of this cleavage explains why the group needed such a strong norm against any portrayal of their employers as (sometimes) gentle persons. In order to protect the women from any controversy about their competencies, the blame had to be assigned unambiguously to a shared opposition. Any more nuanced judgment would have reopened an ambiguity concerning the attribution of guilt.

42. As I have shown in chapter 2, the consumption practices the women had started to practice substantially weakened the group, fragmenting it into several distinct consumption crews. The group itself, however, had made such fragmentation possible. It was its policing against excessive sacrifice that had facilitated and legitimated the creation of the resources for personal expenses.

43. Unsurprisingly, personal networks and peer groups play an important role in this regard. The role of ambition, and the critical role of significant others in shaping it, has traditionally been at the center of the so-called "Wisconsin model" of socioeconomic status attainment in its various versions. See Sewell et al. (1970). Subsequent research has somewhat downplayed the aspirational element, instead stressing the importance—in explaining actual social mobility outcomes—of structural allocation. Motivation has been thus interpreted mostly as a process of progressive adaptation to external conditions, and interpersonal influence has been reinterpreted as a form of communication of the "realistic" expectations available to the individual. Even in this latter version, however, the social psychological dimension is far from negligible. first, it is still important to understand how different individuals "learn" what is "realistic" for them. Second, it is still important to understand what motivates individuals in making their decisions. Third, it is still to be explained why not all actors make the same decisions even when exposed to the same set of structural constraints. For the enduring importance of a social psychology of social mobility, see Kerckhoff (1989).

44. For social closure, see the classical statement by Max Weber (1978). For the importance of race as a category in Soviet and post-Soviet societies, see Zakharov and Law (2017) and Matusevich (2007).

APPENDIX

1.  This was one of the main differences between my previous experience and theirs. As a refugee, I have never technically been an irregular migrant in Italy. They, like most of the women I met subsequently, had entered the country with tourist visas, bound to expire after ninety days. Although many of them were not "irregular" when I met them, they all knew they would lose their legal status soon. A second equally important difference was that, having grown up in a mixed family in the Istrian March, I could count Italian among my mother tongues, well enough to pass as a native in most circumstances.

2.  In fact, the same had happened to me many years before. When I received my degree at the local university, their information system apparently had not yet been updated to include the existence of the newly born Croatian state. Years later, looking at the historical statistics of my alma mater, I discovered I had actually received my degree as a citizen of Kazakhstan.

3.  Alpinetown is far from peculiar. Ukrainians, nearly absent until 2000, are now among the top five nationalities of foreign residents in Italy. Moldovans, whose presence was negligible until 2000, are now among the top ten. Moreover, 79 percent of Ukrainians, 81 percent of Russians, and 67 percent of Moldovans in Italy are women.

4.  The "justification" of ethnographic research is particularly tricky. In contrast to other research methods, which produce knowledge that would be unavailable to the reader in any other way, ethnographers produce knowledge that, in principle, any layperson could acquire. They struggle to understand and describe to other audiences a form of knowledge that the subjects of their studies already possess. On the warrants for ethnographic research, see Katz (1997; 2012).

5.  The study of migratory events within the broader life course of individuals and family is an important aspect of long-term studies of migration related changes. See Kulu and Milewski (2008).

6.  Among the exemplars of long-term migration ethnographies that I have found especially inspiring for thinking about the specificities of long-term fieldwork with immigrant groups, see Black (2010), Bloch (2018), Chamberlain (1997), Gonzales (2015), and Smith (2006).

# References

Adams, Caroline. 1987. *Across Seven Seas and Thirteen Rivers: Life Stories of Pioneer Sylhetti Settlers in Britain*. London: THAP Books.

Aguilar, Filomeno V., Jr. 1999. "Ritual Passage and the Reconstruction of Selfhood in International Labour Migration." *Sojourn: Journal of Social Issues in Southeast Asia* 14 (1): 98–139.

Ahmad, Jamal. 2003. "Marketing in a Multicultural World: The Interplay of Marketing, Ethnicity and Consumption." *European Journal of Marketing* 37 (11/12): 1599–620.

Aidis, Ruta. 2003. "Officially Despised yet Tolerated: Open-Air Markets and Entrepreneurship in Post-Socialist Countries." *Post-Communist Economies* 15 (3): 461–73.

Aktar, Cengiz, and Nedim Ögelman. 1994. "Recent Developments in East-West Migration: Turkey and the Petty Traders." *International Migration* 32 (2): 343–54.

Alexander, Jeffrey C. 2012. *Trauma: A Social Theory*. Cambridge, Polity.

Ambrosini, Maurizio. 2000. "Immigrazione e politiche sociali: Il ruolo peculiare del terzo settore nell'esperienza italiana." In *L'azione del volontariato nei confronti degli immigrati stranieri: Analisi di casi e proposta di modelli organizzativi*, edited by Maurizio Ambrosini, 1–13. Milano: Fondazione Cariplo.

Andall, Jacqueline. 2000. *Gender, Migration and Domestic Service: The Politics of Black Women in Italy*. Aldershot, UK: Ashgate.

Anghel, Remus. 2013. *Romanians in Western Europe: Migration, Status Dilemmas, and Transnational Connections*. Plymouth, UK: Lexington Books.

Anthias, F., ed. 2000. *Gender and Migration in Southern Europe*. Oxford: Berg.

Ashwin, Sarah, ed. 2000. *Gender, State and Society in Soviet and Post-Soviet Russia*. London: Routledge.

Baganha, I. Maria, and Maria Lucinda Fonseca, eds. 2004. *New Waves: Migration from Eastern to Southern Europe*. Lisbon: Luso-American Foundation.

Bakewell, Olivier, Hein de Haas, and Agnieszka Kubal. 2011. "Migration Systems, Pioneers and the Role of Agency." Working paper 48/2011, International Migration Institute, Oxford.

Barbagli, Marzio, Asher Colombo, and Giuseppe Sciortino, eds. 2004. *I sommersi e i sanati: Le regolarizzazioni degli immigrati*. Bologna: Il Mulino.

Barrett, Betty Jo, Nazim Habibov, and Elena Chernyak. 2012. "Factors Affecting Prevalence and Extent of Intimate Partner Violence in Ukraine: Evidence from a Nationally Representative Survey." *Violence Against Women* 18 (10): 1147–76.

Bartolomei, Maria Rita. 2010. "Migrant Male Domestic Workers in Comparative Perspective: Four Case Studies from Italy, India, Ivory Coast, and Congo." *Men & Masculinities* 13 (1): 87–110.

Bashi, Vilna F. 2007. *Survival of the Knitted: Immigrant Social Networks in a Stratified World*. Stanford: Stanford University Press.

Bernstein, Frances Lee. 2007. *The Dictatorship of Sex: Lifestyle Advice for the Soviet Masses*. DeKalb: Northern Illinois University Press.

Berry, John W. 1997. "Immigration, Acculturation, and Adaptation." *Applied Psychology* 46 (1): 5–34.

Berry, John W. 2001. "A Psychology of Immigration." *Journal of Social Issues* 57 (3): 615–31.

Bettie, Julie. 2014. *Women without Class: Girls, Race, and Identity*. Berkeley: University of California Press.

Bird, Rebecca Bliege, and Eric Alden Smith. 2005. "Signaling Theory, Strategic Interaction, and Symbolic Capital." *Current Anthropology* 46 (2): 221–48.

Black, Timothy. 2010. *When a Heart Turns Rock Solid: The Lives of Three Puerto Rican Brothers on and off the Streets*. New York: Vintage.

Blaschke, Jochen. 2008. "Trends on Regularization of Third Country Nationals in Irregular Situation of Stay across the European Union." Directorate-General Internal Policies, PE 393.282, European Parliament, Brussels.

Bloch, Alexia. 2011. "Intimate Circuits: Modernity, Migration and Marriage among Post-Soviet Women in Turkey." *Global Networks* 11 (4): 502–21.

Bloch, Alexia. 2018. *Sex, Love, and Migration: Postsocialism, Modernity, and Intimacy from Istanbul to the Arctic*. Ithaca: Cornell University Press.

Bommes, Michael. 2013. *Immigration and Social Systems: Collected Essays of Michael Bommes*. Amsterdam: Amsterdam University Press.

Boneva, Bonka S., and Irene Hanson Frieze. 2001. "Toward a Concept of a Migrant Personality." *Journal of Social Issues* 57 (3): 477–91.

Bourdieu, Pierre. 1990. *The Logic of Practice*. Stanford: Stanford University Press.

Bourdieu, Pierre. 2004. *Esquisse pour une auto-analyse*. Paris: Editions Raisons d'agir.

Bren, Paulina, and Mary Neuburger. 2012. *Communism Unwrapped: Consumption in Cold War Eastern Europe*. Oxford: Oxford University Press.

Brettell, Caroline. 2016. *Gender and Migration*. New York: Wiley.

Brubaker, Rogers. 2004. *Ethnicity without Groups*. Cambridge: Harvard University Press.

Cabaniss, Emily Regis, and Abigail E. Cameron. 2018. "Toward a Social Psychological Understanding of Migration and Assimilation." *Humanity & Society* 42 (2):171–92.

Catanzaro, Raimondo, and Asher Colombo, eds. 2009. *Badanti & co.: Il lavoro domestico straniero in Italia*. Bologna: Il Mulino.

CBS-AXA. 2005. *Moldova Migration and Remittances*. Chişinău, Moldova.

Cerrutti, Marcella, and Douglas S. Massey. 2001. "On the Auspices of Female Migration from Mexico to the United States." *Demography* 38 (2): 187–200.

Chamberlain, Mary. 1997. *Narratives of Exile and Return*. London: MacMillan.

Chattaraman, Veena, and Sharron J. Lennon. 2008. "Ethnic Identity, Consumption of Cultural Apparel, and Self-Perceptions of Ethnic Consumers." *Journal of Fashion Marketing and Management* 12 (4): 518–31.

Chauvin, Sébastien, and Blanca Garcés-Mascareñas. 2012. "Beyond Informal Citizenship: The New Moral Economy of Migrant Illegality." *International Political Sociology* 6 (3): 241–59.

Chavez, Leo R. 1992. *Shadowed Lives: Undocumented Migrants in American Society*. Fort Worth: Harcourt Brace.

Chernishova, Natalya. 2013. *Soviet Consumer Culture in the Brezhnev Era*. London: Routledge.

Choldin, Harvey M. 1973. "Kinship Networks in the Migration Process." *International Migration Review* 7 (2): 163–75.

Connell, John. 1993. "Kitanai, Kitsui and Kiken: The Rise of Labour Migration to Japan." Economic & Regional Restructuring Research Unit, University of Sydney.

Connelly, Brian L., S. Trevis Certo, R. Duane Ireland, and Christopher R. Reutzel. 2011. "Signaling Theory: A Review and Assessment." *Journal of Management* 37 (1): 39–67.

Constable, Nicole. 1997a. *Maid to Order in Hong Kong: Stories of Filipina Workers*. Ithaca: Cornell University Press.

Constable, Nicole. 1997b. "Sexuality and Discipline among Filipina Domestic Workers in Hong Kong." *American Ethnologist* 24 (3): 539–58.

Cuc, Milan, Erik Lundback, and Edgardo Ruggiero. 2005. "Migration and Remittances in Moldova." Washington, DC: International Monetary Fund.

Curran, Sara R., and Estela Rivero-Fuentes. 2003. "Engendering Migrant Networks: The Case of Mexican Migration." *Demography* 40 (2): 289–307.

Cvajner, Martina. 2009. "Non solo domestiche: Reti amicali e vita sentimentale delle donne immigrate." In *Badanti & co.: Il lavoro domestico straniero in Italia*, edited by Raimondo Catanzaro and Asher Colombo, 134–64. Bologna: Il Mulino.

Cvajner, Martina. 2011. "Hyperfemininity as Decency: Beauty, Womanhood and Respect in Emigration." *Ethnography* 12:356–74.

Cvajner, Martina. 2012. "The Presentation of Self in Emigration: Eastern European Women in Italy." *ANNALS of the American Academy of Political and Social Science* 642 (1): 186–99.

Cvajner, Martina. 2016. "Il prisma del desiderio: La stratificazione sessuale in emigrazione." *Etnografia e ricerca qualitativa* 3:513–33.

Cvajner, Martina, and Giuseppe Sciortino. 2010a. "Away from the Mediterranean: Italy's Changing Migration Systems." *Italian Politics and Society* 69:15–23.

Cvajner, Martina, and Giuseppe Sciortino. 2010b. "A Tale of Networks and Policies: Prolegomena to an Analysis of Irregular Migration Careers and Their Developmental Paths." *Population, Space and Place* 16 (3): 213–25.

Darii, Mihaela. 2008. *On the Border of Legal and Illegal: Women Open-Air Market Traders in the Republic of Moldova*. Saarbrucken: VDM Verlag.

Davidenko, M. 2017. "Searching for Lost Femininity: Russian Middle-Aged Women's Participation in the Post-Soviet Consumer Culture." *Journal of Consumer Culture*, https://doi.org/10.1177/1469540517714021.

Degiuli, F. 2016. *Caring for a Living: Migrant Women, Aging Citizens, and Italian Families*. New York: Oxford University Press.

Denisova, Liubov N., and Irina Mukhina. 2010. *Rural Women in the Soviet Union and Post-Soviet Russia*. New York: Routledge.

Diner, Hasia R. 1983. *Erin's Daughters in America: Irish Immigrant Women in the Nineteenth Century*. Baltimore: Johns Hopkins University Press.

Dines, Nicholas. 2002. "Urban Renewal, Immigration, and Contested Claims to Public Space: The Case of Piazza Garibaldi in Naples." *GeoJournal* 58 (2–3): 177–88.

Donato, Katharine M. 1992. "Understanding U.S. Immigration: Why Some Countries Send Women and Others Send Men." In *Seeking Common Ground: Multidisciplinary Studies of Immigrant Women in the United States*, edited by Donna R. Gabaccia, 159–84. Westport, CT: Greenwood Press.

Donato, Katharine M. 2010. "U.S. Migration from Latin America: Gendered Patterns and Shifts." *ANNALS of the American Academy of Political and Social Science* 630 (1): 78–92.

Donato, Katharine M., and Donna Gabaccia. 2015. *Gender and International Migration*. New York: Russell Sage Foundation.

Donato, Katharine M., Joseph T. Alexander, Donna R. Gabaccia, and Johanna Leinonen. 2011. "Variations in the Gender Composition of Immigrant Populations: How They Matter." *International Migration Review* 45 (3): 495–526.

Donato, Katharine M., Bhumika Piya, and Anna Jacobs. 2014. "The Double Disadvantage Reconsidered: Gender, Immigration, Marital Status, and Global Labor Force Participation in the 21st Century." *International Migration Review* 48:S335–S376.

Douglas, Mary. 1991. "The Idea of a Home: A Kind of Space." *Social Research* 58 (1): 287–307.

Dreby, Joanna. 2010. *Divided by Borders: Mexican Migrants and Their Children*. Berkeley: University of California Press.

Dreby, Joanna, and Leah Schmalzbauer. 2013. "The Relational Contexts of Migration: Mexican Women in New Destination Sites." *Sociological Forum* 28 (1): 1–26.

Durkheim, Emile. 1951. *Suicide: A Study in Sociology*. New York: The Free Press.

Duvell, Franck. 2006. "Ukraine—Europe's Mexico?" Country Report. Oxford: COMPAS.

Ehrenreich, Barbara, and Arlie Russell Hochschild. 2004. *Global Woman: Nannies, Maids, and Sex Workers in the New Economy*. New York: Metropolitan Books.

Epstein, Gil S., and Ira N. Gang. 2010. *Migration and Culture*. Bingley, UK: Emerald Group Publishing.

Espiritu, Yen Le. 2001. " 'We Don't Sleep around Like White Girls Do': Family, Culture, and Gender in Filipina American Lives." *Signs* 26 (2): 415–40.

Esser, Hartmut. 2007. "Does the 'New' Immigration Require a 'New' Theory of Intergenerational Integration?" In *Rethinking Migration: New Theoretical and Empirical Perspectives*, edited by Alejandro Portes and Josh DeWind, 308–41. New York: Berghahn Books.

Exley, Catherine, and Davina Allen. 2007. "A Critical Examination of Home Care: End of Life Care as an Illustrative Case." *Social Science & Medicine* 65 (11): 2317–27.

Faier, Lieba. 2009. *Intimate Encounters: Filipina Women and the Remaking of Rural Japan*. Berkeley: University of California Press.

Fedyuk, Olena. 2009. "Death in the Life of Ukrainian Labor Migrants in Italy." migrationonline.cz, March. Available at http://aa.ecn.cz/img_upload/6334c0c7298d6b396d213ccd19be5999/OFedyuk_DeathinthelifeofUkrainianlabormigrantsinItaly_1.pdf. Accessed July 7, 2017.

Fedyuk, Olena. 2012. "Images of Transnational Motherhood: The Role of Photographs in Measuring Time and Maintaining Connections between Ukraine and Italy." *Journal of Ethnic and Migration Studies* 38 (2): 279–300.

Fedyuk, Olena, and Marta Kindler, eds. 2016. *Ukrainian Migration to the European Union*. Cham, Switzerland: Springer.

Field, Deborah A. 2007. *Private Life and Communist Morality in Khrushchev's Russia*. New York: Peter Lang.

Fikes, Kesha, and Alaina Lemon. 2002. "African Presence in Former Soviet Spaces." *Annual Review of Anthropology* 31:497–524.

Finotelli, Claudia. 2007. *Illegale Einwanderung, Flüchtlingsmigration und das Ende des Nord-Süd-Mythos: Zur funktionalen Äquivalenz des deutschen und des italienischen Einwanderungsregimes*. Münster: LIT.

Finotelli, Claudia, and Giuseppe Sciortino. 2013. "Through the Gates of the Fortress: European Visa Policies and the Limits of Immigration Control." *Perspectives on European Politics and Societies* 14 (1): 80–101.

Franz, Barbara. 2003. "Bosnian Refugee Women in (Re)settlement: Gender Relations and Social Mobility." *Feminist Review* 73:86–103.

Friedman, Sam. 2015. "Habitus Clivé and the Emotional Imprint of Social Mobility." *Sociological Review* 64 (1): 129–47.

Fussell, Elizabeth, and Douglas Massey. 2004. "The Limits to Cumulative Causation: International Migration from Mexican Urban Areas." *Demography* 41 (1): 151–71.

Gal, Susan, and Gail Kligman. 2000. *The Politics of Gender after Socialism: A Comparative Historical Essay*. Princeton: Princeton University Press.

Gamburd, Michele Ruth. 2000. *The Kitchen Spoon's Handle: Transnationalism and Sri Lanka's Migrant Housemaids*. Ithaca: Cornell University Press.

Garfinkel, Harold. 1952. "The Perception of the Other: A Study in Social Order." PhD dissertation, Department of Sociology, Harvard University.

George, Sheba M. 2005. *When Women Come First: Gender and Class in Transnational Migration*. Berkeley: University of California Press.

Ger, Glintz, and Per Ostergard. 1998. "Constructing Immigrant Identities in Consumption: Appearance among the Turko-Danes." *Advances in Consumer Research* 25:48–52.

Ghodsee, Kristen. 2006. " 'Shopaholic' in Eastern Europe: A Guest Editor's Foreword." *Anthropology of East Europe Review* 24 (2): 7–9.

Goffman, Erving. 1966. *Behavior in Public Places: Notes on the Social Organization of Gatherings*. New York: Free Press.

Goffman, Erving. 1967. *Interaction Ritual: Essays on Face-to-Face Behavior*. New York: Pantheon Books.

Goldthorpe, H. John. 1980. *Social Mobility and Class Structure in Modern Britain*. Oxford: Clarendon Press.

Golovakha, Evhen, Andriy Gorbachyk, and Natalia Panina. 2007. "Ukraine and Europe: Outcomes of International Comparative Sociological Survey." Institute of Sociology, Ukrainian National Academy of Sciences, Kiev.

Gonzales, Roberto G. 2015. *Lives in Limbo: Undocumented and Coming of Age in America*. Berkeley: University of California Press.

González-López, Gloria. 2005. *Erotic Journeys: Mexican Immigrants and Their Sex Lives*. Berkeley: University of California Press.

Gordon, Milton. 1964. *Assimilation in American Life: The Role of Race, Religion and National Origins*. New York: Oxford University Press.

Gorny, Agata, and Paolo Ruspini, eds. 2004. *Migration in the New Europe: East-West Revisited*. London: Palgrave.

Green, Adam Isaiah. 2014. *Sexual Fields: Toward a Sociology of Collective Sexual Life*. Chicago: University of Chicago Press.

Grinchenko, Gelinada. 2015. " 'And Now Imagine Her or Him as a Slave, a Pitiful Slave with No Rights': Child Forced Labourers in the Culture of Remembrance of the USSR and Post-Soviet Ukraine." *European Review of History: Revue européenne d'histoire* 22 (2): 389–410.

Guetto, Raffaele, and Davide Azzolini. 2015. "An Empirical Study of Status Exchange through Migrant/Native Marriages in Italy." *Journal of Ethnic and Migration Studies* 41 (13): 2149–72.

Gurova, Olga. 2018. "Consumer Culture in Socialist Russia." In *The Sage Handbook of Consumer Culture*, edited by Olga Kravets, Pauline Maclaren, Steven Miles, and Alladi Venkatesh, 102–123. London: Sage.

Hagan, Jacqueline Maria. 1998. "Social Network, Gender, and Immigrant Incorporation." *American Sociological Review* 63 (1): 55–67.

Harney, Nicholas D. 2012. "Migrant Strategies, Informal Economies and Ontological Security: Ukrainians in Naples, Italy." *International Journal of Sociology and Social Policy* 32 (1): 4–16.

Harzig, Christiane. 1997. *Peasant Maids—City Women*. Ithaca: Cornell University Press.

Hellerman, C. 2006. "Migration Alone: Tackling Social Capital? Women from Eastern Europe in Portugal." *Ethnic and Racial Studies* 29 (6): 1135–52.

Herrera, Gioconda. 2013. "Gender and International Migration: Contributions and Cross-Fertilizations." *Annual Review of Sociology* 39 (1): 471–89.

Heyse, Petra. 2011. "A Life Course Perspective in the Analysis of Self-Experiences of Female Migrants in Belgium: The Case of Ukrainian and Russian Women." *Migracijske i Etničke Teme* 27 (2): 199–225.

Hine, Thomas. 2002. *I Want That! How We All Became Shoppers*. New York: Harper Perennial.

Hirsch, Jennifer S. 2003. *A Courtship after Marriage: Sexuality and Love in Mexican Transnational Families*. Berkeley: University of California Press.

Hoerder, Dirk. 2002. *Cultures in Contact: World Migrations in the Second Millennium*. Durham: Duke University Press.

Hoerder, Dick, Elise van Nederveen, and Silke Neunsinger, eds. 2015. *Towards a Global History of Domestic and Caregiving Workers*. Leiden: Brill.

Hofmann, Erin Trouth, and Cynthia J. Buckley. 2013. "Global Changes and Gendered Responses: The Feminization of Migration from Georgia." *International Migration Review* 47 (3): 508–38.

Hollifield, James F., Philip L. Martin, and Pia M. Orrenius, eds. 2014. *Controlling Migration. A Global Perspective*. Stanford: Stanford University Press.

Hondagneu-Sotelo, Pierette. 1992. "Overcoming Patriarchal Constraints: The Reconstruction of Gender Relations among Mexican Immigrant Women and Men." *Gender & Society* 6 (3): 393–415.

Hondagneu-Sotelo, Pierette. 1994. *Gendered Transitions: Mexican Experiences of Immigration*. Berkeley: University of California Press.

Hondagneu-Sotelo, Pierrette. 2001. *Doméstica: Immigrant Workers Cleaning and Caring in the Shadows of Affluence*. Berkeley: University of California Press.

Hondagneu-Sotelo, Pierrette, and Ernestine Avila. 1997. "I'm Here but I'm There: The Meanings of Latina Transnational Motherhood." *Gender & Society* 11 (5): 548–71.

Houle, Jason N. 2011. "The Psychological Impact of Intragenerational Social Class Mobility." *Social Science Research* 40 (3): 757–772.

Houle, Jason N., and Molly A. Martin. 2011. "Does Intergenerational Mobility Shape Psychological Distress? Sorokin Revisited." *Research in Social Stratification and Mobility* 29 (2): 193–203.

Houstoun, Marion F., Roger G. Kramer, and Joan Mackin Barrett. 1984. "Female Predominance in Immigration to the United States since 1930: A First Look." *International Migration Review* 18 (4): 908–63.

Huisman, Kimberly, and Pierrette Hondagneu-Sotelo. 2005. "Dress Matters: Change and Continuity in the Dress Practices of Bosnian Muslim Refugee Women." *Gender & Society* 19 (1): 44–65.

Ibarra, M. 2002. "Emotional Proletarians in a Global Economy: Mexican Immigrant Women and Elder Care Work." *Urban Anthropology* 31 (3): 317–50.

Ibroscheva, Elza. 2013. *Advertising, Sex, and Post-Socialism: Women, Media, and Femininity in the Balkans*. Lanham, MD: Lexington.

Iglicka, Krystyna. 2001. "Shuttling from the Former Soviet Union to Poland: From 'Primitive Mobility' to Migration." *Journal of Ethnic and Migration Studies* 27 (3): 505–18.

Ismayilova, Leyla, and Nabila El-Bassel. 2013. "Prevalence and Correlates of Intimate Partner Violence by Type and Severity: Population-Based Studies in Azerbaijan, Moldova, and Ukraine." *Journal of Interpersonal Violence* 28 (12): 2521–56.

Istat. 2014. *Il matrimonio in Italia*. Roma: Istituto Nazionale di Statistica.

Jackson, Pauline. 1984. "Women in 19th Century Irish Emigration." *International Migration Review* 18 (4): 1004–20.

James, William. 1988. *The Manuscript Lectures*. Cambridge: Harvard University Press.

Jasso, Guillermina. 2011. "Migration and Stratification." *Social Science Research* 40 (5): 1292–336.

Jokela, Markus. 2009. "Personality Predicts Migration within and between U.S. States." *Journal of Research in Personality* 43 (1): 79–83.

Jones, Sandra J. 2003. "Complex Subjectivities: Class, Ethnicity, and Race in Women's Narratives of Upward Mobility." *Journal of Social Issues* 59 (4): 803–20.

Kanaiaupuni, Shawn Malia. 2000. "Reframing the Migration Question: An Analysis of Men, Women, and Gender in Mexico." *Social Forces* 78 (4): 1311–47.

Kandel, William, and Douglas S. Massey. 2002. "The Culture of Mexican Migration: A Theoretical and Empirical Analysis." *Social Forces* 80 (3): 981–1004.

Katz, Jack. 1997. "Ethnography's Warrants." *Sociological Methods & Research* 25 (4): 391–423.

Katz, Jack. 1999. *How Emotions Work*. Chicago: University of Chicago Press.

Katz, Jack. 2012. "Ethnography's Expanding Warrants." *ANNALS of the American Academy of Political and Social Science* 642 (1): 258–75.

Kelly, Philip, and Tom Lusis. 2006. "Migration and the Transnational Habitus: Evidence from Canada and the Philippines." *Environment and Planning A* 38 (5): 831–47.

Keough, L. J. 2016. *Worker-Mothers on the Margins of Europe: Gender and Migration between Moldova and Istanbul*. Bloomington: Indiana University Press.

Kerckhoff, Alan C. 1989. "On the Social Psychology of Social Mobility Processes." *Social Forces* 68 (1): 17–25.

Kis, Oksana. 2005. "Choosing without Choice: Dominant Models of Femininity in Contemporary Ukraine." In *Gender Transitions in Russia and Eastern Europe*, edited by I. Asztalos Morell, Helene Carlbäck, and Madeleine Hurd, 105–37. Stockholm: Gondolin.

Kivisto, Peter. 2004. "What is the Canonical Theory of Assimilation?" *Journal for the History of the Behavioral Sciences* 40 (2): 149–63.

Kivisto, Peter. 2014. *Religion and Immigration*. Cambridge, UK: Polity.

Kivisto, Peter, and Vanja La Vecchia-Mikkola. 2013. "Immigrant Ambivalence toward the Homeland: The Case of Iraqis in Helsinki and Rome." *Journal of Immigrant & Refugee Studies* 11 (2): 198–216.

Kofman, Eleonore, Annie Phizacklea, Parvati Raghuram, and Rosemary Sales. 2000. "Migration and Women's Work in Europe." In *Gender and International Migration in Europe*, edited by Eleonore Kofman, Annie Phizacklea, Parvati Raghuram, and Rosemary Sales, 105–33. London: Routledge.

Kon, Igor, and James Riordan, eds. 1993. *Sex and Russian Society*. Bloomington: Indiana University Press.

Kontos, Maria. 2012. "Negotiating the Social Citizenship Rights of Migrant Domestic Workers: The Right to Family Reunification and a Family Life in Policies and Debates." *Journal of Ethnic and Migration Studies* 39 (3): 409–24.

Kuehnast, Kathleen R., and Carol Nechemias. 2004. *Post-Soviet Women Encountering Transition: Nation Building, Economic Survival, and Civic Activism*. Washington, DC: Woodrow Wilson Center Press.

Kulu, Hill, and Nadja Milewski. 2008. "Family Change and Migration in the Life Course: An Introduction." *Demographic Research* 17:567–90.

Kusenbach, Margarethe. 2003. "Street Phenomenology. The Go-Along as Ethnographic Research Tool." *Ethnography* 4 (3): 455–85.

Kuus, Merje. 2004. "Europe's Eastern Expansion and the Reinscription of Otherness in East-Central Europe." *Progress in Human Geography* 28 (4): 472–89.

Lamont, Michelle. 2000. *The Dignity of Working Men: Morality and the Boundaries of Race, Class, and Immigration*. New York: Russell Sage.

Lazarsfeld, F. Paul, and Robert K. Merton. 1954. "Friendship as a Social Process." In *Freedom and Control*, edited by Morroe Berger, Theodore Abel, and Charles H. Page, 18–66. New York: Von Norstrand.

Lee, Everett S. 1966. "A Theory of Migration." *Demography* 3 (1): 47–57.

Leon, David A., Laurent Chenet, Vladimir M. Shkolnikov, Sergei Zakharov, Judith Shapiro, Galina Rakhmanova, Sergei Vassin, and Martin McKee. 1997. "Huge Variation in Russian Mortality Rates 1984–94: Artefact, Alcohol, or What?" *LANCET* 350 (9075): 383–88.

Levi Martin, John, and Matt George. 2006. "Theories of Sexual Stratification: Toward an Analytics of the Sexual Field and a Theory of Sexual Capital." *Sociological Theory* 24 (2): 107–32.

Levinson, Amanda. 2005 *The Regularization of Unauthorized Migrants: Literature Survey and Country Case Studies*. Oxford: COMPAS.

Levitt, Peggy, and Deepak Lamba-Nieves. 2013. "Rethinking Social Remittances and the Migration-Development Nexus from the Perspective Time." *Migration Letters* 10 (1): 11.

Lindstrom, David P., and Adriana López Ramírez. 2010. "Pioneers and Followers: Migrant Selectivity and the Development of U.S. Migration Streams in Latin America." *ANNALS of the American Academy of Political and Social Science* 630 (1): 53–77.

Lintelman, Joy K. 1995. "Making Service Serve Themselves: Immigrant Women and Domestic Service in North America, 1850–1920." In *People in Transit: German Migrations in Comparative Perspective, 1820–1930*, edited by Dirk Hoerder and Jorg Nagler, 249–66. Cambridge: Cambridge University Press.

Luhmann, Niklas. 1976. "Generalized Media and the Problems of Contingency." In *Explorations in General Theory in Social Science*, edited by Jan J. Loubser, Rainer C. Baum, Andrew Effrat, and Victor M. Lidz, 507–32. New York: The Free Press.

Lutz, Helma. 2010. "Gender in the Migratory Process." *Journal of Ethnic and Migration Studies* 36 (10): 1647–63.

Lutz, Wolfgang, Sergei Scherbov, and Andrei Volkov. 1993. *Demographic Trends and Patterns in the Soviet Union before 1991*. London: Routledge.

MacDonald, John S., and Leatrice D. MacDonald. 1964. "Chain Migration Ethnic Neighborhood Formation and Social Networks." *Milbank Memorial Fund Quarterly* 42 (1): 82–97.

Mahler, Sarah J., and Patricia R. Pessar. 2006. "Gender Matters: Ethnographers Bring Gender from the Periphery toward the Core of Migration Studies." *International Migration Review* 40 (1): 27–63.

Mandel, Ruth, and Caroline Humphrey. 2002. *Markets and Moralities: Ethnographies of Postsocialism*. Oxford and New York: Berg Publishers.

Markowitz, Fran. 1993. *A Community in Spite of Itself: Soviet Jewish Émigrés in New York*. Washington, DC: Smithsonian Institution Press.

Marshall, J., and N. Foster. 2002. "'Between Belonging': Habitus and the Migration Experience." *Canadian Geographer* 46 (1): 63–83.

Martinello, Marco, and Andrea Rea. 2014. "The Concept of Migratory Careers: Elements for a New Theoretical Perspective of Contemporary Human Mobility." *Current Sociology* 62:1079–96.

Martsenyuk, Tatiana. (2013). "Ukrainian Societal Attitudes Towards the Lesbian, Gay, Bisexual, and Transgender Communities." In *Gender, Politics and Society in Ukraine*, edited by Olena Hankivsky and Anastasiya Salnykova, 385–410. Toronto: University of Toronto Press.

Massey, Douglas, Rafael Alarcon, Jorge Durand, and Humberto Gonzalez. 1990. *Return to Aztlan: The Social Process of International Migration from Western Mexico*. Berkeley: University of California Press.

Massey, Douglas S., Mary J. Fischer, and Chiara Capoferro. 2006. "International Migration and Gender in Latin America: A Comparative Analysis." *International Migration* 44 (5): 63–91.

Matusevich, M., ed. 2007. *Africa in Russia, Russia in Africa: Three Centuries of Encounters*. Trenton, NJ: Africa World Press.

Mazzacurati, Cristina. 2005. "Dal blat alla vendita del lavoro: Come sono cambiate colf e badanti ucraine e moldave a Padova." In *Stranieri in Italia: Migrazioni globali, integrazioni locali*, edited by Asher Colombo and Tiziana Caponio, 145–74. Bologna: Il Mulino.

McPherson, Miller, Lynn Smith-Lovin, and James Cook. 2001. "Birds of a Feather: Homophily in Social Networks." *Annual Review of Sociology* 27:415–44.

Menjívar, Cecilia. 1999. "The Intersection of Work and Gender: Central American Immigrant Women and Employment in California." *American Behavioral Scientist* 42 (4): 601–27.

Menjívar, Cecilia. 2006. "Liminal Legality: Salvadoran and Guatemalan Immigrants' Lives in the United States." *American Journal of Sociology* 111 (4): 999–1037.

Merton, Robert K. 1987. "Three Fragments from a Sociologist's Notebooks: Establishing the Phenomenon, Specified Ignorance, and Strategic Research Materials." *Annual Review of Sociology* 13:1–29.

Mialon, Hugo M. 2012. "The Economics of Faking Ecstasy." *Economic Inquiry* 50 (1): 277–85.

Mirsky, Julia, V. Slonim-Nevo, and L. Rubinstein. 2007. "Psychological Wellness and Distress among Recent Immigrants: A Four-Year Longitudinal Study in Israel and Germany." *International Migration* 45 (1): 151–75.

Momsen, Janet H., ed. 1999. *Gender, Migration and Domestic Service*. London: Routledge.

Monsutti, Alessandro. 2007. "Migration as a Rite of Passage: Young Afghans Building Masculinity and Adulthood in Iran." *Iranian Studies* 40 (2): 167–85.

Morokvasic, Mirjana. 1984. "Birds of Passage Are Also Women." *International Migration Review* 18 (4): 886–907.

Näre, Lena. 2009. "The Making of 'Proper' Homes: Everyday Practices in Migrant Domestic Work in Naples." *Modern Italy* 14 (1): 1–17.

Näre, Lena. 2011. "The Moral Economy of Domestic and Care Labour: Migrant Workers in Naples, Italy." *Sociology* 45 (3): 396–412.

Newman, Katherine S. 1988. *Falling from Grace: Downward Mobility in the Age of Affluence*. Berkeley: University of California Press.

Nicklett, Emily J., and Sarah A. Burgard. 2009. "Downward Social Mobility and Major Depressive Episodes among Latino and Asian-American Immigrants to the United States." *American Journal of Epidemiology* 170 (6): 793–801.

Nikolova, Marina. 2012. *Ukrainian Migration in Greece: There and Back Again and Straight Ahead for One More Time*. Athens: ELIAMEP.

O'Connell, Paul G. J. 1997. "Migration under Uncertainty: 'Try Your Luck' or 'Wait and See.'" *Journal of Regional Science* 37 (2): 331–47.

Oishi, Nana. 2005. *Women in Motion : Globalization, State Policies, and Labor Migration in Asia*. Stanford: Stanford University Press.

Oliver, Caroline, and Karen O'Reilly. 2010. "A Bourdieusian Analysis of Class and Migration: Habitus and the Individualizing Process." *Sociology* 44 (1): 49–66.

Park, Robert E. 1928. "Human Migration and the Marginal Man." *American Journal of Sociology* 33 (6): 881–93.

Park, Robert E., and Herbert E. Miller. 1921. *Old World Traits Transplanted*. New York: Harper and Brothers.

Parreñas, Rhacel Salazar. 2000. "Migrant Filipina Domestic Workers and the International Division of Reproductive Labor " *Gender & Society* 14 (4): 560–80.

Parreñas, Rhacel Salazar. 2001. *Servants of Globalization: Women, Migration, and Domestic Work*. Stanford: Stanford University Press.

Parreñas, Rhacel Salazar. 2015. *Servants of Globalization: Migration and Domestic Work, Second Edition.* Stanford: Stanford University Press.

Perrotta, Domenico. 2011. *Vite in cantiere: Migrazione e lavoro dei rumeni in Italia.* Bologna: Il Mulino.

Pessar, Patricia R. 1999. "Engendering Migration Studies: The Case of New Immigrants in the United States." *American Behavioral Scientist* 42 (4): 577–600.

Petersen, William. 1958. "A General Typology of Migration." *American Sociological Review* 23:256–66.

Pew Global Attitudes Project. 2009. "Two Decades after the Wall's Fall: End of Communism Cheered but Now with More Reservation." Washington, DC: Pew Research Center. Available at http://assets.pewresearch.org/wp-content/up loads/sites/2/2009/11/Pew-Global-Attitudes-2009-Pulse-of-Europe-Report -Nov-2-1030am-NOT-EMBARGOED.pdf. Accessed February 28, 2019.

Piore, M. J. 1979. *Birds of Passage: Migrant Labor and Industrial Societies.* New York: Cambridge University Press.

Piovesan, Serena. 2011. "Dove danzano i moldavi la terra trema: Etnografia su una pratica culturale in emigrazione." PhD dissertation, Department of Sociology and Social Research, University of Trento.

Piselli, Fortunata. 1981. *Parentela ed emigrazione.* Torino: Einaudi.

Pizzorno, Alessandro. 2010. "The Mask: An Essay." *International Political Anthropology* 3 (1): 5–28.

Porteous, H. 2017. "'A Woman Isn't a Woman When She's Not Concerned About the Way She Looks': Beauty, Labour, and Femininity in Post-Soviet Russia." In *The Palgrave Handbook of Women and Gender in Twentieth-Century Russia and the Soviet Union*, edited by M. Ilic, 413–28. London: Palgrave.

Portes, Alejandro, and G. Ruben Rumbaut. 1996. *Immigrant America: A Portrait.* Berkeley: University of California Press.

Reeder, L. 2003. *Widows in White: Migration and the Transformation of Rural Women, Sicily 1880–1928.* Toronto: University of Toronto Press.

Reid, Susan E. 2007. "Gender and the Destalinisation of Consumer Taste in the Soviet Union under Khrushchev." In *Gender and Consumption*, edited by Emma Casey and Lydia Martens, 49–78. Aldershot, UK: Ashgate.

Remennick, Larissa I. 2007. *Russian Jews on Three Continents: Identity, Integration, and Conflict.* New Brunswick: Transaction Publishers.

Repak, Terry A. 1995. *Waiting on Washington: Central American Workers in the Nation's Capital.* Philadelphia: Temple University Press.

Reyneri, Emilio, and Giovanna Fullin 2011. "Low Unemployment and Bad Jobs for New Immigrants in Italy." *International Migration* 49 (1): 118–47.

Rotkirch, A. 2004. "What Kind of Sex Can You Talk About? Acquiring Sexual Knowledge in Three Soviet Generations." In *On Living through Soviet Russia*, edited by D. Bertaux, P. Thompson, and A. Rotkirch, 90–117. New York: Routledge.

Rubchak, Marian J. 2009. "Ukraine's Ancient Matriarch as a Topos in Constructing a Feminine Identity." *Feminist Review* 92 (1): 129–50.

Ryan, Jake, and Charles Sackrey. 1996. *Strangers in Paradise: Academics from the Working Class*. New York: University Press of America.

Said, Edward. 1979. *Orientalism*. New York: Vintage.

Salzinger, Leslie. 1991. "A Maid by Any Other Name: The Transformation of 'Dirty Work' by Central American Immigrants " In *Ethnography Unbound: Power and Resistance in the Modern Metropolis*, edited by Michael Burowoy, Alice Burton, Ann Ferguson, and Kathryn J. Fox, 130–60. Berkeley: University of California Press.

Samuelson, Paul A. 1954. "The Pure Theory of Public Expenditure." *Review of Economics and Statistics* 36 (4): 387–89.

Saraceno, Chiara, Nicola Sartor, and Giuseppe Sciortino, eds. 2013. *Stranieri e diseguali*. Bologna: Il Mulino.

Sarti, Raffaella. 2004. " 'Noi abbiamo visto tante città, abbiamo un'altra cultura': Servizio domestico, migrazioni e identità di genere in Italia." *POLIS* 18 (1): 17–46.

Sayad, A. 1999. *La double absence: Des illusions de l'émigré aux souffrances de l'immigré*. Paris: Seuil.

Schierup, Carl-Ulrik, and Alexandra Ålund. 1986. "Will They Still Be Dancing? Integration and Ethnic Transformation among Yugoslav Immigrants in Scandinavia." PhD dissertation, Department of Sociology, Umeå University.

Schmalzbauer, Leah. 2009. "Gender on a New Frontier: Mexican Migration in the Rural Mountain West." *Gender & Society* 23 (6): 747–67.

Schmalzbauer, Leah. 2011. " 'Doing Gender,' Ensuring Survival: Mexican Migration and Economic Crisis in the Rural Mountain West." *Rural Sociology* 76 (4): 441–60.

Schmoll, Camille. 2004. "Une place marchande cosmopolite: Circulations commerciales et dynamiques migratoires à Naples." PhD dissertation, Department of Human Geography, Universitè Paris X Nanterre.

Schrover, Marlou. 2013. "Feminization and Problematization of Migration: Europe in the Nineteenth and Twentieth Centuries." In *Proletarian and Gendered Mass Migrations: A Global Perspective on Continuities and Discontinuities from the 19th to the 21st Centuries*, edited by Dirk Hoerder and Amarjit Kaur, 103–31. Leiden: Brill.

Sciortino, Giuseppe. 2012. "Ethnicity, Race, Nationhood, Foreignness and Many Other Things: Prolegomena to a Cultural Sociology of Difference-Based Interactions." In *Oxford Handbook of Cultural Sociology*, edited by Jeffrey C. Alexander, Ronald Jacobs, and Philip Smith, 365–89. Oxford: Oxford University Press.

Sciortino, Giuseppe. 2019. "Cultural Trauma." In *Routledge Handbook of Cultural Sociology*, edited by Laura Grindstaff, M. Lo Ming-Chen, and John R. Hall, 135–43. London: Routledge.

Sewell, William H., Archibald O. Haller, and George W. Ohlendorf. 1970. "The Educational and Early Occupational Status Attainment Process: Replication and Revision." *American Sociological Review* 35 (6): 1014–27.

Shtern, Mikhail, and August Stern. 1981. *Sex in the Soviet Union*. London: WH Allen.

Sik, Endre, and Claire Wallace. 1999. "The Development of Open-Air Markets in East-Central Europe." *International Journal of Urban and Regional Research* 23 (4): 697–714.

Smith, Robert Courtney. 2006. *Mexican New York: Transnational Lives of the New Immigrants*. Berkeley: University of California Press.

Snyder, Timothy A. 2010. *Bloodlands: Europe between Hitler and Stalin*. New York: Basic Books.

Solari, Cinzia. 2006. "Transnational Politics and Settlement Practices: Post-Soviet Immigrant Churches in Rome." *American Behavioral Scientist* 49 (11): 1528–53.

Solari, Cinzia. 2011. "Between 'Europe' and 'Afrika': Building the New Ukraine on the Shoulders of Migrant Women." In *Mapping Difference: The Many Faces of Women in Ukraine*, edited by J. Marian Rubchak, 23–47. Oxford: Berghan Book.

Solari, Cinzia. 2018. *On the Shoulders of Grandmothers: Gender, Migration, and Post-Soviet State Building*. New York: Routledge.

Sorokin, Pitirim A. 1959. *Social and Cultural Mobility*. Glencoe, IL: Free Press.

Sorokov, Vladimir. 1988 [1983]. *The Queue*. New York: Readers International.

Spence, Michael. 1973. "Job Market Signaling." *The Quarterly Journal of Economics* 87 (3): 355–374.

Stella, Francesca. 2015. *Lesbian Lives in Soviet and Post-Soviet Russia*. London: Palgrave.

Stephens, Dionne P., and Layli D. Phillips. 2003. "Freaks, Gold Diggers, Divas, and Dykes: The Sociohistorical Development of Adolescent African American Women's Sexual Scripts." *Sexuality and Culture* 7 (1): 3–49.

Stulhofer, Aleksandar. 2004. *Sexuality and Gender in Post-Communist Eastern Europe and Russia*. London: Haworth Press.

Suarez Orozco, Marcelo. 1997. "The Cultural Psychology of Immigration." In *Health and Social Services Among International Labor Migrants: A Comparative Perspective*, edited by Antonio Ugalde and Gilberto Cardenas, 131–51. Austin: University of Texas at Austin.

Świtek, B. 2016. *Reluctant Intimacies: Japanese Eldercare in Indonesian Hands*. Oxford: Berghahn Books.

Tacoli, Cecilia. 1999. "International Migration and the Restructuring of Gender Asymmetries: Continuity and Change among Filipino Labor Migrants in Rome." *International Migration Review* 33 (3): 658–82.

Thomas, William Isaac. 1923. *The Unadjusted Girl*. Boston: Little & Brown.

Thomas, William Isaac, and Florian Znaniecki. 1918. *The Polish Peasant: Monograph of an Ethnic Group*. Chicago: University of Chicago Press.

Thranhardt, Dietrich. 1996. "European Migration from East to West: Present Patterns and Future Directions." *New Community* 22 (2): 227–42.

Tilly, Charles. 2000. "Transplanted Networks." In *Immigration Reconsidered: History, Sociology, and Politics*, edited by V. Yans-MacLoughlin, 79–95. Oxford: Oxford University Press.

Tilly, Charles. 2007. "Trust Networks in Transnational Migration." *Sociological Forum* 22 (1): 3–24.

Tilly, Charles, and Harold C. Brown. 1967. "On Uprooting, Kinship and the Auspices of Migration." *International Journal of Comparative Sociology* 8:139–64.

Triandafyllidou, Anna, and Mariangela Veikou. 2001. *Immigration Policy Implementation in Italy: Organisational Culture, Identity Processes and Labour Market Control.* Florence: Robert Schuman Centre.

Trigos, Ludmilla A. 2009. *The Decembrist Myth in Russian Culture.* London: Palgrave.

Truman, Sean D., David A. Sharar, and John C. Pompe. 2011. "The Mental Health Status of Expatriate Versus U.S. Domestic Workers: A Comparative Study." *International Journal of Mental Health* 40 (4): 3–18.

Turner, Victor. 1965. *The Ritual Process: Structure and Anti-Structure.* London: Penguin.

Turner, Victor Witter. 1967. *The Forest of Symbols: Aspects of Ndembu Ritual.* Ithaca: Cornell University Press.

Twigg, Julia. 2000. "Carework as a Form of Bodywork." *Ageing and Society* 20 (04): 389–411.

Twigg, Julia, Carol Wolkowith, Rachel Lara Cohen, and Sarah Nettleton. 2011. "Conceptualising Body Work in Health and Social Care." *Sociology of Health & Illness* 33 (2):171–88.

Tymczuk, Alexander. 2013. "The Morality of Transnationalism: Children of Ukrainian Labor Migrants Write About Migration, Homeland and Abroad." *Children's Geographies* 11 (4): 490–503.

Uehling, Greta. 2002. "Sitting on Suitcases: Ambivalence and Ambiguity in the Migration Intentions of Crimean Tatar Women." *Journal of Refugee Studies* 15 (4): 388–408.

Van Gennep, Arnold. 1981. *Les rites de passage (1909).* Paris: Picard.

Vianello, Alice. 2009. *Migrando sole: Legami transnazionali tra Ucraina e Italia.* Milano: FrancoAngeli.

Vignali, Claudio, Ruth A. Schmidt, and Barry J. Davies. 1993. "The Benetton Experience." *International Journal of Retail & Distribution Management* 21 (3).

Waldinger, Roger. 2015a. *The Cross-Border Connection: Immigrants, Emigrants, and Their Homelands.* Cambridge: Harvard University Press.

Waldinger, Roger. 2015b. "The Cross-Border Connection: A Rejoinder." *Ethnic and Racial Studies* 38 (13): 2305–13.

Waldinger, Roger, Eric Popkin, and Hector Aquiles Magana. 2008. "Conflict and Contestation in the Cross-Border Community: Hometown Associations Reassessed." *Ethnic and Racial Studies* 31 (5): 843–70.

Weber, Max. 1978. *Economy and Society: An Outline of Interpretative Sociology.* Berkeley: University of California Press.

Weber, Serge. 2004. "Des chemins qui mènent à Rome . . . Trajectoires et espaces migratoires roumains, ukraniens et polonais a Rome." PhD dissertation, UFR de Geographie, Université de Paris 1.

Wehner, Silke. 1995. "German Domestic Servants in America, 1850–1914: A New Look at German Immigrant Women's Experiences." In *People in Transit:*

*German Migrations in Comparative Perspective, 1820–1930*, edited by Dirk Hoerder and Jorg Nagler, 267–94. Cambridge: Cambridge University Press.

Williams, Allan M., and Vladimir Baláž. 2012. "Migration, Risk, and Uncertainty: Theoretical Perspectives." *Population, Space and Place* 18 (2): 167–80.

Wolff, Larry. 1994. *Inventing Eastern Europe: The Map of Civilization on the Mind of the Enlightenment.* Stanford: Stanford University Press.

World Bank. 2016. *Migration and Remittances Factbook 2016.* Washington, DC: The World Bank.

Yeoh, Brenda S. A., and Shirlena Huang. 1998. "Negotiating Public Space: Strategies and Styles of Migrant Female Domestic Workers in Singapore." *Urban Studies* 35 (3): 583–602.

Yücesoy, Eda Ünlü. 2008. *Everyday Urban Public Space: Turkish Immigrant Women's Perspective.* Amsterdam: Het Spinhuis.

Yükseker, Deniz. 2007. "Shuttling Goods, Weaving Consumer Tastes: Informal Trade between Turkey and Russia." *International Journal of Urban and Regional Research* 31 (1): 60–72.

Zakharov, Nikolay, and Ian Law, eds. 2017. *Post-Soviet Racisms.* London: Palgrave Macmillan.

Zaslavski, Victor. 1981. *Il consenso organizzato: La società sovietica negli anni di Brežnev.* Bologna: Il Mulino.

Zdravomyslova, Helena. 2010. "Working Mothers and Nannies: Commercialization of Childcare and Modifications in the Gender Contract (A Sociological Essay)." *Anthropology of East Europe Review* 28 (2): 201–25.

Zhurzhenko, Tatiana. 2001. "Free Market Ideology and New Women's Identities in Post-Socialist Ukraine." *European Journal of Women's Studies* 8 (1): 29–49.

Zhurzhenko, Tatiana, Kathleen Kuehnast, and Carol Nechemias. 2004. *Strong Women, Weak State: Family Politics and Nation Building in Post-Soviet Ukraine.* Washington, DC: Woodrow Wilson Center Press.

Zolberg, Aristide R. 1987. "Wanted but Not Welcome: Alien Labor in Western Development." In *Population in an Interacting World*, edited by W. Alonso, 36–73. Cambridge: Harvard University Press.

# Index of Participant Pseudonyms

# Index of Subjects